ULTRASONICS

BENSON CARLIN

Executive Vice President, Circo Ultrasonic Corporation

SECOND EDITION

McGRAW-HILL BOOK COMPANY, INC.

New York   Toronto   London

1960

RICHMOND COLLEGE LIBRARY
Staten Island, New York 10301

ULTRASONICS

Copyright © 1960 by the McGraw-Hill Book Company, Inc.

Copyright, 1949, by the McGraw-Hill Book Company, Inc. Printed in the United States of America. All rights reserved. This book, or parts thereof, may not be reproduced in any form without permission of the publishers. *Library of Congress Catalog Card Number:* 59-14438

IV

09849

THE MAPLE PRESS COMPANY, YORK, PA.

To Vivian, Robert and Richard

PREFACE

Thanks are due to all the many people who read the first edition, many of whom have corresponded with me about problems in the field. Helpful suggestions and criticisms have been received from engineers in many parts of the world. So far as possible, these have been incorporated into the second edition.

The confidence I had in the growth of ultrasonics has been more than justified, and in the years since the first edition appeared ultrasonics have become a recognized technique with many accepted industrial applications. Not only in testing materials, but in cleaning and degreasing, soldering, plating, and many other fields it has made significant advances. I have been particularly fortunate in being active in many of these, and I look forward to much greater growth in the future.

In addition, new transducer materials and the further development of old ones have been made. This has made practical applications of what were formerly only laboratory curiosities. In this field also, the future looks particularly promising.

As in the first edition, the new revised volume will stress the engineering application of ultrasonics, emphasizing practical equipment design rather than theory.

Since this work is not primarily a historical one, no attempt has been made to include mention of all the workers in the field or to compile prior work. Well-known theories and works are therefore presented as statements of fact, without derivations and histories of development.

It is possible that credit may not always be given where it is due, since much material became known to me anonymously. Such slights are entirely unintentional and will be corrected gladly when called to my attention.

Naturally much of the material, especially the theoretical parts, is well known in the art, and it can have but little claim to originality, but I personally carried out almost all the practical experimentation, both in repeating the investigations of prior workers and along original lines as they suggested themselves to me. It is, of course, very likely that other workers in the field have carried out similar investigations. Full credit has been given wherever I was familiar with such work. It is hoped that further studies will be suggested by the information contained here.

The applications of ultrasonics are so numerous that they merit special attention.   These include among them the following:

1. The mixing of ordinarily immiscible liquids.
2. The dispersion of metals in liquids.
3. The breaking up of some polymers.
4. Coagulation of certain suspensions.
5. Production of heating effects.
6. Production of chemical reactions.
7. Precipitation of smoke.
8. Homogenization.
9. Emulsification.
10. Transformation of chemical compounds and crystal structures.
11. Destruction of bacteria.
12. Stimulation of plant + growth.
13. Killing of small animals.
14. Formation of the basis for systems of television, underwater signaling, depth sounding, communication, etc.
15. The testing of materials and seismic exploration.

The ability to produce a highly directive and focused beam of vibration and to concentrate high powers in a small area makes most of these applications possible.

I worked at the University of Michigan as a visiting engineer for a period during the development of the ultrasonic Reflectoscope and later as a senior research and product engineer for the Sperry Products Corporation.   Particular thanks are due to the many engineers whose advice during these years was often invaluable, and to my present associates at Circo Ultrasonics Corporation.

Benson Carlin

CONTENTS

face waves in solids. Beam interrupter. Tanks. Beam-limiting devices. Coupling the crystal to the work. Matching the crystal. Holders for agitating liquids. Submarine signaling transducers. The cable connection. Lenses and reflectors. Holders for resonance testing. Interoferometry. Holders for microscope use. Glues.

History. Miscellaneous effects. General. Controlling device for oscillators. Materials. Systems (the magnetostriction oscillator). Dimensions and frequency. Shapes. Diaphragms. Temperature coefficient (drift). Curve temperature. Limits. Power available. Designing the magnetostrictive unit (cores: rod, tube and slit tube, laminated bar, slotted bars, ring or cylindrical transducers; lamination cutting, bonding, annealing, nickel anneals, Permandur anneals, oxides, coils). Effect of load (effect of loading one or both ends). Tool design. Resonance. Use. Rod tools. Cones with straight tapers. Step tools. Exponential cones. Choice of tool. Materials. Tips. Determining the center of mass. Insulating tools. Diaphragms. Backing. Cooling. Bending transducers. Magnetostrictive delay lines. Distributed amplifiers.

General. Whistles (Galton whistle, Hartmann whistle, Vortex whistle, jet-edge system—Pohlmann whistle). Sirens. Electromagnetic transducers (moving-coil systems). Miscellaneous mechanical vibrators. Hydrodynamic valve transducer. Thermal. Singing flames.

Detection of ultrasonic waves—pressure (theory, mechanical devices, other mechanical means). Tanks. Diffraction of light. Diffraction systems. Striation. Wavefront effects. Bragg reflection. Light diffraction in solids. Microphones. Barium titanate. Magnetostriction. x-cut Rochelle salt. Capacitive probes. Hot-wire instruments. Interferometers (fixed path, variable path). Thermocouple probes. Shadowgraphs. Electrokinetic effect. Bleach-out. Starch plate. Direct photographic effects (luminescence, chromotropism, labile compounds, reaction). Photographing cathode-ray screens.

High-power ultrasonics. General. History. Crystal generators. Holders and containers. Power output. Coupling to the crystal. Magnetostrictive transducers. Electronic generators for magnetostrictive use. Pulsed or continuous generators.

Continuous wave. History. General continuous-wave system. The ultrasonic oscillator. The ultrasonic receiver. Transmission at an angle. Wobbulated systems (varying the oscillator frequency). Methods of indication. Shielding. Sonic or ultrasonic signaling. Signaling by ultrasonic carriers. Factors that control transmission. Methods of use. Signaling in the ocean. Tuning the transducers. Resonance. Testing materials by resonance. Exciting resonance. Resonance thickness measurement. Standing waves. Acoustic impedance. Matching impedances. Standing-wave ratio. History—submarine apparatus. Interferometry. Indicating resonance. Complete resonance system.

The oscillator. Magnetostrictive resonance system. The Reflectogage. Drop tests. Pulsed resonance systems. Limitations of resonance. Testing bond. Ultrasonic liquid-level sensors.

Testing materials with pulsed ultrasonics. Hughes ultrasonic instrument. Pulsed systems—electronic considerations. The pulsed ultrasonic unit (sweep, sweep operation, delay circuits, differentiation, marker circuits, cathode-ray tube, pulse forming, pulse generator: gas tubes, high-vacuum pulse; ultrasonic receivers for pulsed energy, methods of gating the receiver, other means of presentation). Pulse technique applications (attenuation measurements).

General. Physical effects (cavitation, thermal, fog production, degassing). Biological effects. Chemical effects (frequency, intensity, duration of time, pressure, temperature). Electrochemical effects. Emulsion and dispersion. Medical effects (therapy, diagnosis, neurosonic surgery). Metallurgical effects (grain refinement, dispersion, welding). Precipitation (in gas, in liquid). Photographic effect.

Pulse technique (testing distance, testing materials), type and size of flaw: size, orientation; wall thickness, shape, surface, fatigue testing, absorption testing technique for close testing, setting standards for ultrasonic testing. Resonance technique (bond testing). Transmission of continuous ultrasonics. Medical equipment (diagnostic: diagnostic equipment; therapy, surgery). Soldering and brazing (soldering pots, applications). Welding (welding equipment). Cleaning (evaluation of cleaning, surface decontamination). Drilling (tool wear, finish, abrasive-water ratio, milling). Dental cutting. Burglar alarm. Miscellaneous devices (ultrasonic trainer, blind guidance, microscopes and telescopes, fish and depth finders, tank-level indicator, viscosity-measurement devices, flowmeter, radar targets, sonic gas analyzer, vibration pickup. Ultrasonic signaling in the ocean. Ultrasonic propagation in air. Propagation through waves. Television. Ultrasonic delay lines (miscellaneous considerations: insertion losses, delay times, frequency, bandwidth, temperature). Phase systems. Miscellaneous pulse applications.

CHAPTER 1

ULTRASONIC WAVES

Ultrasonic waves have become of great importance in recent years. Their unique properties have been applied to industry, signaling, medicine, and many other fields.

Ultrasonics. Vibrational waves of a frequency above the hearing range of the normal ear are referred to as *ultrasonic*, and the term therefore includes all waves of a frequency of more than about 20,000 cps. Actually, however, frequencies in the sonic range may also be used for certain ultrasonic applications; and when this is done, they are sometimes also referred to loosely as "ultrasonic." Also, high-amplitude ultrasonic waves are sometimes referred to as "sonic." Since frequencies of as much as 500×10^6 to 1×10^9 cps[1] have been generated, it is readily apparent that the term defines a tremendous range in both frequency and wavelength. Some vibrations of the same order of frequency as audible ones act essentially in the same manner as the latter; others in the minimum order of wavelength behave like light in many ways. Many phenomena, especially those occurring in these higher frequency ranges, are still unexplained; there are also numerous places where the classic theory and the observed facts do not agree.

In the minimum frequency range, the length of ultrasonic waves in solids is about 8 in., in liquids about 2.4 in., and in air about 0.63 in.

In the maximum frequency range the wavelengths approach a value in solids of 3.2×10^{-4} in., in liquids 1×10^{-4} in., and in gases 0.24×10^{-4} in. It is possible that waves of even greater frequency and therefore shorter wavelength may be produced in the future.

Frequencies of 10,000 to 100,000 cps are used for industrial applications, sound ranging, submarine signaling, and communication. Those of 10,000 to 20,000,000 cps are used in testing materials for flaws, chemical treatment, medical therapy, etc. All frequencies are suitable for investigation of the physical properties of matter. A more complete spectrum of frequencies and phenomena is shown in Table 1-1.

[1] L. Bergmann, "Der Ultraschall," VDI Verlag, Berlin, 1942; translated by H. S. Hatfield, "Ultrasonics and Their Scientific and Technical Applications," Wiley, 1944; G. B. Devey, *Radio & Tel. News, Radio-Electronic Eng. Section*, **20** (February, 1953) 8.

1

TABLE 1-1. ULTRASONIC SPECTRUM

Frequency, kc	Action
Under 1 kc	Sonic altimeter, early underwater navigation, ship's propeller
16–20	The upper limit to average human hearing—the boundary between sonics and ultrasonics; common frequency for magnetostriction units for underwater work. Low-frequency underwater signaling, aerosol reactions, and agitation of liquids occur at or below this frequency; also drilling and soldering, industrial cleaning, whistles, etc.
19.2	Alarm systems for burglar detection, etc.
25	Ultrasonic control apparatus, door opening, etc.
30	Upper limit produced by friction
40	Common for underwater signaling, cleaning, etc.
60	Practical limit to generation by magnetostriction, blind-guidance devices
90	Top limit for tuning forks
100	Limit for Galton whistle
120	Limit for gas whistles in air (resonant cavity)
300	Thick limit on resonance testing by fundamental means; limit to generation by spark discharge; emulsion formation
400	Common frequency in emulsion and agitation work
500	Low limit, pulsed material testing; upper limit to underwater signaling; testing of material of large grain of poor homogeneity; hydrogen whistle
600	High polymer reactions
750	Experimental biological work, Poulsen arc in gas
1,000	Common test frequency for materials with ordinary metallic structures; production of oil jets; medical therapy, mixing, cleaning, etc.
2,250	Common test frequency for material with fine grain structure
5,000–25,000	Testing of fine homogeneous material
6,000	Approximately 0.025 in. in steel; resonance method
7,500–30,000	Mercury delay lines
15,000	Radar trainer, absorption measurements, delay lines
1,000,000	Highest ultrasonic frequency reported attained at present

The minute size of the ultrasonic wavelength is the factor that has made possible the application of these waves in many cases.

Wave Motion. Study of any recent text on physics or acoustics will give the modern concept of wave motion. The term connotes a condition that is somehow transmitted so that it can be experienced at a distance from where it was originally generated. Ultrasonic waves are special forms of these general ones, in which the condition being propagated is a displacement of the particles of the medium in which the wave travels.

By placing a source of vibration in a bell jar and gradually evacuating the jar, it can readily be shown that these waves will not travel unless there is a medium through which they can be propagated. It can therefore be stated that the presence of a medium is essential to the transmission of ultrasonic waves.

Almost any material that has elasticity can propagate ultrasonic waves. The propagation takes the form of a displacement of successive elements of the medium. If the substance is elastic, there is a restoring force that tends to bring each element of material back to its original position. Since all such media also possess inertia, the particle continues to move after it returns to the position from which it started and finally reaches another different position, past the original one. From this second point it returns to its starting position, about which it continues to oscillate with constantly diminishing amplitude. The elements of material will therefore execute different movements or orbits as the wave passes through them. It is the differences in these movements which characterize basic types of ultrasonic waves; but no matter what the wave type, the general properties of ultrasonics[1] remain.

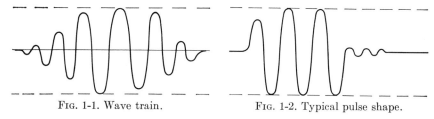

FIG. 1-1. Wave train.   FIG. 1-2. Typical pulse shape.

As the wave travels through the material, successive elements in it experience these displacements, each such element in the wave path moving a little later than its neighbor. In other words, the phase of the wave, or vibration, changes along the path of wave transmission. This displacement can be plotted, and the graph is descriptive of the wave.

Wave Train. A wave train refers to a short group of waves before or after which there are no waves (Fig. 1-1). Such a group is usually called a *pulse* and may be of several different shapes. For one thing, the individual waves in such a pulse may be of about the same amplitude, and it may stop and start very rapidly, so that its envelope, i.e., the locus of points on its extremes, is essentially a square wave (Fig. 1-2). The pulse may also be such that it builds up and decays gradually, in which case the locus will look like a half cycle of a sine wave. The pulse may also build up rapidly and decay exponentially (Fig. 1-3), in which case it is called a *decayed* or *damped train* and takes the form familiar in exponential damping. This last case is the most common.

All these types of wave trains are used extensively. All are rich in harmonics, and analysis of a wave train by the Fourier method or by

---

[1] We use the term *ultrasonics* freely to refer to ultrasonic waves, as well as to the general subject.

other means will therefore show a great number of frequency components. Waves may also be continuous, i.e., each wave may be followed by another exactly like itself or modulated in various ways.

Types of Waves. An ultrasonic wave being transmitted through a substance may be any of several types. Each type causes a specific movement in the elements of the medium, and the paths that these elements follow as they move in response to the wave are called their *orbits*. These orbits may be essentially parallel to the line of propagation, in which case the wave is *longitudinal*. On the other hand, they may be executed normal to the direction of propagation. Such waves are called *transverse* or *shear* (usually shear). They may travel within a very short distance of the surface, and are then called *surface waves*. In a thin diaphragm, *flexural waves* may exist. The particle motion in them is similar to shear or surface waves but extends throughout the medium.

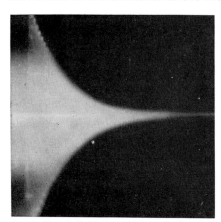

Fig. 1-3. Damped wave train.

Waves are also sometimes described on the basis of whether or not they change the volume of the material in which they are propagated. If they do, they are called *waves of dilatation;* and if they do not, they are classed as *waves of distortion*. Waves of dilatation are also usually classified as irrotational. This term defines a condition in which there is no element of rotation.

Longitudinal or shear waves may theoretically be either dilatational or distortional. However, a material cannot always support the propagation of all these types of wave motion, and those longitudinal waves used in ultrasonic applications are experimentally determined to be almost exclusively distortional. Therefore, longitudinal, dilatational, irrotational waves may be referred to as simply *longitudinal*, while shear, distortional waves may be called simply *shear*.

The type of wave should not be confused with the modulation impressed upon it. Any of these types may be continuous, modulated, or pulsed. They can be produced or detected by various means. None of these factors affects the general type. Moreover, the generation of most types is by means of the same or very similar apparatus and transducers.

Longitudinal Waves. Longitudinal waves exist when the motion of the particles in a medium is parallel to the direction of wave propagation. This kind of wave is often referred to as the L wave. The L

type has been most often used in ultrasonics up to the present, since it will travel in liquids, solids, or gases and is easily generated and detected. Longitudinal waves have a high velocity of travel in most media, and the wavelengths in common materials are usually very short in comparison with the cross-sectional area of the transducer, the element that produces the waves. This property allows the energy to be focused into a sharp beam from which it diverges only slightly.

The L wave should not be confused with the total vibration of a part in which ultrasonic or sonic waves are traveling. Such vibrations are characteristic of the geometry of the part and are caused by the action of the waves within it (Fig. 1-4).

Since longitudinal waves exist within a comparatively small section of a part, they may or may not extend to the surfaces parallel to the direction of travel. However, it is not usual for them to reach such a boundary. Such waves are diagrammatically represented in Fig. 1-5.

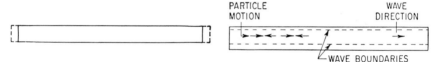

FIG. 1-4. Total vibration of a part due to internal waves.

FIG. 1-5. Longitudinal waves traveling through a medium.

Longitudinal waves may be generated within a medium by the vibration of any one of its surfaces in a normal direction at an ultrasonic frequency. If the energy is to remain in a beam, the frequency (and therefore the wavelength) must be the proper ratio to the area of the surface that is being vibrated.

In order to make use of these oscillations, since they travel with very great velocities and since their frequencies are generally high, the systems that are used with them must be capable of responding to such frequencies and of resolving signals following each other closely in time. In those cases where time intervals are to be determined, means of measuring to the nearest microsecond are necessary.

Shear Waves. When shear waves are used, the movement of the particles in the medium is at right angles to the direction of wave propagation. If the wave movement is in the x direction, the particle displacement is in the y direction. These waves may also exist either in a limited area of or entirely throughout a body. Usually, however, they are in the form of a beam of small cross section in comparison with the cross-sectional area of the piece in which they travel. The beam does not ordinarily extend to a surface parallel to the direction of travel. Shear waves, which will also be referred to hereafter as S waves, have a velocity that is approximately one-half of that of the L waves. Because of this lower velocity, the wavelength of shear waves is much shorter than that of L waves. Figure 1-6 illustrates the particle motion in a shear wave.

Shear waves have certain advantages, because their lower velocity makes the electronic timing circuits with which they are used less critical. However, the shorter wavelength makes them more sensitive to small inclusions, and they are therefore more easily scattered within a material. Moreover, since the vibration is in a specific direction, rotation of the sending element changes this direction, and therefore polarization effects may be noticed. In other words, the results in a material that is not absolutely uniform may differ with rotation of the transducer. Shear waves will not travel in liquids or gases, since there is little or no elasticity to shear in such materials.

FIG. 1-6. Particle motion and wave directions of a shear wave.

FIG. 1-7. Total shear motion of a part.

Shear waves are generated by applying a shearing force to the face of a material, i.e., rocking it back and forth in a direction parallel to the surface. The whole part may also vibrate in a shear manner (Fig. 1-7).

Polarized Waves. The particle motion of a shear wave is at right angles to the direction of travel and parallel to the X axis in the case of a y-cut crystal (see Chap. 2). Rotating the transducer will therefore rotate this direction of motion, although the same path of travel is followed. When this beam is received, a maximum signal results where the receiver is rotated similarly (i.e., X axes parallel), and minimum (or zero) when crossed. The fact that such polarizations exist is of importance in cases where the reflected wave must be entirely shear—which it is in any case where the incident wave is normal to the reflector—or when the incident wave is at any angle so long as the line of vibration is at right angles to the incident surface.

The velocity of polarized waves may differ according to the relationship between the X axis and the physical characteristics in the material of propagation, i.e., grain orientation, etc., or according to the polarization of the shear wave (in certain solids).

Surface or Rayleigh Waves. Waves can be propagated over the surface of a part without penetrating below that surface to any extent. These waves are roughly analogous to water waves which travel over a body of water. Their velocity depends upon the material itself and is about nine-tenths of S-wave velocity.

Surface waves can be generated by shaking an area of a surface back and forth in a manner similar to that by which S waves are generated. However, the area is oblong in shape.

The wavelength of a surface wave is always extremely short, and the plate on which it travels is at least several wavelengths thick. Under such conditions the displacement of particles a few wavelengths below the surface is negligible. Surface waves consist of both L and S types of particle motion. Figure 1-8 is a representation of surface waves traveling over a plate.

FIG. 1-8. Surface waves traveling over a plate.

Any of these wave types can be used for exploration of materials for defects, for measuring thickness by resonance or other methods, for measuring characteristics of the material in which the wave travels, or for performing any of the other functions of which ultrasonic waves are capable, although longitudinal waves are exclusively used for cleaning and other industrial power applications.

Basic Properties. *Longitudinal Waves.* The longitudinal waves common to ultrasonics are defined as those in which the particle velocity is restrained to a motion in the direction of the wave propagation. They are dilatational and irrotational; i.e., there is a change in the body volume; and to state it crudely, particle motion consists of strain without rotation.

The equations for such waves in the x direction reduce to

$$(x + 2G) \frac{\partial^2 u}{\partial x^2} = \rho \frac{\partial^2 u}{\partial t^2}$$

Physically, this equation states that the particle displacement is a function of x and a function of t. In other words, if it were plotted as a function of x for a constant value of t, the shape of the displacement would be proportional to the plot of u as a function of time. The proportion is that of $\lambda + 2G : \rho$.

The terms λ and G are elastic constants; i.e., they are determined by the characteristics of the material; and ρ is the mass density, i.e., the mass per unit volume. These characteristics are physical entities that can be measured in a material.

Essentially, this equation states that the only possible particle velocity is in the x direction. This is the ideal condition in the propagation of L waves. However, in actuality, although the greatest motion is in this direction, there is always some shear stress, since the edges of the path cannot move back and forth quickly.

Shear Waves. Shear waves have been defined as those whose particle motion is perpendicular to the direction of wave travel. In such a case when the volume expansion e is zero, the equation is

$$G \frac{\partial^2 u}{\partial y^2} = \rho \frac{\partial^2 u}{\partial t^2}$$

This is known as a wave of distortion. In other words, the volume of the entire body does not change, although its boundaries may. (It may be noticed that the condition of no volume change is set by definition.)

Considering this case physically, it may also be noted that the displacement at a particular point in space corresponds exactly to the displacement at any other point, each in its own time over the entire wave, with the scale factor $\sqrt{G/\rho}$. This means that a particle will occupy a particular point in space at periodic intervals of time.

Rayleigh or Surface Waves. These are waves which travel over the surface of the part without any essential penetration into it. Lord Rayleigh[1] bases his description of these waves on two assumptions:

1. There is a combination of two waves existing on the surface: one distortional and the other dilatational.

2. Both types exist on the surface only.

When the conditions above are solved for, the wave velocity depends on μ, since both λ and G are functions of μ, and they in turn control the velocities of the two types of waves. The quantity μ represents the displacement normal to the pressure. The velocity of a surface wave can be solved for when the physical characteristics are known.

Many interesting phenomena may be associated with surface waves. In ultrasonic work it is very often difficult to separate out various types of waves, since many forms of receivers and indicators cannot distinguish, for example, longitudinal from shear waves. They merely indicate the presence of energy, which may be of any type. In working with large masses of metal, reflections will occur, which can be damped out at certain points by the passage of the hand or some other damping medium over the surface. This would, of course, occur with any type of wave if it were hitting the surfaces at that point. However, in certain cases reflections may be observed that seem to return from the edge of a large object, and the time elapsed between the sending of the pulse and this reflection seems to coincide with what would be expected of surface waves.

If a thin film of oil or similar material is spread over such a surface, waves may travel in the oil and reflections will occur even when the film is only a few molecules thick. Exactly what type of wave exists in such a case is questionable. Although the wave obviously travels within a fraction of the wavelength of the surface, it would not necessarily be a surface wave even though it is described as a wave traveling within a wavelength of the surface.

[1] Lord Rayleigh, *Proc. London Math. Soc.*, **17** (1885) 4.

Figure 1-9 shows the amount of energy in a surface wave while the distance from the surface is increasing, as well as the means for measuring it.

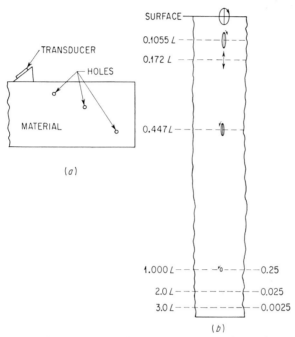

(a)

(b)

Fig. 1-9a. Means for measuring the penetration of a surface wave.
Fig. 1-9b. Amount of acoustic energy as a function of depth below the surface.

Reflection between Two Materials. When a wave traveling through one material impinges on a boundary between it and a second medium, part of the energy travels forward as one wave through the second medium while part is reflected back into the first medium, usually with a phase change.

The characteristic that determines the amount of reflection is known as the *specific acoustic impedance* and is the product of the density and velocity. The amplitude (pressure) of the reflected wave is related to the incident wave as

$$A_r = \frac{R_1 - R_2}{R_1 + R_2}$$

where $R_1 = \rho_1 c_1$
$R_2 = \rho_2 c_2$
ρ = density of each material
c = velocity
A_r = ratio between reflected and incident amplitudes

The subscripts 1 and 2 indicate two media. Any system of units can be used.

As long as the wave travels in the same medium, the energy is proportional to the amplitude squared. Therefore,

$$R = R_0 \left(\frac{\rho_1 c_1 - \rho_2 c_2}{\rho_1 c_1 + \rho_2 c_2} \right)^2$$

where R = reflected energy

R_0 = incident energy

In the case of an air-solid boundary, practically 100 per cent of the energy is reflected.

It should be remembered that in a reflection system, the energy passes through an interface twice, once in each direction of travel (see Chap. 9).

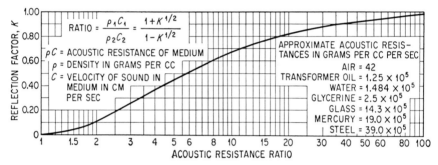

FIG. 1-10. Reflection of waves at a boundary.

For a liquid-steel interface about 88 per cent is reflected each time. Thus the energy received after two transmissions through the boundary is 12 per cent of 12 per cent, or 1.4 per cent.

All these calculations are entirely independent of attenuation and scattering. The amount of energy actually reflected may differ considerably from that calculated theoretically. Energy may be dissipated at a boundary or in a material in several ways. The formulas given refer only to a perfect boundary between two infinite media. If there is any discontinuity, no matter how minute, these relationships no longer apply. It is accordingly difficult to get actual values of reflected energy except by experiment.

A list of values of reflection between two media is shown in Table 1-2 and a graph of per cent reflection in Fig. 1-10.[1]

Strong reflections take place when transmitting from any liquid to any solid. However, the usual way of getting ultrasonic waves into a solid

[1] F. W. Smith and P. K. Stumpf, *Electronics*, **19** (1946) 116.

TABLE 1-2. PERCENTAGE REFLECTION OF ULTRASONIC VIBRATIONS NORMALLY INCIDENT ON THE BOUNDARIES BETWEEN MEDIA PERFECTLY JOINED AT INTERFACE

Material or medium	Specific acoustic impedance × 10⁶	Aluminum	Steel	Nickel	Magnesium	Copper	Brass	Lead	Mercury	Glass	Polystyrene	Bakelite	Water	Oil	Air
Aluminum	1.70	0	21	24	9	18	14	3	1	2	50	42	72	74	100
Steel	4.76		0	0.2	43	0.3	1	9	16	31	77	76	88	89	100
Nickel	4.98			0	47	0.8	2	12	19	34	79	75	89	90	100
Magnesium	0.926				0	40	36	20	12	2	27	19	54	58	100
Copper	4.11					0	0.2	7	13	19	75	71	87	88	100
Brass	3.61						0	5	10	23	73	68	86	87	100
Lead	2.73							0	1	9	62	55	79	80	100
Mercury	1.93								0	4	8	6	75	76	100
Glass	1.805									0	40	32	65	67	100
Polystyrene	0.294										0	1	12	17	100
Bakelite	0.363											0	18	23	100
Water	0.143												0	0	100
Transformer oil	0.128													0	100
Air	0.0000413														0

is by using thin films of couplants (usually liquids), since air boundaries reflect almost 100 per cent. In such a case the energy equation becomes

$$\frac{R}{R_0} = \frac{(R_1/R_2 - R_2/R_1)^2}{4 \cot^2 (2\pi L/\lambda) + (R_1/R_2 + R_2/R_1)^2}$$

where
$R = $ reflected energy
$R_0 = $ incident energy
$L = $ thickness of material
R_1 and $R_2 = $ specific impedances of materials concerned

The thickness of films capable of reflecting different amounts of energy can be calculated from this for various wavelengths, and optimum thicknesses chosen for coupling layers.

Most reflections in a medium take place from obstacles of irregular shape, size, and orientation. Some of the considerations in such a case are discussed elsewhere. However, it is impossible to calculate most such effects. If the surface is flat and large with respect to the wavelength, the reflection is essentially specular. A flat surface may be considered one where the irregularities are not greater than about $\frac{1}{20}\lambda$. When the surface is very irregular, the energy is broken up and reflected haphazardly.

Reflection from an Obstacle. When an ultrasonic wave meets an obstacle, it may be reflected in various ways depending upon both the nature of the obstacle and its size. The action seems to depend upon the relation of the wavelength to the size of the obstacle. If the obstacle is large compared with the wavelength, there is a strong reflected wave that returns from it. A definite shadow is cast behind the obstacle or defect, and there may or may not be some diffraction of the wave around its edges. If the obstacle, however, is very small and only a small fraction of a wavelength, there will be no real reflection and no shadow. The ultrasonic energy seems to pass around the obstacle and to come together behind it and pass along as though there were no interference. Of course, if there are enough of these small inclusions or obstacles, a large proportion of the energy may be scattered but there will still be no reflection. The energy will merely disappear inside the piece, and it is difficult to say exactly why this is so.

One possible explanation of the phenomenon of such reflection is as follows: The wavelength of any ultrasonic vibrational wave represents the distribution of particle displacement within a certain limit: i.e., it represents the amount of compression or expansion in any particular interval of the entire range covered by one wave. Thus, in a 1-Mc wave the amount of compression covers an area of a half wavelength, or approximately $\frac{1}{16}$ in. in aluminum, while in a 5-Mc wave the amount of compression covers an area of a half wavelength, or approximately $\frac{1}{80}$ in.

in aluminum. The ratio of the size of the flaw to this wavelength represents the fraction of this compression which is interfered with by the obstacle. If an obstacle is $\frac{1}{50}$ in. in dimension, it will interrupt the entire 5-Mc wave but only approximately $\frac{1}{16}$ of the 1-Mc wave.

The dimensions mentioned so far are in the direction parallel to the propagation of the wave. Now, if this same flaw or obstacle has a very small cross-sectional area, this smallness coupled with the fact that it has a minute effect on the 1-Mc wave will give negligible reflection. The greater the cross-sectional area of the flaw the more energy it will interrupt and the larger the reflected signal will be.

In other words, there are two important facts that influence the reflection. One is the dimension in the direction along the propagation path; the other is the cross-sectional area. It is the dimension along the propagation path that interrupts the wave, but it is the cross-sectional area that determines the amount of reflection.

Orientation. The orientation of a reflecting surface is important, since it is essentially the projection of the interface on a plane perpendicular to the beam that determines the amount of reflection. A very regular interface, however, may act as a perfect reflector and direct the beam away at an angle, in the same manner that a beam of light is reflected by a mirror. Irregular surfaces almost always return some of the energy along the path by which it reached the obstacle.

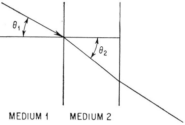

MEDIUM 1   MEDIUM 2

FIG. 1-11. Refraction at a boundary.

Refraction. It is sometimes advisable to send ultrasonic waves into a medium at angular incidence. Materials or liquids of a wedge shape can be used for such purposes. When this is done, the ray is introduced at an angle θ_1 and travels within the material at another angle θ_2, the difference being caused by refraction at the interface (Fig. 1-11).

The angle of this refracted wave is

$$\frac{\sin \theta_1}{\sin \theta_2} = \frac{c_1}{c_2}$$

where θ_1 = angle of incidence
θ_2 = angle of refraction
c_1 = velocity in first medium
c_2 = velocity in second medium

When these angles are small, θ_1 may be considered equal to $\sin \theta_1$, and θ_2 equal to $\sin \theta_2$. Small angles of inclination will therefore be greatly magnified.

Total reflection at the interface occurs for values equal to or greater than 90 deg. At that point

$$\sin \theta_1 = \frac{c_1}{c_2}$$

For liquids and solids θ_1 is about 15 deg. Therefore when the angle of incidence is greater than this value, no energy at all enters the part.

When shapes are complex, refraction patterns become extremely hard to interpret. For example, in a part flat on one side and curved on the other, the ray enters the flat side with no refraction but exists from the curved one broken up so that various parts of it travel at different angles.

Lenses can therefore be designed to affect the ultrasonic rays in the same manner as they are used in light. These lenses can be used to focus the waves in liquids or in gases and may be formed of plastics, metals, or liquids.

Diffraction. Ultrasonic waves do not always propagate in a rectilinear manner. For example, a wave passing near the edge of an object has a tendency to become bent toward and around it. This bending of the wave is called *diffraction*. Ultrasonic signals that would normally be received at a certain point may be diverted by diffraction and received at some other position.

Velocity. There are a number of different types of velocity that can be discussed. The most significant are referred to as phase velocity, group velocity, and signal velocity.

Each of these terms covers a complex phenomenon, and they should not be confused with each other or with the velocity of the particles in the waves as they execute their orbits.

The phase velocity may be defined as the speed with which a phase is "propagated" along a wave. It refers to a condition existing along the line of propagation that seems to show a change in phase traveling along with and superimposed on the wave itself.

Group velocity is a term used to indicate the velocity with which the envelope of a wave is propagated when the wave is amplitude-modulated. The basic or carrier frequency must be high for such a condition to manifest itself.

The group velocity is most often considered in ultrasonic work. Whenever the term *velocity* is used without a modifier, group velocity is intended. Phase and group velocity may have the same or different values. In the first case the material is not dispersive, and in the second it is.

A material is dispersive when signals of different frequencies travel with different velocities. It is not entirely established whether or not ultrasonic signals are dispersive under all possible conditions. However, the weight of evidence so far is that they are dispersive in solids and liquids.

Signal velocity is a very complex condition existing only when a medium is dispersive. In such a case different signals seem to travel with different velocities, and the actual speed of travel of a particular signal is its signal velocity. The time of travel may differ with the transmitting power; and changing the sensitivity of a particular receiver may change the apparent signal velocity.

The velocity of the wave and that of the individual particles of material are not the same. In all cases it is the velocity of the propagation of the wave that is referred to. The group velocity is also referred to as *bulk velocity* in some contexts.

Measurement of Velocity in Solids. A number of investigators, including the author, have experimentally measured the velocities of ultrasonic waves in various media. However, there are differences in published results. These may be due either to the equipment used, to the material tested, or to phenomena that are so far unexplained. Apparatus that can be adapted to making such measurements will be described in the following chapters.

There is a possibility that velocity varies somewhat with intensity. Experiments indicate that velocity may be higher near the source, where the intensity of ultrasonics is very great. Under such conditions velocities as much as three times normal have been reported.[1] However, the frequency is not affected by the intensity.[2]

The velocity of longitudinal waves is given by the relation

$$c = \sqrt{\frac{E}{d} \frac{1 - \mu}{(1 + \mu)(1 - \mu)}}$$

where E = Young's modulus
c = velocity
μ = Poisson's ratio
d = density

Examination of this formula shows that velocity depends on the density and elastic constants of the medium. Young's modulus may be defined as a relation between the stress intensity and the resulting strain. Poisson's ratio is the relation between a change in width and the change in length that causes it.

Common velocities of longitudinal waves in solids, liquids, and gases are given in Table 1-3.

[1] E. v. Angerer and E. Fadenburg, *Ann. Physik*, **66** (1933) 293.
[2] R. W. Boyle and G. B. Taylor, *Trans. Roy. Soc. Canada*, **19** (1925) 197.

TABLE 1-3. ULTRASONIC PROPERTIES OF COMMON MATERIALS

Material	Temperature, °C	c Velocity, cm/sec (bulk) $(\times 10^5)$	d Density, g/cm³	Specific acoustic impedance, $\rho c \times 10^6$ (bulk)
Air	0	0.331	1.293	0.00000428
	20	0.343	1.205	0.00000413
Alcohol	.....	1.44	0.79	0.11
Aluminum	.....	6.22	2.65	1.70
Ammonia (gas)	0	0.415	0.771	0.000032
Antimony	3.40	....	6.68	2.27
Argon	0	0.319	1.781	0.000056
Bakelite	.....	2.59	1.4	0.363
Bismuth	.....	2.18	9.80	1.75
Brass	.....	4.25	8.55	3.61
Cadmium	2.40	2.78	8.64	2.07
Carbon dioxide	0	0.259	1.977	0.000051
Carbon monoxide	0	0.388	1.250	0.000042
Chlorine	0	0.266	3.214	0.000066
Concrete	.....	....	2.6	
Constantan	.....	5.24	8.88	3.82
Copper	.....	4.60	8.93	4.11
Cork	.....	....	0.24	
Ethane	10	0.308	1.357	0.000041
Ethylene	0	0.317	1.260	0.000040
German silver	3.58	4.76	8.70	3.12
Glass	.....	3.4–5.9	2.5–5.9	1.2–2.1
Glycerin	.....	1.9	1.26	2.42
Gold	2.03	3.24	19.32	3.92
Granite	.....	3.9	2.75	1.09
Helium	0	0.97	0.179	0.000017
Hydrogen	0	1.28	0.090	0.000011
Hydrogen bromide	0	0.200	3.645	0.000073
Hydrogen chloride (gas)	0	0.296	1.640	0.000048
Hydrogen iodine	0	0.157	5.789	0.00009
Hydrogen sulfide	0	0.289	1.539	0.000044
Iridium	.....	....	22.41	10.70
Iron	.....	5.85	7.87	4.07
Ivory	.....	....	1.85	0.557
Lead	.....	2.13	11.4	2.73
Magnesium	.....	5.33	1.74	0.926
Manganese	.....	4.66	7.39	2.83
Marble	.....	....	2.65	1.01
Mercury	.....	1.46	13.6	1.93
Methane	.....	0.43	0.717	0.0000308
Neon	.....	0.435	0.900	0.0000392
Nickel	.....	5.6	8.9	4.98
Nitrogen	0	0.33	1.25	0.0000418
	20	0.35	1.16	0.0000408

TABLE 1-3. ULTRASONIC PROPERTIES OF COMMON MATERIALS (*Continued*)

Material	Temperature, °C	c Velocity, cm/sec (bulk) ($\times 10^5$)	d Density, g/cm³	Specific acoustic impedance, $\rho c \times 10^6$ (bulk)
Oxygen.................	0	0.316	1.42	0.0000452
	20	0.328	1.32	0.0000436
Petroleum...............	.....	1.33	0.7	0.93
Platinum................	.....	3.96	21.5	6.02
Polystyrene.............	.....	2.67	1.1	0.294
Potassium bromide (x).....	.....	3.5	2.75	0.93
Quartz (x)...............	.....	5.75	2.65	1.52
Rochelle salt (x)...........	.....	....	1.77	0.566
Rock salt (x).............	.....	4.78	2.17	0.979
Silver...................	.....	3.80	10.50	3.9
Slate...................	.....	4.5	2.60	1.17
Steel....................	.....	5.81	7.8	4.76
Sulfur dioxide............	.....	0.213	2.92	6.23
Tantalum................	.....	3.3	16.6	5.56
Tin.....................	.....	3.32	7.29	1.99
Tourmaline (z)............	.....	7.54	3.10	2.23
Transformer oil...........	.....	1.39	0.02	0.128
Tungsten................	.....	5.46	19.30	8.32
Turpentine..............	.....	1.37	0.881	1.21
Water (fresh)............	.....	1.43	1.00	0.143
Water (salt).............	.....	1.51	1.025	1.55
Water vapor.............	.....	0.401	0.0048	0.19
Wood...................	.....	4.17	0.5, 0.8	0.17–0.35
Zinc....................	.....	....	7.10	2.71

The velocity of shear waves is

$$c = \sqrt{\frac{G}{d}}$$

where G = modulus of rigidity.

This velocity is about 48 per cent of that of the longitudinal one. Tables of shear-wave velocities can be computed from the longitudinal ones using this factor.

The velocity of Rayleigh or surface waves is (about)

$$c = 0.9 \sqrt{\frac{G}{d}}$$

It can be shown that the constant (numerical) multiplier changes with the properties of the medium.

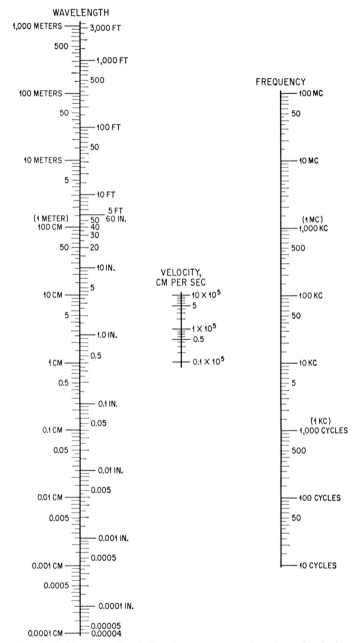

F$_{IG}$. 1-12. Nomograph relating frequency, wavelength, and velocity.

Velocities in Liquids and Gases. Only L waves can be transmitted in liquids and gases. In such cases it is usually assumed that the vibrations take place too rapidly for heat to exchange. The velocity in either a liquid or gas is then[1]

$$c = \sqrt{\frac{K}{\rho B_{is}}} = \sqrt{\frac{1}{\rho B_{ad}}}$$

where K = ratio of specific heats

B_{is} = compressibility at a constant temperature

B_{ad} = adiabatic compressibility

Measurements of velocities are made in liquids in order to get an idea of their chemical and physical characteristics. A large number of such measurements have been made and will be found in the literature.

Two main methods of measurement are used. The interferometer is used for both liquids and gases.[2] Pulse methods have been more recently applied, and the time of travel of a pulse measured.[3] In any of these formulas any consistent system of units may be used.

Frequency and Wavelength. The usual relation among frequency, velocity, and wavelength holds for ultrasonic waves. They are related as

$$\lambda = \frac{c}{f}$$

where λ = wavelength

c = velocity

f = frequency

Common wavelengths are given in Table 1-4 and a nomograph of the formula in Fig. 1-12, from which the third value can be read when two are known.[4]

Superposition. It can be shown theoretically that the same section of a medium may concurrently transmit a number of different waves, which do not interfere with each other in motion and which travel individually. These can therefore be considered as completely independent and separate.

Moreover, in addition to superposition, there appears to be some evidence that each wave traveling in the material acts to affect others in the same area by producing areas of compression and expansion.

Scattering. Attenuation losses result whenever ultrasonic waves pass through a material, due to reflection and scattering at the grain boundaries (especially in metals). This loss may be an important source of attenuation and is proportional to grain volume and the fourth power of

[1] L. Bergmann, *op. cit.*

[2] G. W. Pierce, *Proc. Am. Acad. Arts. Sci.*, **60** (1925) 271.

[3] F. A. Firestone, U.S. Patent 2,398,701 (1946).

[4] B. V. Henvis, Wavelengths of Sound, *Electronics*, **20** (1947) 134.

ULTRASONICS

TABLE 1-4. WAVELENGTHS IN COMMON MATERIALS (20°C)

Material	Frequency, Mc			
	½	1	2¼	5
	Wavelength, cm			
Air....................	0.0688	0.0344	0.0153	0.00688
Aluminum..............	1.244	0.622	0.277	0.124
Bakelite...............	0.518	0.259	0.115	0.0518
Brass..................	0.886	0.443	0.197	0.0886
Copper.................	0.924	0.462	0.206	0.0924
Glass..................	1.040	0.520	0.231	0.104
Lead...................	0.426	0.213	0.0947	0.0426
Magnesium.............	0.533	0.267	0.119	0.533
Mercury...............	0.284	0.142	0.0631	0.0284
Nickel.................	0.952	0.476	0.211	0.095
Polystyrene............	0.534	0.267	0.119	0.0534
Quartz.................	0.150	0.575	0.255	0.115
Steel..................	0.162	0.581	0.259	0.116
Transformer oil........	0.278	0.139	0.0618	0.0278
Water................. ...	0.290	0.115	0.0645	0.0290

frequency in accordance with Rayleigh's calculations. As the frequency is raised, losses become attributable to diffusion (when $\lambda \gg$ grain size). Scattering appears most important up to $\lambda <$ [(grain size)/3].[1]

In diffusion-type losses, the attenuation is a function of the waves' free path between grain boundaries. The phenomenon appears similar to heat transfer, but the theory is incomplete.

Plane and Spherical Waves. Ultrasonic waves may usually be considered as essentially plane; i.e., the amplitude of motion over a plane perpendicular to the direction of wave travel is uniform. As a result, the orbits of the elements are in a straight line instead of being elliptical or circular. The size of the vibrating area and the distance that the waves have traveled both affect the shape of the wavefront. Generally as the distance of propagation increases, the wave becomes more nearly plane.

A purely spherical wave is one produced by a point source, from which it spreads out evenly in all directions. Since the control of wave direction is important, such waves are rarely used in practice except in the theoretical consideration of ultrasonic effects and in certain specialized applications. The difference between a plane and a spherical wave is illustrated in Fig. 1-13.

[1] W. P. Mason and H. J. McSkimmim, *J. Appl. Phys.*, **19** (1948) 940.

Rectilinear Propagation. Rectilinear propagation is a characteristic exhibited by ultrasonic waves because of their short wavelength. In such a case the wave motion is transmitted in a straight line. Therefore, energy cannot travel around sharp discontinuities. It is this property which makes it possible to use these waves for locating small objects, since any such small inhomogeneity will cast a sharp shadow behind it.

As the wavelength becomes shorter and shorter, the wave motion more closely approaches the ideal condition of absolute rectilinear propagation. However, the characteristic is pronounced enough to be noticeable at almost all ultrasonic frequencies.

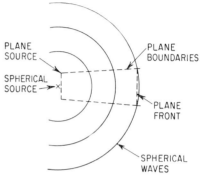

Fig. 1-13. Path of plane and spherical waves.

Beams. A beam of ultrasonics is propagated through a material with very little divergence. Although such a beam can be considered to be confined to the projection of the face of the transducer, in reality there is always some spreading. This spread is a function of the ratio λ/D, where λ is the wavelength of the ultrasonic wave and D is the distance across the transducer face.

In an ordinary circular quartz plate the energy is located in a cone whose half angle of spread is given by

$$\sin A = 1.2 \frac{\lambda}{D}$$

This formula will not give exact experimental results, because the way in which the crystal is mounted affects its beaming characteristics. For example, edge effects may produce secondary beams.

These secondary rays are not determined by the relation above but have greater angles of spread. However, in practical work the basic beam is the only one of consequence.

When ultrasonic waves hit the face of a material in which they are to be propagated, only the main beam will be transmitted through the interface and actually enter the medium, since the transmitted energy depends on the angle at which the waves hit. There is such great refraction in the ordinary case of an oil-to-metal surface that any beam diverging at more than a comparatively small angle is totally refracted. This angle is about 15 deg from the normal and is determined by the ratio of the velocities of the ultrasonics in the two media: the one from which the waves are transmitted and the one that they enter (Fig. 1-14). The figure shows how parts of a beam hitting at an angle greater than the critical value are bent so much that they do not cross the interface. In the figure, *A* represents such a refracted ray.

The beam may be scattered in other ways than by its normal divergence. For example, if the medium in which it travels is full of small dispersed discontinuities or is of very large grain size, the ultrasonic energy will be broken up and reflected and refracted in a haphazard manner. This may occur even between neighboring crystals

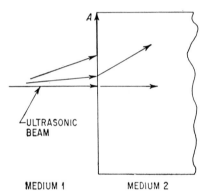

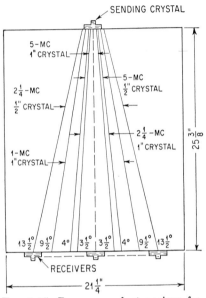

FIG. 1-14. Action of a wave at a boundary.

FIG. 1-15. Beam spread at various frequencies from a given transducer size.

of different elastic properties. In this way the energy may be diffused by continuous reflection.

This difficulty can be minimized by lowering the frequency of transmission, thus initially widening the beam. However, because of the now longer wavelength, the energy will not be affected by the small discontinuities but will pass through them without reflection. In other words, with a given transducer size, the beam spread becomes greater as the frequency goes down but the internal scattering becomes less. However, the usual transducer is large enough so that the sharpness of the beam is still maintained even at the lower frequency.

Figure 1-15 shows the way in which beams of ultrasonic energy of different frequencies fan out from a vibrating body. Figure 1-16 shows the possible effects of the mounting in producing secondary lobes. Besides the normal beaming effect, many special means have been tried for focusing the beam of ultrasonics more sharply. Some of these are discussed in the later context.

Experimental Examination of the Beam.   The distribution of the ultrasonic energy in a beam can be explored experimentally in several ways. One such way is shown in Fig. 1-17.   In this case the energy is sent out by a crystal and is transmitted through a medium.   A second crystal is used as a receiver on the opposite side of the medium to explore the field and determine its intensity.   The amplitude can then be read at several points and plotted.   By changing the thickness of the medium, the beam can be explored at various distances from the sending crystal.

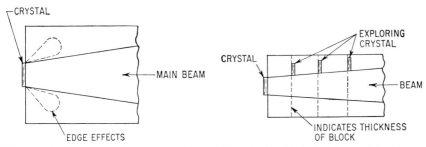

FIG. 1-16. Secondary beams resulting from mounting effects.   FIG. 1-17. Method of exploring beam spread.

Transmission through Thin Plates.   In the case of ultrasonic waves traveling through a thin plate, Lord Rayleigh showed that the plate might or might not be transparent to the passage of the waves, depending upon its dimensions and physical properties.   Such a situation is significant in ultrasonics, since there are certain thicknesses of materials (in the case of thin parts) that cannot be penetrated by the waves.   This action was experimentally verified by Boyle and Lehmann.[1]

The case will be considered only where the waves are perpendicular to the part.   Work was also done by Shraiber[2] on this problem.   It was shown that transmission was greatest when the part thickness was a whole number of half wavelengths (or a suitable number of quarter ones).

When a thin sheet whose thickness is gradually changing is ultrasonically scanned, certain regions may appear to be opaque, which may be due to defects in the material or to the phenomena described.   The part is impenetrable when

$$\frac{t}{2n-1} = \frac{c}{4f}$$

where f = frequency
c = velocity
t = plate thickness
n = integer

[1] R. H. Boyle and J. F. Lehmann, *Trans. Roy. Soc. Canada*, **21** (1927) 115.
[2] D. S. Shraiber, Testing of Metals by the Use of Ultrasonics, *Z. Lab.*, **9** (1940) 1001.

since

$$\frac{c}{f} = \lambda \qquad t = \frac{2n - 1}{4}$$

The amount of variation of frequency to get a maximum transmission is

$$\frac{f}{f_1} = \frac{2n}{2n - t}$$

where f is the original frequency and f_1 the one it is changed to. Shraiber decided that a frequency variation of 7 per cent would cause a sheet to be always penetrable.

This reasoning is partly responsible for the use of variable-frequency ultrasonic generators in the through type of material testing. The frequency of generation is varied over the above range. The same effect can be accomplished by the transmission of several frequencies concurrently.

It is sometimes important to design plates for minimum or maximum transmission. For example, backing plates of suitable dimensions may be designed to reduce back radiation to a negligible amount.[1] This can be done by using a plate of metal of about a half wavelength.

The calculations are based on the assumption that all the standing waves exist only within the plate and the transducers are coupled directly to it. Methods for accomplishing such variations in frequency over a given range will be discussed in Chap. 8.

Other applications are numerous, and the case is very important in designing efficient reflecting and transmitting plates.

Absorption. *Theoretical Considerations.* There have been a number of investigations of the amount of absorption in various solids, liquids, and gases. The results have not been uniform, and in most cases the theoretical and practical results have not agreed.

Most of the later investigations made in the field of absorption depend upon the measurement of sound radiation pressure at various points along the ultrasonic path. These measurements may be carried out by using a torsion balance, which twists a given amount for a certain degree of radiation pressure. In order to accomplish these experiments accurately, all other disturbances, except those to be measured, must be eliminated. Such disturbances, for example, may take the form of motion of the liquid. The motion can be eliminated by placing the torsion balance in an enclosure made of a thin film of celluloid or similar material which does not allow it to pass through but does transmit the ultrasonic waves. The measurements cannot be made entirely exact, since the presence of the balance itself affects the radiation field.

---

[1] W. P. Mason, U.S. Patent 2,415,832 (1947).

For this reason optical methods have been applied. In these methods a beam of light is transmitted through the liquid under test and the absorption estimated from the intensity of the diffracted rays.

More recently, the amount of absorption has been investigated by the pulse method. In this system a pulse of given amplitude is sent through the medium that it is desired to investigate and the peak-to-peak amplitude of the pulse is measured at various points along the path. The energy at each point is proportional to the size of the pulse, and the decrease in size is a measure of absorption.

Methods of making absorption measurements are considered at length in Chap. 6.

Classic Theory. The common classical explanation of the absorption of ultrasonic energy is contained in the following description by Stokes. Stokes[1] and Kirchhoff[2] ascribed the absorption of sound to heat conduction and internal friction. The resultant equation is

$$2\alpha = \frac{4\pi^2 f^2}{c^3 \rho_0}\left(\frac{4}{3}\eta + \frac{K-1}{C_p}k\right)$$

where η = coefficient of viscosity
f = frequency of the wave
ρ_0 = mean density
c = velocity of sound
K = ratio of the specific heats
C_p = specific heat at constant pressure
k = thermal conductivity

The quantity 2α is the intensity absorption coefficient of a plane wave and is defined by

$$I = I_0 e^{-2\alpha x}$$

where the intensity I_0 falls to a value I after traveling a distance x.

Stokes defined the viscosity contribution as

$$\alpha_1 = \frac{8\pi^2 f^2 \eta}{3c^3 \rho}$$

and Kirchhoff the amount due to heat conduction as

$$\alpha_2 = \frac{2\pi^2 f^2}{c^3 \rho}\frac{K-1}{C_p}k$$

Generally speaking, the amount of absorption is not a problem in any ultrasonic system used for testing, measurement, or agitation. However, it is very important in signaling systems where large distances are

[1] G. G. Stokes, *Phil. Trans.*, **8** (1845) 287.
[2] G. Kirchhoff, *Pogg. Ann.*, **134** (1868) 177.

to be transversed by the ultrasonic waves. Experimental values are usually several hundred times those computed from these formulas.

Motional Impedance. The electrical impedance of a circuit driving an ultrasonic transducer is influenced by the vibration of the transducer. Because of this vibration a back emf is generated and impressed on the circuit, just as in the electrical case. This back emf will act to oppose the impressed one, and as a result there will be a change in the circuit impedance. The change is referred to as the *motional impedance*, and the amount that is generated is an indication of the efficiency with which the transducer is vibrating.

Beats. Beats can be produced by having two sources of energy of nearly the same frequency physically close to each other. The resulting ultrasonic wave will be the result of superposition. The energy of the two waves is added, and a resultant wave produced whose amplitude varies with that addition. The difference in frequency between the two sources is the number of beats produced.

Beats may occur between electrical and ultrasonic signals in certain cases, i.e., between electrical oscillations themselves and those signal variations caused by the ultrasonics. It is important to realize this when designing instrumentation, since the beats may vary in intensity so that a signal is produced which is very similar to that produced by a discontinuity in the ultrasonic path itself. This is especially true in continuous-wave systems when tanks containing liquids are used.

Although the two waves beating with each other are of high frequency, the beats produced may actually be sonic if the frequency difference is of that order. Beats are sometimes used as a method of indicating the presence of energy or to measure the frequency of an unknown wave.

Doppler Effect. It can be demonstrated that the frequency of a source of energy seems to vary when either the source or its receiver is moving with respect to the other. This is known as the *Doppler effect* and has many interesting manifestations in nature. If the receiver moves toward the source, the frequency rises; and if the motion is away from the source, the frequency lessens. The amount of increase or decrease is

$$f = 2f_0 \frac{v}{C}$$

where f_0 = original frequency
v = amplitude of motion
c = velocity of sound in medium

The Doppler effect can be used as an indicator of the presence of ultrasonic waves by noting the change in frequency as an ultrasonic source approaches a reflecting surface or vice versa. Such a change may be in the form of an audible or an ultrasonic indication.

Cancellation Effects. Like other types of waves, ultrasonic ones exhibit cancellation effects. In other words, waves of the correct phase may add up to zero displacement. Such effects can be noted experimentally if two sets of holes are drilled a quarter wavelength apart in a block of material and the amount of reflecting surface is balanced by drilling more holes in one or the other group until there is no reflection indicated from the combination. The energy reflected from each is then canceling out that from the other.

Cancellation effects do not ordinarily occur in natural situations to such an extent that absolutely no resultant energy is reflected, since the reflecting surfaces are usually not perfectly regular or spaced exactly the proper distance apart.

Cavitation. Cavitation originally was used as a term to describe erosion of parts caused by the action of cavities in liquids. This is now referred to as *cavitation erosion*, and cavitation is defined as the formation and collapse of cavities in liquids, either gas or vapor filled.[1] The cavities are caused by a pressure drop in the liquid. The bubbles then collapse as the pressure is increased. Rosenberg[2] lists numerous bibliographies on the subject.

Cavitation bubbles may be broadly divided into several forms:

1. Those formed by several smaller bubbles coming together
2. Those formed by degassing the liquid
3. Those formed by the addition of gas (previously dissolved in the liquid) due to the alternating pressures (gaseous cavitation)
4. Those formed by the decrease in pressure (vaporous type)

The last two are most commonly referred to in the literature. Since the vapor-filled bubbles cause erosion and are at the basis of many "sonic" phenomena such as cleaning, they are of more interest and are therefore more widely considered. The gaseous type are larger than the vaporous.

As ultrasonic waves of high intensity pass through a liquid, bubbles may be observed to collect at certain points. These bubbles seem to be due to gas that is expelled from the medium.

The bubbles will tend to form where the ultrasonic waves have their nodes and may be very well defined. Generally, the more volatile the liquid the larger the volume of bubbles that collect. Hydrostatic pressure[3] seems to be a controlling factor of the action.

---

[1] M. D. Rosenberg, *Tech. Mem.* 26, *ONR Contract N*50 *ri*-76; F. G. Blake, *Tech. Mem.* 12, Harvard Univ. Acoustic Research Lab.

[2] Rosenberg, *loc. cit.*

[3] R. W. Boyle, *Sci. Progr.*, **7** (1928) 89.

The amount of energy necessary to cause cavitation can be measured experimentally. The gas expelled from the medium has been determined to be either wholly air or a very high percentage of it.

The action does not seem to indicate any actual rupture of the liquid itself, but the forming and destruction of these bubbles have a strong effect upon agitation systems and form the basis of many of the phenomena associated with them.

Cavitation may be produced by either thermal, chemical, or mechanical action. Ultrasonics will also produce cavitation. When the cavities are small and essentially empty, their collapse produces shock waves of great intensity. Cavitation may destroy solid objects, such as ship propellers, or cause chemical or other action in liquids.

An attempt to treat cavitation mathematically is complicated by the nature of the problem which is very involved and is influenced by the characteristics of the medium, such as viscosity, surface tension, compressibility, etc.

When cavitation is produced ultrasonically it often causes bubble formation on the face of the transducer. When the transducers are of the focusing type, the cavitation may also appear at the focus. These bubbles may interfere with the transfer of energy from the transducer to the liquid.

The effects of sonically induced cavitation have been extensively studied,[1] especially in connection with biological and emulsification effects. It is generally agreed that the removal of dissolved gases from the liquid greatly curtails the effect. It also appears likely that particles in the liquid act as nuclei for the cavitation bubbles.

The onset of cavitation is influenced by all the characteristics of the system, i.e., temperature, hydrostatic pressure, type of excitation, viscosity, etc.

Cavitation Nuclei. Many experimentors have pointed out that the presence of a particle or bubble in a liquid seems to act as the nucleus for cavitation. The theory has been extensively explored in connection with exploration of the tensile strength of liquids.[2] These cavitation nuclei may come from small amounts of gas which remain in cracks or elsewhere in the liquid, or from dust particles with a diameter of about 5×10^{-5} to 10^{-3} cm which themselves have a surface roughness which allows for cracks (mean diameter about 10^{-6} cm). Dust particles of this size always seem to be present.

When an acoustic signal occurs, a few cycles evidently result in a

[1] H. B. Briggs, J. B. Johnson, and W. P. Mason, *J. Acoust. Soc. Am. (JASA)*, **19** (1947) 664.

[2] H. M. V. Temperley and L. L. G. Chambers, *Proc. Phys. Soc. London*, part I, **58** (1946) 428; part II, **58** (1946) 436; part III, **59** (1947) 199.

movement of the liquid surface and a small bubble results, which in turn acts as a nucleus.

After a liquid has cavitated, it takes several hours to recover.

Cavitation Noise. As cavitation occurs streamers of bubbles are formed. A characteristic hissing noise occurs which is easily audible. In addition, noises may be picked up on a hydrophone.

Pressurization. An increase in pressure may suppress cavitation. The pressure acts as a sort of bias on it. However, increasing the pressure does not increase the violence of cavitation which is determined by the ratio of the radii of the bubbles R_m (maximum) to R_0 (initial size).

Erosion. As indicated, destruction of a solid immersed in a cavitating liquid occurs. In some cases this is detrimental and in others is the basis of ultrasonic tools, i.e., soldering, etc. Action is pronounced using water and other liquids.[1] Some studies have been made of the amount of material removed from various materials under differing conditions. However, much remains to be done in this connection. This effect has been suggested as a means of measuring ultrasonic fields.

Transformation of Waves. When a wave of any kind strikes a boundary between two media of different acoustic impedances at any angle other than 90 deg, a transformation may take place and the wave may be changed into another type. The theoretical conditions for such a transformation are discussed below.

A common example would be an L wave passing from a liquid to a solid and hitting the solid at an angle. At the boundary between the liquid and the solid, reflected L and S waves and transmitted L and S waves may form with different amplitudes and different angles of travel, depending on the angle at which the wave hits and also on the impedances of the materials. Since S waves will not travel in liquid, only the reflected L wave and the transmitted L and S waves remain. Thus, under certain appropriate conditions, the type of wave may be changed. Figure 1-18 shows diagrammatically what may happen when an L wave undergoes such a transformation, in this case traveling within a solid and hitting a boundary between the solid and a gas (i.e., as a metal block in air).

Changes such as these can be very misleading if all the types of waves which may appear at such a boundary are not taken into account. It should also be noted that in the case of liquids incident on solids, the results will be misleading unless the liquid wets the solid. Wetting agents may be included to assist in obtaining intimate contact.

The case of liquids incident upon solids is of practical interest in studying earthquakes and in the design of transducers where a volume of liquid is imprisoned between the transducer and the medium. It is also of

[1] T. C. Poulter, *The Frontier*, **10** (1947) 7.

concern in testing objects that are inspected in a liquid bath, in delay lines, etc.[1]

As indicated, waves traveling in a metal or solid part supported in air exhibit the same tendency, and a number of signals may be observed, which are caused by the originally generated wave hitting a boundary at an angle. This results in the generation of different types of waves,

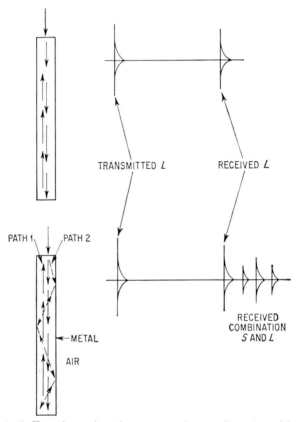

Fig. 1-18. Transformation of wave types in a medium (metal in air).

which, in turn, again hit a boundary and repeat the phenomenon. In this way a large number of extraneous signals may be generated, each traveling at its own velocity and in a different direction. When observed on a receiver, the resulting signal is so confused that it is impossible to interpret.

A part whose dimensions are such that waves are likely to strike a boundary at an angle will cause the transformation of wave energy.

[1] J. B. Macelwaine and F. W. Sohon, "Introduction to Theoretical Seismology," Wiley, 1936; C. G. Knott, *Phil. Mag.*, **48** (1899) 64.

Thin or irregularly shaped sections are particularly apt to produce such an action.

Types of Ultrasonic Waves and Their Velocities. As already mentioned, several types of ultrasonic waves can exist. Such waves are the *L*, *S*, surface, and flexural waves briefly described heretofore.

The theoretical discussion of these types of motion is important, since it correlates the several fields (sound, vibration, ultrasonics, etc.) of which ultrasonics is a part, and gives a more specific view of what is occurring. The treatment is necessarily very brief and discursive. These waves may occur in any of the forms of modulation already mentioned. *The type of ultrasonic wave refers only to the particle motion, not in any way to the waveshape.*

Theory. A particle in any material can obviously experience three distinct displacements: one in the *x* direction (usually called *u*), one in the *y* direction (called *v*), and one in the *z* direction (called *w*). Any particle motion can therefore be resolved into a combination of three displacements.

From any test on elasticity,[1] equations describing the motion of these particles are given as

$$(\lambda + G) \frac{\partial e}{\partial x} + G\Delta^2 u - \rho \frac{\partial^2 u}{\partial t^2} = 0$$

$$(\lambda + G) \frac{\partial e}{\partial y} + G\Delta^2 v - \rho \frac{\partial^2 v}{\partial t^2} = 0$$

$$(\lambda + G) \frac{\partial e}{\partial z} + G\Delta^2 w - \rho \frac{\partial^2 w}{\partial t^2} = 0$$

where λ = Lame's constant
G = modulus of rigidity (shear modulus)
e = volume expansion
Δ^2 = Laplacian operator

These are equations of motion and represent types of displacement in which the body in question remains continuous, i.e., in one piece, in equilibrium, so that it does not move as a whole and obeys Hooke's law, that the strain is proportional to the stress. They also represent the motion of the body about a static state in which the forces acting are due only to the internal stresses and shears and to the particle acceleration forces. From these equations, linear types of ultrasonic wave motion of small amplitude can be derived.

The above equations completely describe all the possible types of motion of a particle, subject to the given boundary conditions. Phys-

[1] S. Timoshenko, "Theory of Elasticity," McGraw-Hill, 1936; Lord Rayleigh, "Theory of Sound," Dover, 1945.

ically, however, experimental conditions may not allow the realization of all these motions. The equations to follow are derived from these and represent typical periodic wave motions. The equations represent the theoretical case and may be difficult to apply directly to a practical experiment. They therefore act more as a guide to the experimenter than as an actual exact explanation of a particular phenomenon.

Angular Transmission. The transmission of ultrasonic energy into a medium at an angle other than the normal is of particular importance,[1] and the theory will therefore be briefly considered. This type of transmission has been widely discussed in connection with earthquakes, and any good text on seismology is of interest in connection with it.

When energy is transmitted into a medium at an angle to its face, it must always be first transmitted through a coupling medium. Placing, for example, a piece of the same material to act as the coupling between the crystal and the medium does not meet this requirement, and transmission is then considered to be at right angles to the front surface.

The material that forms the angle may be gas, liquid, or solid as long as the medium into which the energy passes is different. However, in ultrasonic work, transmission from a gas to a solid or vice versa has never been carried out successfully enough to merit special consideration. The other two cases are of great importance in all phases of ultrasonics and seismology.

From what has already been said, it may be readily seen that angular transmission assumes refraction of the wave at the interface between the two separate media. The transformation of types of waves makes angular transmission more complicated than it would otherwise be. However, even in those cases where the beams are not transmitted at an angle, internal reflections or beam spread may cause part of the energy to hit a surface at a glancing incidence. Such an occurrence will bring about a transformation of the wave. A more detailed consideration of this transformation is therefore advisable.

The Law of Angular Transmission. The basic formula for the transmission at angular incidence is known as Snell's law and states:

$$\frac{\sin \theta_L}{c_L} = \frac{\sin \theta'_L}{c'_L} = \frac{\sin \theta'_S}{c'_S}$$

where θ_L = angle of incidence of longitudinal waves in one medium
θ'_L = angle of transmission of L waves in second medium
θ'_S = angle of transmission of S waves in second medium
c_L = velocity of L waves in first medium
c'_L = velocity of L waves in second medium
c'_S = velocity of S waves in second medium

[1] B. Carlin, *J. Am. Welding Soc.*, **27** (1948) 438.

Wave Transformations at Angular Incidence.   In the case of an L wave which is to be transmitted ultrasonically, it can be seen from Fig. 1-19 that when this wave is incident upon an interface between two materials at certain angles, four resultant waves may appear, of which two are transmitted.   One of these two in each case is an L wave, and the other is an S wave.   All these waves may not exist in practice, but they are theoretically possible in certain cases.

The complete action is as follows: When an L wave is incident in the normal direction, it is transmitted through as a 100 per cent L wave. As the angle is rotated from 90 deg, a point comes that is known as the *first critical angle.*   Between 90 deg and this first critical angle the L wave is transmitted into both L and S waves of various percentages.   As the angle continues to rotate, a second point is reached, which is known as the *second critical angle.* In that portion of the rotation between the first and second critical angle only S waves are produced. For those points between the second critical angle and grazing incidence no waves enter the material.   There-

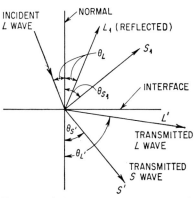

FIG. 1-19. Waves produced at a boundary by an incident L wave.

fore, by choosing the angle of incidence it is possible to choose one of the following conditions:

1. Both S and L waves are produced at the surface, the angle of refraction of the L wave being greater than that of the S wave in every case.

2. Between the critical angles only S waves are produced, and the angle of refraction of the L wave is sufficiently great so that the L wave exists only theoretically and is outside the boundaries of the material.

3. All angles of refraction are so great that there are essentially no waves entering the material.

The case of L waves incident on the material is the more important one, since shear waves cannot be transmitted through liquid and are therefore rarely used in ultrasonic work.   Moreover, it is difficult to couple shear waves into a solid, since a stiff couplant is necessary.

To recapitulate, the critical angles are those angles bounding the regions where only one type of wave, the S type, exists.   The first critical angle (see Fig. 1-20) exists where the transmitted L waves graze the interface; i.e., critical angle = 90 deg.   Between this angle and the second critical angle all the energy is in the form of a transmitted S wave. The L wave no longer exists.

The second critical angle is the one where the S wave first grazes the surface; i.e., $\theta'_S = 90$ deg. Beyond this point there is a total reflection, and no energy is transmitted through the interface.

The critical angles can be calculated from the formula if the velocities are known. The sine of 90 deg, i.e., 1, is then substituted for one sine, and the equation solved for the other. Both critical angles are found in this manner.

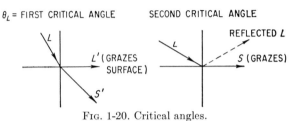

FIG. 1-20. Critical angles.

In a like manner, the equation can be solved for any angle of transmitted S wave or L wave, for a given angle of incident L wave (as long as both exist).

These conditions may exist between two solids when the velocities of various types of wave are defined as in the following paragraphs and as shown in Fig. 1-21. In the case of most liquids incident on solids this is true, and it also may be true with many solids on solids. It is rarely true with solids incident on liquids. The transformations do not occur to any extent between a solid or liquid and a gas because of the very great reflection at an interface.

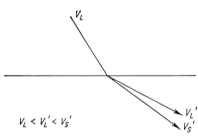

FIG. 1-21. Conditions for wave transformation.

Equations can therefore be set up for these cases and are valuable in determining what happens to the wave types during transmission at angular incidence. Critical angles normally run from about 20 to 60 deg with solid materials incident on other solids.

In choosing two materials it is possible to choose such angles that they will follow the laws of refraction already specified, viz., having two critical angles between which all L waves are transposed into S waves, if the velocities of the media are defined by the following relation. If the velocity of the entering L wave is taken as V_L, the velocity of the refracted L wave as V'_L, and the velocity of the refracted S wave as V'_S, then the condition for the production of total S waves from an incident L wave will be specified only when V_L is greater than V'_L which is in turn greater than V'_S.

Between Two Solids. In the case of an incident L wave on an interface, Knott's equations give

$$S_1 + a(L - L_1) = S' + a'L'$$
$$bS_1 + (L + L_1) = -b^2S' + L'$$
$$-2bS_1 + (b^2 - 1)(L + L_1) = 2\frac{G'}{G}b'S' + \frac{G'}{G}(b'^2 - 1)L'$$
$$(b^2 - 1)S_1 - 2a(L - L_1) = \frac{G'}{G}(b'^2 - 1) - 2\frac{G'}{G}a'L'$$

These four equations with four unknowns give the properties of the waves.

The power equation is

$$adL^2 = adL_1{}^2 + bdS_1{}^2 + a'd'L'^2 + b'd'S'^2$$

where L = amplitude of incident L wave
L_1 = amplitude of reflected L wave
S_1 = amplitude of reflected S wave
S' = amplitude of transmitted L wave
L' = amplitude of transmitted S wave
G and G' = coefficients of rigidity
$a = \cos\theta_L$
$b = \cot\theta_S$
$a' = \cot\theta'_L$
$b' = \cot\theta'_S$
d = density

In other words, the incident power equals the sum of the resultant powers. There will be two critical angles in such cases (as defined before).

From these equations the power at an angle can be computed for any type of wave.

Liquids to Solids. The second most important case is that of transmission of waves from a liquid to a solid. Only L waves exist in the liquid, and both L and S in the solid. The sine law as already stated is, of course, still effective. Knott's equations for this situation are

$$S' = \frac{2a}{b'^2 - 1}L'$$
$$L - L_1 = \frac{a'}{a}\frac{b'^2 + 1}{b'^2 - 1}L'$$
$$L + L_1 = \frac{d'}{d}\left(\frac{4a'b'}{b'^4 - 1} + \frac{b'^2 + 1}{b'^2 + 1}\right)L'$$

The power is $adL^2 = adL_1{}^2 + a'd'L'^2 + b'd'S'^2$. In other words, the incident power must equal the sum of the powers in the resulting waves.

Solids to Liquids. In this case, the equations are as follows:

$$S + S_1 = \frac{2a'}{b^2 + 1} L'$$

$$S - S_1 = \left(\frac{1 - b^2}{2b}\frac{a'}{a}\frac{1 - b^2}{1 + b^2} + \frac{d'}{d}\frac{1 - b^2}{2b}\right) L'$$

$$L_1 = \frac{1 - b^2}{1 + b^2}\frac{a}{a'} L'$$

The power equation is

$$bdS^2 = bdS_1^2 + adL_1^2 + a'd'L'^2$$

There will be two critical angles as usual in most cases.

Solids to Gases (Free Surface). Knott's equations (for *L* waves) are

$$L + L_1 = \frac{2b}{b^2 - 1} S_1$$

$$L - L_1 = \frac{b^2 - 1}{2a} S_1$$

Power is

$$adL^2 = adL_1^2 + bdS_1^2$$

(for *S* waves)

$$\frac{L_1}{S_1} = \frac{4b(b^2 - 1)}{2ab + (b^2 - 1)^2}$$

The direction of travel of any wave and its amount of power can be calculated for any angle of transmission from the formulas given. In some cases waves may be imaginary and therefore cannot actually be measured experimentally. However, the experimental measurement of other types of waves existing at the same time will show excellent agreement with the theoretical results.

Although the discussion has mainly been concerned with the generation of *L* and *S* waves in the material, surface waves may also be generated at the proper angles.

Standing Waves. When a wave traveling in a medium meets a reflecting boundary, it is reflected back to the source. If energy is continuously sent out and reflected, the two waves may reach a state of equilibrium in which the sum of the energy becomes stable. The amount of energy at various points in the path of travel, however, may differ and points of maximum and minimum may be set up.

In some cases standing waves are desirable (for example, when agglomeration of particles is desired). They are, however, undesirable in flaw detection where the indication from the standing wave hides the desired signal. Standing waves are the basis for certain optical effects of ultrasonics and provide means for dramatic demonstrations of the presence of ultrasonics.

Methods of Generating Ultrasonics. There are a number of ways in which ultrasonics can be generated. The method chosen depends upon the power output necessary and the frequency range to be covered. Generators of the mechanical type such as tuning forks or Galton whistles can be used up to about 10,000 cps. Power-driven whistles are capable of producing large amounts of energy. One special type of whistle sometimes used is the gas current generator. Another mechanical method of producing ultrasonic waves is the vibration of a rod of glass or metal.

With the possible exception of whistles and sirens, few of these mechanical methods are used in the generation of ultrasonics for practical purposes. The frequency range mechanically attainable is extremely limited, and all high-frequency ultrasonics are generated by other means.

Some ultrasonic generators use a spark gap or an arc of direct current to produce vibrations. Units such as these are based upon thermal principles and are not commonly used at present.

The most common and the simplest method of producing high-frequency ultrasonics is by the use of magnetostriction or crystal transducers. Magnetostriction is used when frequencies of the order of about 30,000 cps are needed, while crystals are used for most frequencies above that and can be easily driven in the megacycle range to generate frequencies as high as about 15 Mc. Much higher frequencies can be obtained by vibrating the crystal at one of its harmonics. Recently, motor generators have been used at the lower ultrasonic frequencies.

All practical methods will be extensively discussed hereafter.

Analogies. In some cases procedures for solving problems in certain fields are more complete than in others, and if equations or structures in the latter can be identified with those in the former, common procedures can then be used to get problem solutions. This identification of mutual similarity between fields is known as *analogy*. Analogies may be between electrical and mechanical characteristics, or between acoustical and electrical or acoustical and mechanical ones. The application may be made in either direction.

In acoustics, analogy to electrical systems is common. Pressure difference is analogous to voltage, acoustic flux, or volume velocity. The acoustic resistance is the real component of the acoustic impedance (dissipates energy), and the acoustic reactance is the imaginary component (results from stiffness, etc.). Acoustic inertance is analogous to electrical inductance; and acoustic compliance is the analogue of capacitance and is the volume displacement produced by unit pressure.

CHAPTER 2

CRYSTALS FOR ULTRASONIC USE

There are several possible means of producing ultrasonic waves. Of these, one of the most common is the crystal transducer, where "crystal" refers to a number of natural and synthetic materials which exhibit piezoelectricity or similar phenomena.

Types of Crystals. The most popular types of electromechanical converting systems are the piezoelectric and magnetostrictive ones, although there are also other types, viz., the mechanical, electromagnetic, electrostatic, etc. These last types have not been extensively used in generating acoustic waves and are not of much interest in ultrasonics at present except possibly in sound ranging. However, they will be separately considered in Chap. 5, since it appears likely that improvement in transducer design could change this situation.

The piezoelectric effect is of great importance in certain types of ultrasonic work, although the magnetostrictive is also widely used and will therefore be discussed separately. The former effect occurs in several natural and artificial crystals and is defined as a change in the dimensions when an electric charge is applied to the crystal faces. For purposes of consideration here the electrostrictive effect is included under piezoelectric. *Electrostriction* refers to a distortion which is proportional to the square of the electric displacement. Crystals such as barium titanate exhibit this effect to a marked degree. Once polarized, however, they may be included in the piezoelectric type.

In the past, quartz crystals have been almost exclusively used for generating ultrasonic vibrations in solids and liquids. They are still widely used for sending and receiving at low powers and will therefore be described first. Attempts to use them at high powers have not been entirely successful owing to difficulties in holder design because of the high voltages required.

Especially in ultrasonic work at the higher frequencies, where there may be contact between the transducer and a solid medium or where great power is not important, longitudinally or shear vibrating quartz crystals are still most commonly used.

Frequencies produced by quartz blanks cover a range from a few hundred kilocycles to about 25 Mc when vibrating in a fundamental mode and can extend to very much higher frequencies when operating at a harmonic frequency.

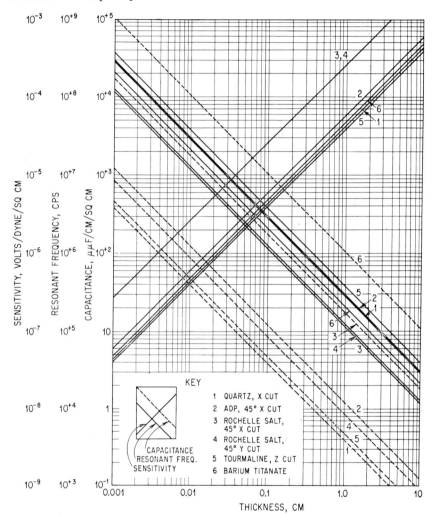

FIG. 2-1. Chart for determining electromechanical characteristics of various crystals. [*A. I. Dranetz, G. N. Hewatt, and J. W. Crownover, Barium Titanate as Circuit Elements, Tele-Tech, **8** (1949) 28.*]

History. Langevin was one of the first to apply piezoelectric effect to the problem of ultrasonic generation when he was commissioned by the French government during the First World War to find a means of locating enemy submarines which at the time were attacking French vessels. He found, after considering the problem, that the piezoelectric effect

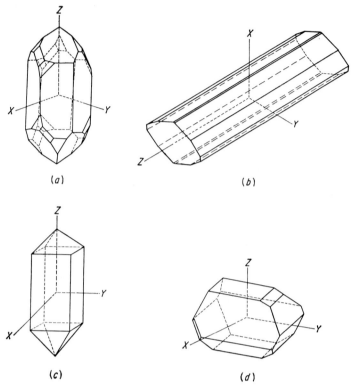

(a) (b)

(c) (d)

FIG. 2-2. Crystallographic axes. (a) Quartz; (b) Rochelle salt; (c) ammonium dihydrogen phosphate; (d) lithium sulfate.

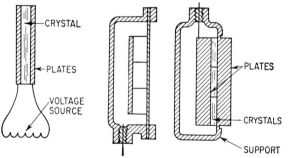

FIG. 2-3. Langevin transducers.

made the quartz crystal useful for this purpose, and his patent[1] discloses the idea of a mosaic of crystals cemented between steel plates (Fig. 2-3) and used to generate and receive ultrasonic waves.

The quartz crystal has the property of expanding and sending out an ultrasonic wave when a voltage is applied to it, and it can also produce an

[1] P. Langevin, British Patent 145,691 (1921).

electrical signal when it is mechanically vibrated. The device was not used during the war of 1914 to 1918 to any extent, since its development was not completed soon enough. However, since that time, quartz and other crystals have become the basis of many underwater detecting and signaling means, of listening systems, and of depth-finding devices. Of course, since the date of Langevin's patent a huge number of additional experiments has been carried out.

Besides quartz, Rochelle salt is one of the principal materials used in the generation of ultrasonics, especially in the low-frequency ranges and for use submerged in a liquid, as in submarine signaling.

A. M. Nicolson[1] of the Bell Laboratories did pioneer work with the Rochelle salt crystal at about the same time that Langevin was working. The piezoelectric effect in Rochelle salt is considerably greater than it is in quartz. However, the units are much softer and therefore more subject to breakage and damage than quartz. On the other hand, in submarine work the transducer is protected by its housing, and Rochelle salt can therefore be used.

During the Second World War several other artificial crystals were developed, mainly for submarine work. These crystals have characteristics especially adapted to such applications. More recently, barium titanate and lithium sulfate have come into common use in industrial applications.

From every point of view—durability, economy, ease of manufacture, and simplicity—the quartz crystal is one of the most desirable of all the types of generating units that may be chosen for ultrasonic work. The x-cut crystal is the most commonly used, since it generates longitudinal or L waves. For the production of shear waves, y-cut crystals are used; but this type of wave motion will not travel through liquids or gases, in which there is no shear elasticity. Also for use with solids y cuts must be coupled to the work by special means. For these reasons y-cut crystals are not widely applied.

The Quartz Crystal. Natural quartz is an extremely stable material, both chemically and physically, and very hard (7 in Mohs' scale). It is usually found in the shape of a six-sided prism with a pyramid attached to each end. If the points of these pyramids are joined by a line, that line is defined as the *optical* or Z axis.

The X axes are also called the *electrical* ones and are defined by lines passing through the opposite corners of the crystal. There are therefore three X axes to each natural piece of quartz. The Y axes are perpendicular to the sides of the figure. There are therefore three of these also. Both of these axes are perpendicular to the Z or optical axis.

[1] A. M. Nicolson, *Proc. Am. Inst. Elec. Engrs.*, **38** (1919) 1315.

Plates or blanks can be cut to either of these axes (or in many other ways), and in each case they have certain definite characteristics. Blanks can be cut for fundamental vibration up to about 10 to 15 Mc. Beyond this range they become so thin that they develop a tendency toward mechanical failure. Accordingly, crystals for higher frequencies are cut at a subharmonic frequency.

The crystals must have parallel faces and be polished free of all kinds of chips or cracks; otherwise they will not vibrate freely. Optical emery finish is usually satisfactory for ultrasonic work.

The Piezoelectric Effect. The fact that certain crystals will develop an electric charge when a mechanical pressure or tension is applied was discovered in 1880 by the Curie brothers.[1] This phenomenon was later named the *piezoelectric effect.* Their experiments showed that there was a direct proportion between the mechanical pressure and the resultant charge. Moreover, the sign of the charge changed when pressure changed to tension or vice versa.

The effect is present in many types of crystals, but it is most useful in quartz and Rochelle salt. However, as mentioned, a number of artificial crystals were developed during the late war, which were mainly designed for submarine signaling and are not suited for the transmission of ultrasonics into solids.

The polar axis of a quartz crystal is the direction in which the maximum charge will appear. It is therefore also called the *piezo axis.* This axis can be identified by rotating the crystal. When the rotation is carried out about an axis perpendicular to the polar axis, the crystal is not symmetrical.

The polar axis is important because the blanks used in ultrasonics are cut at right angles to it to get the maximum effect. Moreover, the crystal differs at the ends of this axis optically, chemically, and physically. Etching produces different patterns, and stresses produce charges of different signs.

When a crystal is cut in the x or y direction, it has the characteristic that pressure on the X axis produces a charge on the crystal surfaces perpendicular to that axis. This is known as the *longitudinal direct effect.* The transverse direct effect will produce the same charges that pressure on the X axis would produce but will do it as the result of tension on the Y axis.

When tension is changed to pressure or vice versa, the sign of the effect changes, but otherwise there is no other electrical change. Therefore, if an alternating charge is applied at high frequency to the crystal, and if the crystal is properly designed to oscillate at that frequency, it will

[1] P. Curie and J. Curie, *Compt. rend.,* **91** (1880) 383.

follow the applied field. The faces of the crystal will move with respect to each other; and if one face is pressed against the surface of a medium, ultrasonic waves will be produced, enter the medium, and then travel through that medium (if, of course, the medium is able to support the propagation of ultrasonics).

It is not theoretically necessary for a crystal to vibrate or oscillate at its resonant frequency. Crystals can be driven at any frequency whatever; however, the amplitude of crystal oscillation is so much greater at resonance that crystals are rarely used at any other frequency except when there is some definite reason for doing so. A typical reason would be the necessity for thick plates at comparatively high frequencies in agitation. In such a case a low-frequency plate is driven at a higher harmonic frequency. In a like manner high-frequency crystals can be driven at lower frequencies. This is commonly done in resonance work where a crystal is driven over a range covering a group of frequencies all below its natural or resonant one.

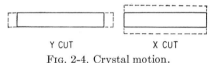

Y CUT   X CUT

FIG. 2-4. Crystal motion.

In this manner resonances in the medium are made to indicate without being influenced by resonance in the crystal.

Quartz crystals can be very sharply tuned to a particular frequency. The logarithmic decrement is about 1×10^{-4}. Any material in contact with the quartz increases the damping, i.e., broadens the tuning of the blank.

A crystal will vibrate in different directions or manners depending on its cut. These modes have been widely studied and can be understood by examination of Fig. 2-4. The first sketch shows the way in which a y-cut crystal vibrates, and the second, the way in which an x-cut crystal does. The crystal may also oscillate at any harmonic, usually an odd one. In harmonic vibration, even more complicated patterns result.

Crystals do not ordinarily vibrate in one direction only, even though designed to do so. There is always sufficient movement in the other dimensions to be of practical importance. Thus, a crystal that is to vibrate in the X direction must not be clamped rigidly about its edges, since in that case its vibrations will be strongly damped. For this reason crystals are ordinarily relieved in all dimensions other than the one in which vibrations take place. This may be accomplished by careful design of the support. In the case of resonance measurements just the opposite is true, since only one type of wave must be allowed to exist. The crystal is therefore rigidly clamped in such a manner that all other types are prevented. For these and other reasons the pattern of vibration on the face of the crystal may be extremely complex. These are referred to as *Chladni patterns*.

The Reverse Piezoelectric Effect. Lippmann predicted the reverse effect in 1881 and pointed out that not only will vibrating the crystal mechanically cause electric charges but that placing electric charges on the crystal will produce mechanical vibrations. This action is sometimes called the *longitudinal reciprocal* or *transverse reciprocal effect,* depending upon whether the crystal acts in the x or y direction. Moreover, when the sign of the applied charge is changed, contraction changes into expansion and vice versa. The amount of contraction and expansion was calculated by Voight,[1] who showed that the longitudinal effect in quartz is dependent on the voltage applied, but not on the crystal dimensions. For 3,000 volts applied in the x direction, the expansion is 6.36×10^{-7} cm/cm.[2] Such a small effect is naturally very difficult to measure. However, methods of doing this have been worked out in the literature.

The entire action of a crystal transducer therefore consists of the direct effect, i.e., the production of electrical signals when mechanical forces are applied to it and vice versa. These two effects form the basis of many ultrasonic systems.

Some Theoretical Considerations. The classic theory of the piezoelectric effect may be found in the literature. However, a few facts that may be of interest are abstracted here.

As indicated, when a crystal is subject to a compression or expansion in the proper dimension, an electric charge appears on it. This charge is directly proportional to the pressure.

The amount of charge that appears is also determined by a characteristic of the crystal, known as *piezoelectric modulus,* that has been experimentally measured. If δ is the modulus for quartz, it is

$$\delta = 6.32 \times 10^{-2} \text{ esu/kg}$$

In both the direct and reverse effect this modulus is an indication of the efficiency of electromechanical conversion. The modulus is a constant and remains identical for any one material.

However, although the charge is proportional to both the force and the modulus, it is essentially independent of the crystal thickness, temperature, and area over a wide range. In other words, the basic relationship is that the field intensity is directly related to strain. This is very fortunate, since variations in temperature or area often occur in practical work and it is preferable that the variation in ultrasonic energy caused by these factors be a minimum.

---

[1] W. Voight, Grundlagen zu einer allgemeinen Theorie der piezo und pyroelektrischen Erscheinungen an Kristallen, *Abhandl. Ges. Wiss. Göttingen,* **36** (1890) 51.

[2] L. Bergmann, "Der Ultraschall," VDI Verlag, Berlin, 1942; translated by H. S. Hatfield, "Ultrasonics and Their Scientific and Technical Applications," Wiley, 1944.

Ny Tse Ze[1] examined the limitations of the piezoelectric effect. He discovered that the changes in the dimensions in quartz were proportional to the applied voltage until an application of about 3,000 volts/cm. Above this point the change in dimensions reached a limit. He also discovered that the temperature should not exceed 300°C. Piezo activity is practically constant between the temperatures of 20 and 300°C, but above that upper limit the piezoelectric modulus falls off sharply. The maximum value of the modulus occurs at about 200°C. At about 573°C, this entire piezoelectric effect stops. When crystals are used under extreme heat, they must be heated gradually; otherwise they will shatter.

Ny Tse Ze also stated that the highest possible frequency using a quartz plate as its fundamental was 50 Mc, for which the plate thickness was 0.055 mm. Higher frequencies are possible if partials (harmonics) were used. Crystals of this order of thickness are very fragile; and unless the crystal is faced with a protective material, a more practical limit is 10 Mc.

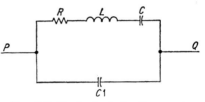

FIG. 2-5. Equivalent circuit—quartz.

These limitations dictate where crystals can be used. It is sometimes desirable, for example, to send vibrations into masses of hot steel. Granted that the materials by which the crystals are mounted will allow it, work up to these limitations is possible. Generally the crystal mounting is more critical in respect to temperature than the quartz itself.

Resonance and Antiresonance. The equivalent circuit of a crystal is composed of L, C, and R values which, when substituted for the crystal, act like it. Owing to the nature of crystals this is possible only for limited frequency ranges, and it is usually chosen near resonance. In general a different circuit is necessary for each mode of vibration (or at least different values for the constants in the circuit).

Figure 2-5 shows the equivalent circuit of a crystal. It is unusual to tune crystals by means of gaps (between the crystal and the plating) in ultrasonics, and the ungapped case is therefore pertinent. Luckily this is the simpler situation.

If the crystal is now activated by a generator of low internal impedance it will vibrate at two frequencies, the series and parallel resonance (antiresonance). These frequencies are essentially determined by the values of C and C_1.

$$\omega_s = 2\pi f_s = \frac{1}{\sqrt{LC}}\left(1 + \frac{R^2 C_1}{2L}\right)$$

$$\omega_p = 2\pi f_p = \frac{1}{\sqrt{LC}}\left[1 + \frac{C}{2C_1} - \frac{R^2(C_1 + C)}{2L}\right]$$

[1] Ny Tse Ze, *Compt. rend.*, **184** (1927) 1645.

In other words as C_1/C becomes smaller, the two resonant frequencies approach each other.

For quartz C_1/C is over 100; for Rochelle salt and other artificial crystals it is much less.

For parallel resonance the series reactance would become infinite if the resistance were zero. This is the reason for the shape of the curve of series reactance (Fig. 2-6).

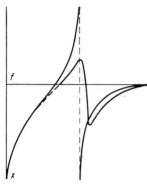

FIG. 2-6. Series reactance vs. frequency for a crystal.

Crystal characteristics may be measured by various methods. One of the most commonly used is based on antiresonance. By means of a signal generator and oscilloscope the resonant and antiresonant points are measured. Generally no calculations are necessary since this in itself is the information wanted. However, if necessary, piezoelectric characteristics can be obtained.[1]

The Circle Diagram. The impedances of resonators may be represented by a circular locus.[2] This represents the operation over a limited frequency range (or over one equivalent-circuit set of values for R, L, and C). Figure 2-7a represents impedance, and 2-7b admittance. R remains constant as the frequency varies, but X changes and so does Z. Similarly g (conductance) remains constant; b (susceptance) and Y (admittance) vary with

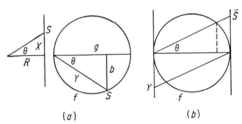

(a)   (b)

FIG. 2-7. Circle diagrams, R, L, C in series; admittance and impedance combined.

frequency. It may be shown that $Y = \cos \theta / R$, which is the equation of a circle with a diameter $1/R$, whence the figure.

Using proper scale values, the two diagrams may be superimposed.

More complete discussions of this technique will be found in the literature.

Design of the Quartz Crystal. *Longitudinal Waves: x-cut Crystals.* An x-cut crystal is usually mounted with an electrode on each face for

[1] W. G. Cady, "Piezoelectricity," McGraw-Hill, 1946.
[2] A. E. Kennelley, "Electrical Vibration Instruments," Macmillan, 1923.

impressing the exciting voltage on the blank and for making contact with the charge produced by vibrating the crystal by ultrasonic waves. This electrode may be either a plating or an actual plate of metal. For the fundamental frequency a longitudinal vibration occurs in the thickness dimension of the crystal. If λ is the wavelength of the stationary wave that is excited in the quartz crystal because of its natural resonance, then the thickness of the plate

$$t = \frac{\lambda}{2}$$

The density of quartz is 2.654 g/cm³; Young's modulus is 770×10^9 g/cm/sec². The velocity of ultrasonic waves in quartz in this direction is

$$c = \sqrt{\frac{E}{d}} = 540 \times 10^3 \text{ cm/sec}$$

However, $\lambda = c/f$ and $t = \lambda/2$. Therefore

$$f = \frac{c}{t} = \frac{2,700}{t} \text{ kc/sec}$$

where t is the thickness in millimeters.

Experimental values do not agree exactly with this statement, but come closer to

$$f = \frac{2,870}{t \text{ (mm)}} \quad \text{kc/sec}$$
$$= \frac{0.1126}{t \text{ (in.)}} \quad \text{Mc/sec}$$

This difference is probably due to the fact that there is movement in other dimensions than the X. These movements produce shear waves and other effects not considered in the original formula.

Shear Waves: y-cut Crystals. In the case of shear-wave crystals, the theoretical and experimental design formulas agree well, since there is little effect on the oscillations in the y direction due to thickness vibrations. The formula is therefore

$$f = \frac{2,700}{t \text{ (mm)}} \quad \text{kc/sec}$$

where t is the dimension in the y direction. Or

$$f = \frac{0.0771}{t \text{ (in.)}} \quad \text{Mc/sec}$$

Shear waves may also be produced by x-cut crystals used with plastic wedges, as indicated on page 48. A list of crystal thicknesses and frequencies is given in Table 2-1.

TABLE 2-1. CRYSTAL THICKNESS

f, Mc/sec	t, in.
x cut: $f = \dfrac{k}{t} = \dfrac{0.1126}{t}$	
0.1	1.126
0.300	0.375
0.600	0.188
1.0	0.113
2.0	0.05763
3.0	0.0377
4.0	0.0282
5.0	0.0226
6.0	0.0188
12.0	0.0095
y cut: $f = \dfrac{k}{t} = \dfrac{0.0771}{t}$	
1.0	0.0788
2.0	0.0394
3.0	0.026
4.0	0.0197
5.0	0.016
6.0	0.013
12.0	0.0065

Surface-wave Crystals. In order to produce surface waves, a special y-cut crystal may be used. The thickness of this crystal is computed in the usual manner for y crystals. However, the x dimension is designed to be about seven times that thickness. Rayleigh waves will then be sent out over the surface of the part parallel to the X axis (Fig. 2-8). This type of crystal may propagate other types of waves as

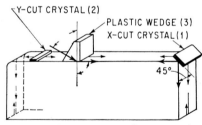

FIG. 2-9. Arrangements for generating surface waves.

FIG. 2-8. Surface wave crystal.

well, especially shear ones. However, crystals designed to these considerations operate satisfactorily for measuring and testing purposes.

A second method of generating surface waves is by means of an x-cut crystal held at a 45-deg angle against a corner of the medium. A third way is by means of an x-cut crystal used with a plastic wedge at a suitable angle. This last method is obviously more practical to handle and also produces more usable power. The design of wedges is considered in Chap. 3. These typical methods are shown in Fig. 2-9.[1]

[1] E. G. Cook and H. E. Van Valkenburg, *ASTM Bull.* 198 (May, 1954).

Tourmaline. Tourmaline lends itself to the production of higher-frequency ultrasonic waves than quartz. The thickness of a plate for producing a particular frequency can be computed from

$$t = \frac{364,000}{f}$$

where t = thickness, cm

f = frequency

This results in a plate about 35 per cent thicker than quartz for the same frequency. The wavelength of the energizing electric wave is accordingly

$$\lambda = 82.5t \qquad mm$$

where t is the thickness of the tourmaline plate. Plates that have a fundamental frequency of 150 Mc have been reported. The piezoelectric modulus of tourmaline is

$$5.78 \times 10^{-8} \text{ cm}^{\frac{1}{2}} \text{ g}^{\frac{1}{2}}$$

The main limitation to the use of tourmaline is its scarcity in nature in usable sizes.

Barium Titanate. Barium titanate is a generic term covering a number of components which may be molded into crystals with electrostrictive properties. The physical dimensions of the barium titanate bar or disk will change in proportion to the applied voltage, at least as long as that voltage is small compared to the voltage used for prepolarizing the crystal. Prepolarizing is necessary to make the material piezoelectric, since it does not have this property as formed. The prepolarization is carried out by placing an electric field across the crystal at temperatures above the Curie point of about 120°C and then gradually cooling it. This voltage is about 2,000 volts/cm of thickness. There results a crystal which performs many of the functions of quartz, but its electric impedance is low, and therefore the voltage which must be placed across it to make it operate is also low. The ratio of voltage between quartz and titanate is about 100, i.e., $\frac{1}{100}$ of the voltage will produce the same power. The material may be cast, pressed, or extruded into many different shapes, the most common of which are flat disks, bars, hollow cylinders, and sections of spheres. Silver faces are painted or baked on the surfaces to which electric voltages are to be applied. Two typical shapes, the bar and disk, are shown in Fig. 2-10. For the bar, the bar length mode refers to the changes in dimension along the axis marked 1. Change in dimension along the axis marked 3 is known as the *bar thickness mode*. In the case of the disk, the *radial mode* is the name given to changes along the axis of the radius, while changes in the thickness are called the *thickness mode*.

Dielectric Constants. The physical constants of the material are shown in Fig. 2-1. These constants are the usual ones also given for quartz, that is, density, dielectric constant, Young's modulus, Poisson's ratio, and piezoelectric coefficient. These constants are defined elsewhere.

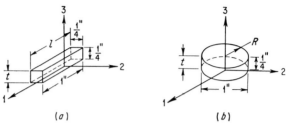

Fig. 2-10. Barium titanate units.

The addition of lead to the barium titanate seems to improve the aging and possibly the temperature characteristics. Figure 2-11 shows various types of titanate transducers and the types of mechanical motion in the various common shapes.

The resonant frequency of titanate elements depends on their size and shape, and on the mode of polarization and vibration. Most elements have multiple resonances; thus a hollow tube is resonant radially in length and in wall thickness. Common tubes would have resonant frequencies at about 20, 40, and 400 kc. Liquid may be passed through such transducers for treatment.

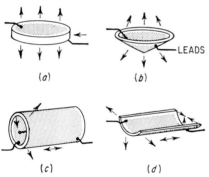

Fig. 2-11. Motion of common shapes.

Bowls have been used where small concentrated areas can be covered at fairly high frequencies. However, the trend toward low frequencies and high coverage have made these units less popular, except in laboratory applications. These units are resonant in wall thickness.

Low-frequency units may easily be bonded to plates by epoxy or similar cement. Higher-frequency units lose considerable energy when this is done because the dielectric constant of the glue is similar to that of the crystal. They are also more critical as to facing dimensions and generally require resonant facings to get usable power.

Aging. After barium titanate is polarized its activity will fall off at a fairly sharp rate for about 48 hr. After that period, the coupling coefficient will remain more or less constant, although a gradual deterioration takes place.

TABLE 2-2. CRYSTAL CHARACTERISTICS

Type of crystal	Bulk velocity V, cm/sec	Density ρ	Piezo strain coefficient e, coulombs/cm²	Young's modulus $E = V_c{}^2 \rho z,{}^a$ dynes/cm²	Elastance (compliance) $S = 1/E$, cm²/dyne	Piezo stress coefficient $d = es,{}^a$ coulombs/dyne	Specific dielectric constant K	Unit capacitance $C_0 = 8.85 \times 10^{-14}K$ farads/(cm²)(cm)	Unit open-circuit output $V = d/C_0$, volts/cm per dyne/cm²
Quartz, z-cut	5.7×10^5 [b]	2.65 [b]	0.176×10^{-4} [b]	8.61×10^{11}	0.116×10^{-11}	0.0204×10^{-15} [g]	4.5 [b]	0.398×10^{-12}	0.512×10^{-4}
ADP, 45-deg, z-cut	4.92×10^5 [b]	1.80 [b]	0.493×10^{-4} [b]	4.37×10^{11}	0.229×10^{-11}	0.113×10^{-15}	14 [b]	1.24×10^{-12}	0.91×10^{-4}
Rochelle, 45-deg, r-cut	2.4×10^5 [d]	1.77 [b]	5×10^{-4} [e]	1.04×10^{11}	0.961×10^{-11}	4.81×10^{-15} [h]	200 [f]	17.7×10^{-12}	2.72×10^{-4}
Rochelle, 45-deg, y-cut	2.7×10^5 [c]	1.77 [b]	0.307×10^{-4} [b]	1.29×10^{11}	0.775×10^{-11}	0.238×10^{-15}	10 [b]	0.885×10^{-12}	2.69×10^{-4}
Tourmaline, z-cut	7.54×10^5 [b]	3.0 [b]	0.333×10^{-4} [b]	17.0×10^{11}	0.059×10^{-11}	0.0196×10^{-15}	5.5 [b]	0.487×10^{-12}	0.403×10^{-4}
Polycrystalline barium titanate	4.2×10^5 [g]	5.55	....	8.0×10^{11}	....	6.3×10^{-15} [j]	1,200 [k]	106×10^{-12}	0.595×10^{-4}

A. I. Dranetz, G. N. Hewatt, and J. W. Crownover, *Tele-Tech*, **8** (1949) 28.

[a] True if cross-coupling coefficients are neglected.
[b] W. J. Fry, J. M. Taylor, and B. W. Henvis, "Design of Crystal Vibrating Systems," p. 173 Dover, 1948.
[c] *Ibid.*; bulk velocity estimated from given value of longitudinal velocity.
[d] *Ibid.*, p. 4; highly temperature dependent.
[e] *Ibid.*, p. 60; highly temperature dependent.
[f] *Ibid.*, p. 61; highly temperature dependent.
[g] W. G. Cady, "Piezoelectricity," p. 219, McGraw-Hill, 1946, gives $d = 6.9 \times 10^{-8}$ statcoulomb/dyne, or 0.023×10^{-15} coulomb/dyne.
[h] Handbooks give values up to 20 times this figure.
[i] Estimated from longitudinal velocity $V_c = 3.8 \times 10^5$ cm/sec.
[j] Determined by static compressional method; dynamic values differ.
[k] Constant over normal temperature range.

Temperature. The temperature characteristic of barium titanate varies greatly with the particular composition and since there are hundreds of compositions being used, it is difficult to say from any one sample what its temperature coefficient will be. However, many titanates are usable up to a temperature of about 130°C.

Resonant Frequency. Most barium titanate crystals are used in the thickness mode and therefore the frequency is a function of the thickness. The thickness of a barium titanate disk is about 0.1 in. at 1 Mc and 1 in. at 100 kc. Since the relation is a linear one, any other frequency may be calculated from this.

Lithium Sulfate. Lithium sulfate is beginning to be used for ultrasonic apparatus. A megacycle blank is about 0.107 in. thick, making 2.25 Mc about 0.045 in. thick, and 5 Mc, 0.0214 in. thick. Other thicknesses may be computed from this. One of the main disadvantages of the material is that it is soluble in water and must therefore be operated in a holder which completely protects it.

However, lithium sulfate has greater amplitude efficiency than quartz, giving much greater gains (35 times has been quoted). Its acoustic impedance is lower than quartz, giving better coupling. Since the gain is greater, the crystal can be loaded with backings which achieve greater bandwidth. Considerable work has been done using these crystals in medical applications.

General Crystal-design Considerations. *Temperature Coefficient.* Within the limits of temperature already cited, there are variations in frequency due to temperature changes (besides the change in the piezoelectric modulus). The amount of variation is usually expressed as a coefficient and gives the frequency excursion caused by the change in temperature of 1°C. It is desirable that there be a minimum amount of frequency variation caused by temperature.

TABLE 2-3. TEMPERATURE RANGE

Material	Lower limit	Lower working limit	Upper working limit	Upper limit
Rochelle salt.......	Unknown below −160°C	−30°C	45°C	Melts at 55°C
Ammonium phosphate	Disintegrates at −118°C	Unknown	Becomes electrically conductive 68 to 80°C	Unknown (over 100°C)
Barium titanate....	Unknown	Unknown	110°C	Loses piezoelectric properties at 120°C

A. I. Dranetz, G. N. Hewatt, and J. W. Crownover, *Tele-Tech*, **8** (1949) 28.

When the change is in the direction of higher frequency, it is called *positive;* and when it is in the direction of lower frequency, it is called *negative.* Most x-cut crystals have a negative temperature coefficient of about 15 to 25 cps/Mc/°C. y cuts vary more widely, from -20 to $+100$ cps. Other cuts have been developed with a much lower coefficient, but they are not widely used in ultrasonics, since they are not efficient as transducers.

The change in frequency is a function of the change in dielectric constant; and these changes are shown in Fig. 2-12 for various materials.

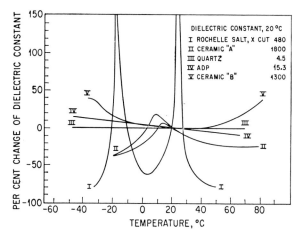

FIG. 2-12. Percentage change of dielectric constant vs. temperature. (*Brush.*)

The change in frequency is not a serious problem in ultrasonic generators, since most of them work satisfactorily within wide frequency variations. A few hundred or even thousand cycles of frequency variation will not affect either the ultrasonic output or any other characteristic of the waves to an appreciable extent.

However, as indicated in the previous section, ultrasonic output may drop with increase in temperature. Such an increase may often occur in agitational systems or in test systems where the crystal is placed on hot steel, etc. Under those conditions serious loss of energy may result.

The crystal is usually cemented in some way to its mounting. If the cement is affected by heat, it may become loose, and the crystal dislodged.

The temperature coefficient is given by the formula

$$\text{Temperature coefficient} = \frac{\Delta f}{f_0 T_{max} - T_{min}}$$

The coefficient is solved for in cycles per second per megacycle per degree centigrade. The change in cycles between the maximum and minimum temperature is Δf. The nominal frequency of the crystal in megacycles is f_0.

There are also cases where the frequency of generation must be controlled very closely, as in systems for the measurement of the physical properties of materials. In such cases the temperature of the whole ultrasonic system must be closely regulated.

Harmonics. The thickness of the crystal blank is inversely proportional to frequency; i.e., it becomes thinner at higher frequencies. As already indicated, when it is desirable to operate at more than about 10 to 15 Mc, a crystal of a lower resonant frequency must be used at one of its harmonics or partials in order to get mechanical strength. Under such conditions the amount of energy supplied by the crystal becomes appreciably less. However, since the crystal is thicker and therefore more sturdy, it can be excited more heavily than one resonant at the frequency, and the loss in energy can be partially compensated for in that manner. This is true, however, only in high-power systems. In test and signaling systems, the crystal is driven at such a low-power level that there is never any question of a power limitation because of the thickness of the crystal. Moreover, it can be shown both theoretically and practically that only the odd harmonics can be excited very strongly because of cancellation of the even ones in the crystal itself.

Harmonics may be of some value where it is desirable to operate a setup at several frequencies without changing crystals. One crystal can then be driven at several different frequencies. Experimentally, it seems easier to drive a high-frequency crystal at low frequencies than a low-frequency crystal at high ones. It is also possible to shock a crystal with a sharp step of voltage and allow it to oscillate or ring at its own natural frequency.

In resonance systems the crystal is always operated over a wide frequency range and the resonance points noted. In such cases the crystal should always be above the highest frequency at which it is desirable to operate. The output will naturally vary with frequency, but the resonance points are sufficiently well marked to make them apparent. The crystal should not have any resonances, either fundamental or harmonic within the operating range. x cuts are used.

For example, a crystal of about 3 Mc is satisfactory for work resonant at about 1 Mc, one of 6 Mc for work at $2\frac{1}{2}$ Mc, etc.

Crystal Shape. Square and round crystals have been most widely used because they are easily procured and handled and operate satisfactorily. Round crystals are probably somewhat superior from the point of view of breakage, since they do not have sharp corners which may chip off. Round crystals also radiate more strongly, since the corners of a square crystal do not seem to put out much power. Holders are easier to make, and polarization effects are less apparent. When the crystals are made very long and thin, other types of vibration may become apparent. The blanks are moreover very fragile.

The Straubel contour[1] is the name given to a special type of cut that is supposed to give greater output. In this type the shape of an x-cut plate is designed so that the edge of a blank is always at a distance from its center which is proportional to the square root of the elastic modulus. Such a plate is shown in Fig. 2-13.

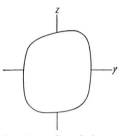

FIG. 2-13. Straubel contour.

The cross-sectional dimensions of a crystal plate are not usually considered in designing crystals for low-power systems, although such dimensions do have some influence on the crystal.

However, this influence is so slight that it can be ignored and satisfactory results obtained. In other words, a 5-Mc crystal may be $\frac{1}{2}$ or 1 in. square or have a diameter of 1 or 2 in. but be designed (in thickness) by the same considerations.

Directional Characteristics. The directional characteristics of crystals have already been considered under ultrasonic-wave characteristics. These characteristics are integral to the crystal dimensions. The mounting of the crystal also strongly influences its directional characteristics (see Chap. 3).

Crystal Plating. Quartz crystals may be plated with faces of metal, usually aluminum, silver, gold, or chromium. These are deposited for physical protection and also to give surfaces on which the electric potentials can be impressed. The films distribute the charge over the face of the blank evenly. The geometry of the films should be such that the two faces do not come close enough to each other for electrical flashover to take place.

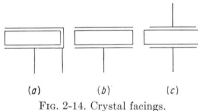

(a) *(b)* *(c)*

FIG. 2-14. Crystal facings.

The facing on the front face of the crystal can be returned to ground either by some form of connection to the work (if it is metal) or by a metal foil (when the medium is nonconducting). The front face can also be returned by bringing the plating around one of the corners of the crystal (Fig. 2-14). In some cases the plating is not extended to the end of the crystal, thus lengthening the voltage breakdown path (Fig. 2-14c).

There are various methods of depositing such films; but for most ultrasonic uses in which a tough surface is necessary, chrome surfaces are best.

[1] H. Straubel, *Z. Hochfrequenztechn.*, **38** (1931) 19.

These are deposited by evaporation in the following manner (similar to that used on astronomical mirrors).[1] First a thin coat of chrome is evaporated, then a coat of copper. The crystal is then removed from the vacuum apparatus and electroplated first with copper and then with chromium. The exact thicknesses are not critical. However, the films should be kept as thin as possible. The parallelism of the plates should be carefully checked. The edges of the crystal can then be cleaned by grinding with an abrasive.

The final film should be checked for adhesion by scoring it with a sharp instrument. If it shows any sign of separation, it should be removed, and the blank replated.

The cleaning of the crystal is very important. Platings will not adhere to a blank that is imperfectly cleaned. Techniques for satisfactory cleaning are therefore indicated in the context.

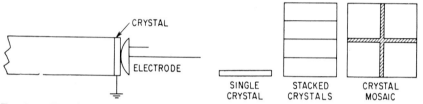

FIG. 2-15. Use of partial electrodes to produce single mode.

FIG. 2-16. Crystal combinations.

Foils may also be fastened to the crystal by gluing or cementing. A thin aluminum foil is sometimes fastened in this manner. Duco cement is satisfactory for such use. When this is done, it is important that the foil be fastened over the entire surface smoothly and evenly and that all excess cement between foil and crystal be removed. The foil should be porous, so that the cement thinner can evaporate. Silver plating of cemented coverings will decrease the vibration of the crystal, in some cases to an extent which will make them useless. Silver paints are also available which provide satisfactory contact.

Leads may be fastened to the foil or plating by soldering or by spring contact.

It has been shown[2] that putting a full electrode on a crystal causes an interference pattern to occur in reflected pulses. This is caused by addition or subtraction of two or more modes, if the phase between successive pulses varies. It is due to the fact that the full coverage generates a fundamental waveguide mode as well as higher modes which travel in the material with a higher phase velocity. It is possible to reduce the effect by using smaller electrodes or by a back contact of the sort shown in Fig. 2-16, which does not touch the crystal over its entire surface. This type

[1] R. C. Williams, U.S. Patents 2,079,784 (1934), 2,151,457 (1939).

[2] W. P. Mason and H. J. McSkimin, *JASA*, **19** (1947) 464.

of electrode drives the crystal at its surface, and the transmitted wave will therefore approximate a phase-mode Bessel function. From a practical point of view, this means that the pulse will die out in an exponential manner rather than becoming larger and smaller. The effect is particularly noticeable with longitudinal waves.

Cleaning Quartz. Before a crystal can be plated, it must be very carefully cleaned, and often individual cleaning processes must be worked out. Dirt on crystals will be found to have individual characteristics depending on the blank's source, history, location, etc. One such cleaning process is as follows: Quartz crystals are placed in a solution of sulfuric acid and potassium dichromate, which is made up in a ratio of 40:1. The solution is then brought to a boil and allowed to continue boiling for 5 min. It is then cooled, and the crystals rinsed in distilled water.

The crystals are then boiled in potassium hydroxide for about 3 min and rinsed again in distilled water. The crystals are then boiled in distilled water, then in ethyl alcohol. Finally they are dried on a wire screen.

It will be seen that the cleaning procedure is involved. However, its importance warrants the care taken. As already indicated, individual variations in the procedure suggest themselves to each experimenter.

Facings of Crystals. Having a face of steel or some other material over the front of the crystal is obviously of great value in prolonging its life. The use of such plates covering the face of a mosaic of crystals has been common practice in the field of submarine signaling, where various types of mosaics were used as early as the First World War.

The covering plates are generally of two basic types. In the first type the steel facing and the crystal are cemented together in such a way that they form a single vibrating system that operates at a certain specific frequency. These are described as *compound oscillators*.

In the second type a piece of steel is placed over the crystal or behind it. However, the crystal continues to oscillate at its original resonant frequency, or at least very near it. This gives the system much greater physical strength but somewhat less ultrasonic output, although not so much less as to be useless. The plates are fastened onto the crystal by soldering or by a cement or wax such as de Khotinsky. Wax is easy to use and is completely satisfactory. The wax is melted on a hot plate, while the holder and crystal are both heated gradually to the melting point of the wax. It is advisable to have a minimum thickness of cement between the holder and the crystal. The crystal and plate are then pressed together while hot and gradually brought back to room temperature. Care should be taken that there are no bubbles in the cement or spots where crystal and plate do not adhere.

Crystal faceplates may normally be designed to be resonant at the frequency of operation for maximum transmission of power. They would therefore be approximately one wavelength thick at the frequency of operation.   Such faceplates are usually used in medical apparatus and in other types of apparatus where the front face of the crystal cannot rest directly on the material being agitated.   The thickness of the plate is therefore very close to twice that of the crystal.   Barium titanate and similar materials may have to be reactivated after facings are connected to them (see Chap. 3).

In addition to metals, quartz plates are sometimes used as faceplates over quartz transducers.

Ultrasonic Output. Sokolov made an investigation of various frequencies of oscillation from 10,000 cps to 130 Mc to determine their use in agitating molten metals ultrasonically in the metal industries.   The results immediately following are partially his.

A crystal transducer has an ultrasonic output that is proportional to the square of the amplitude of oscillation and, of course, to the cross-sectional area of the crystal.   Sokolov stated that the greatest possible mechanical output was obtained from plates of 16 to 20 cm^2.   Plates from 4 to 8 cm^2 were also tried.   The larger the plate the more easily it is destroyed by excessive vibration because of its more inhomogeneous nature.   Limitation to the output is set by the point at which the crystal ruptures.   For maximum output the faces of the crystal should be polished and the edges square.   (This does not refer to the shape of the blank.)   A minimum of damping should exist in the support.

For quartz, an oil with high insulating properties to voltage such as a transformer oil is the optimum medium in which to apply the energy. From 2 to 3 kv can be applied in such a medium to a plate only 1 mm thick.

It is possible to get 150 to 200 watts of ultrasonic energy from a crystal plate 5 mm thick, with other dimensions optimum.   The energy is measured either as heat output in the bath itself or by measurement of the power used in the plate circuit of the agitating oscillator.

The oil above the plate itself is thrown up in a jet about 10 to 15 cm high.   Occasionally, drops of oil will be thrown as high as 40 cm.   The size of the droplets and the shape of the jet of oil are a function of the frequency.   As the frequency gets higher, the jet of oil becomes narrower and narrower, and the size of the droplets becomes smaller.   At 1 Mc the oil becomes very fine mist.

Small bubbles of gas form in the center of the oil bath, and intense heat is generated there.   A test tube of material can be inserted there for agitation and will be violently shaken.

In order to keep the voltage from jumping between plates, the plating is usually kept back from the very edges of the crystal.   Supporting the crystal is the biggest problem.   In order to have intense agitation in the oil, the electrodes should be sputtered or evaporated and as thin as possible.

Bergmann mentions other experiments in which 300 watts of ultrasonic energy was generated and measured calorimetrically. Since no energy can escape from the oil, it is entirely turned into heat, and the measurements are therefore possible. In those experiments 39 kv was impressed on the crystals.

As far as testing or signaling is concerned, the power output problem is a minor one, since only a small amount of power is needed, and therefore no special design is required. More considerations of power output will be discussed under agitation systems.

Barium Titanate. Using barium titanate, powers of as high as 100 watts/cm^2 have been reported. Such powers are possible only where the temperature can be held within the operating range. Focusing naturally raises the amount of power per square centimeter. Experimentally, about 10 to 20 watts per blank (1- by 2-in. face) seems to be average for barium titanate.

Crystal Breakdown. The crystal has certain limits to the amount of power possible to put on it.[1-3] The practical limits seem to be experimentally about 50 watts/cm^2; and the breakdown is in the mounting rather than the crystal, which can take 10^4 watts/cm^2 computed from elastic data. These powers are continuous and pulsed outputs[3] of about 10^3 watts/cm^2 have been reported. When instantaneously higher powers are required, pulsing is therefore valuable.

Crystal Combinations. Crystals can be mounted singly or in mosaics. They can also be stacked for greater output. When they are stacked, they are cemented together with the faces of the same polarity in the same direction. In stacked crystals the output seems to add, i.e., four crystals give four times the output.

The systems are shown in Fig. 2-16. If the crystals are not aligned correctly as to polarity of vibration, the unit will not operate efficiently. All faces in the same direction must be positive or negative simultaneously, and all vibrations in the same direction occur at the same instant. Experimentally, stacked crystals do not add their power output arithmetically, but very great increments of power nevertheless occur.

Mosaics of crystals add to the directional qualities as well as to the power output, since the spreading of the beam is computed for a mosaic as if it were a single crystal. Moreover, since the cross-sectional area is greater, the output is proportionately greater.

[1] T. F. Hueter, *JASA*, **23** (1951) 590.

[2] L. F. Epstein, W. M. A. Anderson, and L. R Harden, *JASA*, **19** (1947) 248.

[3] C. F. Teeter, *JASA*, **19** (1947) 286.

However, the stacked crystals give a more concentrated beam, at least when close to the transducer, since the beam starts as the projection of only one crystal rather than as that of several. It is only when the wavelength becomes of an order of size comparable to the area of the transducer (or greater) that larger areas, i.e., mosaics, result in more concentrated beams.

Compound Oscillators. A compound oscillator is a transducer made up of a combination of steel or other plates and quartz crystals. Usually the steel is fixed to both faces of the quartz. Either a single crystal or any combination of crystals can be used.

When the system is correctly fastened together with very thin layers of glue and with no discontinuities or air bubbles, it may be considered as a unit following the general rules of crystal design. Both longitudinal and shear waves can be produced by compound oscillators.

The material chosen for plates should have an ultrasonic velocity rating as close as possible to that of quartz. Naturally, there should be a minimum of damping in the entire system. Mosaics of crystals may be used for greater output. Generally, the larger the surface the greater the output.

The design formula for a compound oscillator is

$$f = \frac{c}{2t}$$

where f = frequency
c = velocity
t = thickness

Steel plates have been satisfactorily used in combination with quartz to form compound oscillators. Experimental values coincide well with formula.

In other words, a compound oscillator for 5 Mc would have a thickness that is the same as a 5-Mc crystal if the velocity in the metal plates were the same as that in the quartz. When the plate velocity is different, corrections in dimensions must be made, so that the whole unit is a half wavelength thick.

Sokolov[1] investigated both the frequency characteristics and spectra of such oscillators and explored their surfaces, mapping the face patterns by connecting those points which showed equal amounts of oscillation. Fundamental frequencies agreed with the values calculated. He also found evidence of complex partials that were different for different types of facings. The complex frequency response caused by the metal plates

---

[1] S. Sokolov, "Ultrasonic Oscillations and Their Application," Electrotechnical Institute, Leningrad, June 25, 1935.

is due to the fact that they affect both the over-all transducer density and also its modulus of elasticity.

The equivalent circuit of such a transducer may be deduced and consists of a capacitor in series with a parallel combination of a capacitor across an inductance, resistance, and capacitance in series (the same as for a crystal alone).

Compound systems can be driven with such great power that the crystal and plates will be torn apart. However, this is unlikely except in agitational systems or submarine signaling. The compound plate is used only in high-power ultrasonic generators.

Curved Crystals to Fit the Work. Many parts into which it is necessary to transmit ultrasonics have peculiar shapes and forms. For example, they will very commonly be curved. Such parts as pipes, tanks, and shafts fall into this category. In many cases where the piece of material is of radically broken shape, the physical dimensions make it difficult, if not impossible, to make satisfactory contact with the work, except by immersion.

However, in other parts there are smooth curves or changes of contour on which it is impossible to place a flat crystal but which can be compensated for by fillers or by curving the crystals. For example, a crystal may be ground to fit a shaft with an OD (outside diameter) of 10 in. and will transmit ultrasonic energy into it very well.

As the curvature becomes sharper, it is more difficult to grind the crystal to fit. Grinding can be

FIG. 2-17. Curved crystals to fit the work.

carried out satisfactorily on a lathe by mounting a piece of metal of the required diameter and grinding the crystal against it with fine abrasive material. The energy is propagated in essentially the same fashion as with flat crystals. There is, however, a focusing effect from the curved crystal.

A rule of thumb is as follows: If the medium is concave and 24 or more in. in diameter or is convex and 18 or more in. in diameter, flat crystals can be used. Otherwise the crystal must be curved to fit the work (see Fig. 2-17).

The design of curved crystals is essentially the same as that of flat ones of the same frequency. The crystal may be curved on both surfaces or flat on one and curved on the other. The former situation is preferable. The diameter of the crystal should always be slightly greater than that of the work in order to provide a loose press fit.

Focusing Ultrasonics with Curved Crystals. Gruetzmacher[1] made the original experiments with the use of curved crystals for focusing a beam of

[1] J. Gruetzmacher, *Z. Physik*, **96** (1935) 342.

ultrasonics. He was able to get greater ultrasonic action because of the focused, and therefore more concentrated, beam.

The crystal blanks were ground so that the emitting face was concave. This caused the ultrasonic waves to focus at a point in the same way that a lens brings light to focus. Gruetzmacher also made the statement that the ultrasonic energy measured at the focal point of such a crystal was about 150 times that measured at a random sampling of points before the crystal.

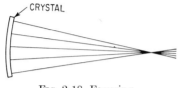

FIG. 2-18. Focusing.

A concentrated beam would presumably be very valuable for agitational work, where a great amount of ultrasonic output is necessary and where the amount of electrical voltage applied must be limited by considerations already mentioned. Figure 2-18 shows how ultrasonic energy is focused.

More recent investigations[1] indicate that the energy measured in front of the crystal face depends not only on this factor of beam spread but also, for a given voltage, on the distance at which the measurements are taken. The energy at a given distance in front of a curved crystal is greater than that at the same distance from a flat one, because the curved crystal actually produces more ultrasonic output. At the sample point the angle of spread of the beam from the curved crystal might actually be greater than that from the flat crystal.

In other words, the greater concentration of energy in front of a curved crystal is due to two factors: (1) the focusing action and (2) the experimental fact that a curved crystal seems to give somewhat greater amplitude of ultrasonic output than a perfectly flat one for a specific voltage impressed. When a crystal is convex, however, there does not seem to be any evidence of greater output. Nevertheless, convex crystals are sometimes used to radiate wider beams. This char-

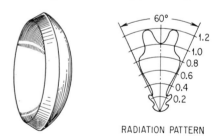

RADIATION PATTERN

FIG. 2-19. Wide-beam crystal.

acteristic is valuable in such fields as submarine signaling, where it is necessary to cover a wide field of search. Figure 2-19 shows a system for spreading the submarine search beam.[2]

The focusing action of crystals, like that of lenses, may be expressed in *diopters*. This is an arbitrary term referring to a lens of 1-m focal length.

[1] L. W. Labaw, *JASA*, **16** (1945) 237.

[2] A. R. Morgan, U.S. Patent 2,399,820 (1946).

Diopters can therefore be transformed into inches of focal length by a simple conversion:

$$\text{Diopters} = \frac{40}{\text{inches}} \quad \text{(focal length)}$$

This terminology is also used in calculating lenses for light.

The design of curved crystals for focusing applications is exactly the same as that of lenses for the same purpose. A suitable text on optics will give such design procedures. The design of separate lenses for focusing ultrasound is considered in Chap. 3.

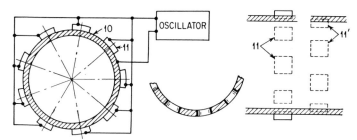

FIG. 2-20. System for flow processing.

Tubular Transducers. In the processing of liquids it has always been apparent that a greater volume of liquid could be passed through a pipe and be processed more conveniently than that handled in a vessel. Such a system has been suggested and is now widely used in various forms (Fig. 2-20).[1]

More recently ceramic transducers have been molded in the forms of tubes or of sections of tubes to allow this same sort of use. In some cases a tube or pipe is mounted within the transducer, similar to that shown in the figure. Coupling by means of fluids may be used, or the transducer may be bonded directly to the pipe.

Testing Crystals for Ultrasonic Activity. The ordinary tests for crystal activity apply somewhat to testing blanks for ultrasonic activity, but the correlation is by no means perfect.

A crystal may have a good deal of activity for the purposes of oscillator control, but the actual physical vibration will not be great enough to make the ultrasonic output sufficiently high for propagating ultrasonic waves. It is therefore sometimes necessary to test crystals for ultrasonic output, which can be done by placing them in a situation where they are actually used as ultrasonic generators and receivers. One such design is shown (Fig. 2-21). A jig supports the crystal to be tested.

[1] B. Carlin, U.S. Patent 2,578,505 (1951).

The blank under test is used as a transmitter to send ultrasonic energy through a medium of a highly absorbent character. A fixed crystal is cemented to the opposite side of the piece and is used as a receiver. This receiving crystal is then connected to a suitable radio-frequency amplifier, and the output of that amplifier is used to actuate a calibrated meter.

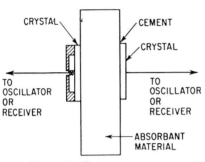

FIG. 2-21. Test arrangement.

This unit may be calibrated against experimental evidence of ultrasonic energy or a known transducer and will provide an excellent indication of the output level. In a like manner, crystals can be rated for their receiving properties when a source of known activity is used. The same arrangement can be used in a tank for high-powered transducers. Other tests will be discussed in the chapter on measurement.

Rochelle Salts. Rochelle salts are probably the most common type of crystal used in submarine signaling. They therefore merit further discussion. These crystals suffer from the fact that their mechanical structure is not sufficiently strong for them to be used in direct contact with anything but liquid media. However, the output of such a crystal is so much greater than quartz that it has found many applications.

Rochelle salt blanks are grown in a chemical solution. The solution is controlled in such a manner that its pressure or temperature changes; and when this is done, crystals form in the bath. Various special methods of producing such crystals have been widely examined and will be found in the literature.

Rochelle salt crystals are so soft that they can be cut with a piece of stretched damp string or with a rubber band pulled back and forth over them.

Any type of electrode can be used on blanks cut from the salt. Electrodes such as fine metal particles, metallic liquids, and foils have been widely used. The most common material is a metallic foil, which is cemented over the faces of the crystal.

Submarine signaling is one of the largest fields for the use of ultrasonics, and Rochelle salts have been widely used up to the present in this field. When most of the units are used in this application, they are driven at a frequency other than the resonant frequency of the crystal. Various special ways of mounting such crystals have been developed; and when they are properly mounted, the crystal is much less subject to critical changes in temperature, etc., than when it is in its free form.

More complete studies of the physical and electrical characteristics of Rochelle salts may be found in the literature. Some of the effects noted are not as yet completely understood. However, these effects are not of great importance in ultrasonic work and will not be considered further here. As far as ultrasonic work is concerned, practical application of the Rochelle salt crystal is limited to the production of waves in liquids, and the special holders necessary for such operations will be discussed elsewhere.

Other Types of Crystals. As indicated, quartz has been the material most commonly used in ultrasonic work done in the past. However, during the war several artificial crystals were developed. For example, the LH type can be used from 100 kc to several megacycles. This crystal is one of a type that produces piezoelectric variations when subjected to hydrostatic changes. The crystal, like certain others, is called pyroelectric because a change in temperature also causes it to develop charges in the same manner that pressure does. In a theoretical sense, the LH crystal has greater activity than Rochelle salts; but because of its capacity effects, it also has very great losses.

The ADP (ammonium dihydrogen phosphate) type is another artificial crystal developed for use under water (at about 50 kc).

Tourmaline would be very valuable ultrasonically except that it is expensive and extremely nonuniform in quality. Owing to this nonuniformity the blanks have a tendency to shatter easily. However, it operates at higher frequencies than quartz, since its thickness at any given frequency is greater, and it is about two and one half times as active as quartz.

Cutting and Grinding Special Crystals. Round crystals can be cut from square ones by means of a circular piece of tubing, with the ends tapered to about 0.010 in. This can be put in a slow drill press or on a lathe, and a grinding compound spread over the face of the crystal. The tubing will slowly cut into the quartz as it is gradually fed downward and as new cutting compound is introduced.

Curved crystals can also be ground on a lathe by cutting a curved template from a metal (see Fig. 2-22) and

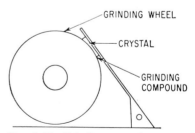

FIG. 2-22. Grinding curved crystals.

grinding the crystal against the template by introducing a grinding compound.

Inside or outside diameters can be ground in the same manner. Both sides of such crystals may be ground, or only one side may be ground and the other left flat.

Curved crystals should be mounted on curved buttons that match them in diameter.   Other than in the amount of curvature, these holders are identical with those described for flat crystals.   Curved crystals are usually a little thinner than flat ones used for producing ultrasonic waves of the same frequency.

Crystals cannot be ground to too sharp a curvature without a great loss in activity.   The exact amount of curvature possible is a matter of experiment.   For test purposes, where the amount of energy is very small, the curvature may be as great as it can be ground.

CHAPTER 3

CRYSTAL HOLDERS FOR ULTRASONIC USE

The design of the crystal is, of course, extremely important in order to get the maximum energy and efficiency from the vibrating system, but often the design of a suitable holder or support within which the crystal will perform its function is at least of equal importance. Since most of the design considerations for such holders have been experimentally rather than theoretically determined, a brief résumé of past experience in this field is of interest.

Many of the first holders were planned for submarine signaling and detection. Since this field is in general outside of the scope of this consideration, these types of holders will be most briefly considered, and only general considerations mentioned.

More recently, holders have been designed for test, agitation, and signal purposes. Very little has been published in these fields, and they are accordingly most completely considered.

Preparing the Crystal. Prior to its mounting in a holder, the crystal is usually plated, both to make electrical contact with the work and also to distribute the charge more evenly over its surface. This process has already been described.

When the transmission is directly into a solid, both faces are usually plated. If the medium is a conductor, it may be grounded to the instrument by a suitable ground pin or clamp. If it is a nonconductor, however, the front face of the crystal must be returned to the ground side of the electrical system that drives it. It is not absolutely necessary that the front face be plated, and in some cases only the rear one is. However, in the case where the medium does not conduct, a foil or facing must be placed over such crystals and returned to ground.

Once the crystal has been plated and suitable leads connected to one or both faces, it is ready for mounting. These leads may be soldered wires, pins, or springs. It is important, when soldering to a crystal or when contacting it in any way, that the contactor does not damp out vibrations by constraining the natural crystal movement. Usually, a single wire soldered to the center of the rear plating provides all the connection necessary. Spring contacts must be designed so that they do not wear away the plating.

Holders.   The simplest way to mount a crystal is merely to lay it on the medium into which it is to transmit ultrasonics and to connect the high-voltage end of a radio-frequency generator to its back face.   A suitable return circuit is provided by grounding the crystal's front face on the medium itself.   This type of mounting works fairly satisfactorily in many cases, but it is awkward to work with and may sometimes be dangerous.   It is therefore rarely used.   The class of mounting is indicated in Fig. 3-1.

However, it is still desirable under certain conditions to have the crystal as free to vibrate as possible.   One way of accomplishing this is to support the blank around its sides by pins or knife edges, which barely constrain it.   This means of mounting is not very convenient, since it is still difficult to handle the unit.   These mountings were originally suggested by Bechmann,[1] who also recommended cutting a groove in the node of the plate for inserting the pins (Fig. 3-2).

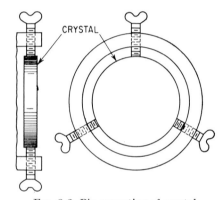

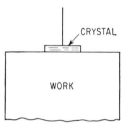

FIG. 3-1. Simple crystal mount.   FIG. 3-2. Pin mounting of crystal.

The most common type of mounting for signaling or test work at the present time is to fix the back face of the crystal to a solid support of some kind, usually referred to in the case of single crystals as a *button* and in the case of a mosaic as a *plate*.   This can be done by solder or by a thin film of cement, such as Duco.   It is important that all excess cement or solder is squeezed out and removed.

When the crystal is entirely free and supported away from any holder, it will oscillate in a harmonic fashion.   However, when it is mounted on a base, it has a tendency to knock against its supports, and oscillations of an uneven character result.   This effect is not serious in most ultrasonic work.   Investigations of the phenomenon were made by H. Becker in Germany.   He also pointed out that a possible shift in the resonance characteristic of the crystal may result from the mounting.

When the crystal is absolutely free, it is almost entirely undamped

[1] R. Bechmann, Entwicklung der Quartzeuerung der Telefunken, Grobsender, *Telefunkenztg.*, **14**, Hf. 63 (1934) 17.

and might not stop vibrating rapidly enough to be satisfactory in a pulsed or modulated communication system. However, the pressure of the front face of the crystal against the medium is generally enough damping to cause free vibrations to die out quickly. On the other hand, when a crystal is very firmly held, the damping may be so great that there is a considerable loss of energy.

In choosing a material on which to mount crystals, it must be remembered that the crystal transmits in both directions perpendicular to its faces, and therefore energy may be radiated into the backing. This energy is, of course, wasted and may cause deleterious effects. It should be avoided by backing the crystal with a material of very small ultrasonic transmission such as air, Bakelite, Catalin, or lead. The crystal cannot then send energy into the button. Air will damp the crystal less than the other substances and is therefore preferable. For this reason, when holders are made of solids, it is advisable to relieve the crystal by an air space behind it. Typical buttons used to mount crystals are shown in Fig. 3-3.

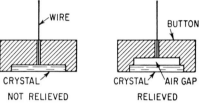

FIG. 3-3. Typical button for crystal support.

In general, crystals will be used for coupling into any of several different media: liquid, solid, or gas. In the case of solids the crystal holder will be held in the hand of the user and slid slowly over the surface of the material under test. For this application the crystal is supported in a holder with one face protruding so that it can be applied more easily to a surface. In the case of liquids or gases the crystal may be supported in any one of a number of ways. One surface must, however, be in contact with the medium, and the other returned to the hot side of the generator. The front facing is connected to ground.

The crystal is either free or clamped at its rear face. These mountings are referred to as *clamped* or *inertia drive*. The latter is the more commonly used. The mathematical derivations and equivalent circuits have been discussed in the literature.

Crystals can be mounted singly, stacked, or arranged in mosaics for greater output and area coverage.

In test and signaling work it is generally desirable to get as much power as possible into a short sharp pulse if the pulsed type of signal is used. In continuous-wave work the holder should always be designed for maximum transfer of power and minimum damping. In pulsed and modulated methods power must be sacrificed, since it is also necessary that the time constant of the crystal, i.e., its time of free vibration after the signal is removed, be less than that of the signal; otherwise it will not follow faithfully. Therefore, damping may actually be added.

In agitation, the crystal is mounted as free as possible. Often the only mounting is to cement its front face to the wall of the tank in which the material to be agitated is contained, while the rest is left in air.

The Holder for Impressing Ultrasonics on Solids. *Longitudinal Waves.* The function of the holder in generating ultrasonics is to support the crystal firmly with its front face far enough advanced so that it makes excellent contact with the material. It should also provide a minimum of damping on the rear face and on the sides so that the crystal can vibrate freely. A protrusion of approximately 0.005 in. is sufficient. The holder must also include a suitable means for grounding the plated face of the crystal and for connecting the high-frequency electrical energy to it without danger of injury to the operators. It must be light and easily held and preferably of a size and shape that will fit into small openings

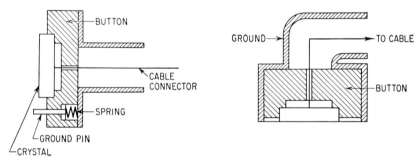

FIG. 3-4. Complete crystal holders.

where testing is to be done or signals impressed. The crystal should occupy the major part of the front face, which should be designed so that the edge of the crystal is near at least one of the edges of the face. This enables the operator to bring the crystal up against fillets or ledges. Figure 3-4 shows common holders used for this purpose.

The holder is merely a support for the button. It may be either straight or bent at any angle. In any case it will usually include a piece of tubing that supports a connector into which a cable can be plugged. Sometimes it is merely a sleeve through which the cable runs. The design of the holder is purely a mechanical one, and there are no real problems associated with it.

The Button. As indicated, the crystal is mounted on a backing referred to as a *button*. The design of this button is of the greatest importance, since it is the item that actually controls the ultrasonic activity of the crystal.

Buttons for test and signal purposes are usually fairly simple and consist of a piece of material that is ultrasonically nonconducting and into which the crystal fits. The crystal is supported about its edges and so mounted that it is constrained a minimum amount. A cutback or shoulder is provided as shown in the illustrations. The crystal is cemented into the button with de Khotinsky or similar cement.

The crystal should fit snugly into the button cutbacks and should be supported in such a way that it does not knock against them. The button should be of material that will not absorb oil or other liquids in which it is operated. Some specific problems of button design are discussed in the following paragraphs.

Air-gap Resonance. Although it is true that ultrasonic propagation in air is heavily damped in a very short distance, it is still possible for air-gap resonance to occur. This term refers to the action that takes place when a crystal is mounted on a button with the back relieved, i.e., with a cutback behind it so that it is supported away from the backing by an air gap. In such a case an ultrasonic wave may travel away from the rear of the crystal through the very small air gap, hit the back wall of the holder, and be reflected back to the crystal. If the total distance traveled compares in certain ways with the ultrasonic wavelengths, interferences may occur. These interferences may either aid or damp the ultrasonic vibration of the quartz, depending upon the specific dimensions.

The velocity of ultrasonics in air is about 1,100 ft/sec. Since the air gap is resonant at one-half the wavelength, the dimensions of a resonant gap differ with the wavelength and can be calculated for any one frequency.

A common ultrasonic test frequency is 5 Mc. At this frequency

$$\frac{\lambda}{2} = \frac{1}{2}\frac{1,100 \times 12 \text{ in.}}{5 \times 10^6 \text{ cps}}$$
$$= 0.0013 \text{ in.}$$

Of course, the effect will cause interference only in the case of generators of L waves, i.e., x-cut crystals.

Physically, the action can be explained as follows. At the moment that the crystal is fully flexed in one direction, a pulse of air starts toward the reflecting surface, hits it, and returns to the crystal. However, the crystal has vibrated in the other direction and is now returning to its starting position. The pulse of air will therefore interfere with its movement, tending to prevent the blank from vibrating as freely as normally. If the action of the crystal is to be reinforced, the pulse of air must return at a time which will push the crystal in the direction of its travel, and therefore gaps of $\frac{1}{4}\lambda$ would be indicated.

In those cases where signal reinforcement is not desired, it is preferable to avoid air-gap resonances. Almost all ultrasonic buttons are designed in this manner. In any case, the distances involved are so small, because of the velocity of travel, that it is extremely difficult to hold design tolerances in terms of fractions of wavelengths.

Another approach is the addition of backings which stop radiation from the back surface. These are more common on high-power systems.

Crystal Damping. It is necessary for the crystal to follow rapid variations not only in order to follow the oscillations themselves but also in order to reproduce the modulation on the electrical or ultrasonic signal. For example, in the use of a crystal with a pulsed ultrasonic system, the crystal should stop oscillating abruptly at the end of a pulse. Otherwise, the original form of the signal is obscured. In order to accomplish this, some loading or damping of the crystal may be necessary. Usually, this damping should be as slight as possible and never more than is absolutely necessary, since it makes the system more inefficient.

However, attempts have been made to fix a mass or load to the back of the crystal in order to damp out any free ringing in the system. Such a

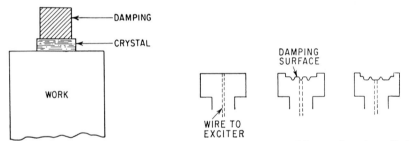

FIG. 3-5. Damping the crystal.   FIG. 3-6. Buttons with different damping effects.

system, disclosed in a U.S. patent,[1] is shown in Fig. 3-5. A material that does not conduct ultrasonically is fastened to the back of the crystal, and a greater bandwidth results, together with a damping of free oscillations. Such systems have the disadvantage that there is a loss in the general amplitude of oscillation and therefore in the over-all sensitivity.

The amount of damping is determined experimentally. Figure 3-6 shows crystals held in buttons in each of which a different area is impressed on the back of the crystal. There is therefore a different damping on each.

These systems may be thought of as varying the bandwidth of the crystals by mechanical means. As the damping becomes greater, the bandwidth also increases. (Damping is sometimes referred to as *dampening.*)

It has already been mentioned that the amount of damping on the crystal can be controlled (at least as far as addition is concerned) by the method of mounting. Generally, the crystal is sensitive to the material to which it is mounted; and if it is firmly held by its backing,

[1] F. A. Firestone, U.S. Patent 2,398,701 (1946).

the amount of damping will vary approximately with the area of cross section that is fastened to the backing and/or comes into intimate contact with it. Thus, if a crystal is held only about its edges and nowhere else touches the back, the damping is minimum, while if the whole area is held firmly, the damping is maximum.

The design of buttons for damping the crystal may be inferred from what has already been said. In each case different amounts are brought into contact with the crystal and cemented firmly.

In high-power units, a minimum of damping is usually desirable.

Standoffs. In testing materials the flaw sometimes falls so close to the test or sending surface that the reflections fall within the body of the transmitted pulse. It is theoretically possible to separate such signals from the pulse by means of either an electrical or mechanical delay between the transmitted pulse and its reflections (see Fig. 3-7.)

Mechanical. A mechanical piece used for this purpose should be long enough to separate the pulse and reflections clearly. Otherwise, secondary reflections from the interface between the standoff and the work may confuse the signals. The diameter of the standoff must be large enough so that waves crossing it and reflecting from the sides will not return during the pulse-signal duration. The sides may also be sintered or corrugated to prevent these reflections.

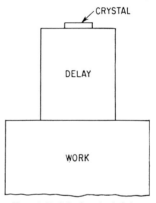

FIG. 3-7. Mechanical delay.

The use of mechanical standoffs of metal for delaying ultrasonic signals is difficult because of internal reflections and the large reflections at the interface.

If no method of separating reflections from the transmitted pulse is used, there is always a minimum distance over which signals can be detected separately; i.e., if a signal only travels for 0.001 μsec and is reflected, it will return so quickly that it is confused with the original transmitted signals. Without special means of delay such as those indicated, the minimum distance that can be easily measured by the echo technique is about ½ in. of steel, i.e., about 4 μsec. However, by special techniques, signals only a fraction of a microsecond away can sometimes be detected.

During the Second World War, standoffs were used to provide delays in ultrasonic echo boxes used in Germany as radar setup devices. In these units the pulse traveled through a piece of material and was reflected and received back after a time interval comparable to those intrinsic to the radar system when actually operating, thus providing a calibrating pulse. Figure 3-8 shows signals provided by mechanical standoffs.

Standoffs may also be used to protect materials, such as lithium sulfate, which cannot be used in direct contact for physical reasons. At the same time they may act to improve impedance matching.

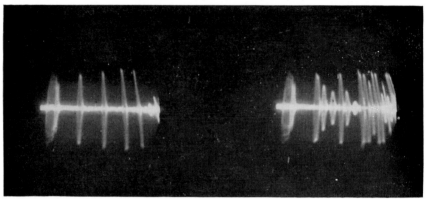

FIG. 3-8. Signals from mechanical delays: (a) delay line only; (b) delay plus additional signal.

Fillers. Where the surface of the medium is slightly curved, in either a convex or concave direction, it is sometimes expensive or impractical to grind the crystal itself to fit the curvature. In order to make contact, a filler may be inserted in the space between the crystal and the work. Any material can be used for a filler, but the closer its acoustic impedance is to that of the crystal the more efficient the results will be. Since aluminum or duraluminum has an acoustic impedance of 1.68×10^6 ohms while quartz has one of 1.52×10^6, there is excellent match between the two materials, and duraluminum is therefore used for fillers. Because of the excellent impedance match, there is a minimum of refraction and reflection. Duraluminum shows less wear and friction than aluminum and is therefore preferable.

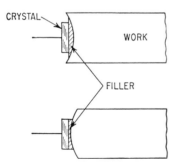

FIG. 3-9. Location of fillers.

Fillers of about 0.050 in. are most satisfactory. As the filler becomes thinner, more energy is transmitted through it but the signal clarity deteriorates. When the filler gets much thicker, there is a strong loss of energy. Figure 3-9 shows the location of a filler between the crystal and the work for both concave and convex curvature.

Liquid fillers can also be used but are not practical because the liquid escapes and must be constantly replenished. Mercury or heavy oils are suitable.

Water Coupling. In some cases, especially when the surface is not perfect or rapid motion is desirable, water coupling may be used. Obviously this is the case where the part under test is immersed in a tank of liquid and the crystal also introduced into the water at a distance from the part. Such a system is shown in Fig. 3-23. The same results may be obtained by having the crystal mounted so that water is trapped in the front of the holder and acts as a couplant (Fig. 3-10).

Such units have been commonly used for material testing. When using the pulse method, the length of the water stream must be sufficient so that the second multiple reflection from the front face of the material under test occurs later than the third or back reflection.

When the liquid is not a conductor and the front face of the crystal not therefore returned to ground, the plating of the front face may be taken around the edge of the crystal to allow a ground wire to contact it at the back. A button (which allows a free access of the stream of water from the sides) should be used to support the crystal itself.

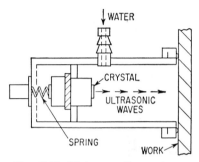

Fig. 3-10. Water-coupling system.

Holders for Transmitting through Liquids into Solids. The liquid-coupling methods already referred to have appeared in various forms. One method of coupling the crystal to the medium is to transmit waves through a small amount of liquid trapped in a container. Such a system is shown in the German Patent 654,673 of December 24, 1937, in which a crystal is supported in a bath in such a way that the energy from it can be focused at some point inside a solid material on which the liquid rests. In this particular case a curved crystal is used. The liquid is kept within the holder by a diaphragm that fits tightly around its bottom and against the medium into which the waves are to be transmitted. Provision is made for continuously adding liquid to the holder. A well or trap may be included to maintain the liquid level.

This type of holder is useful where the surface of the material is very rough or where the contour of the crystal is such that it will not fit directly against the material. The chief disadvantages are its messiness and the difficulty of continuously moving the holder without losing the liquid. Suitable liquids for inclusion are any of those which will transmit ultrasonic vibrations. Of these, mercury is the most suitable, but it is both dangerous and hard to use.

The liquid-containing holder is beginning to have widespread use. It is obviously capable of many variations. The disclosure of the German patent is shown in Fig. 3-11.

Another typical liquid-coupling (flow) type of setup is shown in Fig. 3-12. As indicated before, liquid may be led to the holders through pipes. The crystal is spaced away from the work but a constant ultrasonic contact is maintained by the flow of the liquid. In this figure, the holders are equipped with rollers, which maintain a fixed distance between the

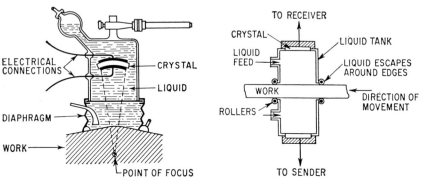

FIG. 3-11. Water-coupling system with curved crystal.

FIG. 3-12. Water-coupling system for through testing.

crystals and the work. The units may be moved in unison over the face of the work.

Support in a Tank. The testing or treatment of parts immersed in a liquid has also been a common ultrasonic approach in the past, and has certain basic advantages since the parts under test can be continuously moved between or in front of the transducers. In such cases, special holders must be designed for the crystals, and, in general, the holder shape is not important, but they must be waterproof and convenient to use. The crystal may be held either perpendicular to the axis of the holder or parallel to it, and the function of the holder is essentially to protect the electrical connections from the liquid and to hold the crystal rigidly. The ultrasonic beams generated in a liquid may be either horizontal or vertical in direction, but the holders should be far enough removed from the surface of the liquid so that troublesome reflections do not occur. Moreover, screens can be placed within the tank either to absorb energy or to protect the holders from stray beams that are reflected back and forth in the liquid. The method of supporting buttons in holders for liquid use is shown in Fig. 3-13.

In certain cases the crystal can be fixed directly to the wall of a tank and radiate through a hole in it. Such an arrangement is indicated in Fig. 3-14. However, this system has a great disadvantage in that it is not sufficiently flexible.   For example, in such a case, when it is necessary to change the frequency of operation, a new tank must be used.   For that and other reasons holders of the types shown in Fig. 3-13 are preferable, except in high-power applications (especially with barium titanate) where the crystal-tank combination is a permanent one and it is only desired to irradiate the material in the tank.   More practical tank arrangements are discussed later.

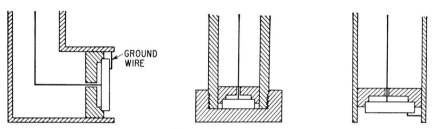

FIG. 3-13. Crystal holders for tank use.

Front Faces.   It is sometimes desirable for mechanical or other reasons to place a metal plate over the face of the crystal.   A typical use would be in the case of a medical transducer consisting of a quartz or other material in a watertight container.   The front face is equal to λ (or a suitable multiple) at the frequency of operation, making allowance for the glue joint which has a tendency to lower the transducer frequency. Figure 3-15 shows a typical unit of this type.

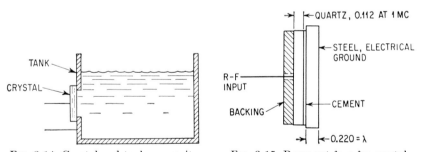

FIG. 3-14. Crystal and tank as a unit.   FIG. 3-15. Resonant face for crystal.

Spring Mountings.   It is sometimes necessary to hold the crystal a fixed distance from the medium, while at the same time moving one with respect to the other.   This can be accomplished by spring-mounting the crystal so that it is positioned before the work by some sort of gauging device.   A desirable feature of spring mount is that the crystal is always held at the same specific pressure.

Spring mounting is especially important for the crystal when it is hand held, since variations in pressure will cause variations in the signal

strength.   A unit that can be used for this purpose is shown in Fig. 3-16.
The high-frequency voltage may be impressed upon the crystal either by
the spring itself or by a separate lead.   The crystal may be sprung within
the holder, or the entire holder may be sprung within an external casing.
When the button is sprung, it should also be keyed so that it will not turn.
Rotation of the unit results in damage to plating and crystal.

Moreover, in cases where it is desirable for the receiver head itself to
follow variations in the contours of a part and rest upon the part, the
crystal can be placed in a flexible head, such as the one shown in Fig.
3-17.   A diaphragm, either of rubber or of a similar material, allows
limited movement of the crystal so that it is always pressed to the part

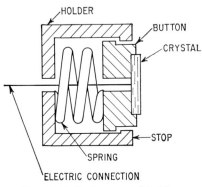

FIG. 3-16. Spring crystal holder.

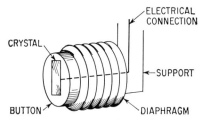

FIG. 3-17. Flexible holder.

no matter what the contour.   This system was first suggested by Shraiber,
who used it to test curved surfaces.   Rubber is attacked by oil, so synthetic substitutes are preferable.

The design of spring mountings is obvious, and mechanical considerations predominate.   However, care must be taken that the button or
other spring member does not bind as it progresses over the work, since
erratic indications will then result.   The spring must not touch the
case or other metal parts of the unit.   A minimum spring pressure is
preferable.

Magnetic Holders.   When working with materials that have magnetic
properties, a magnetic shell may be placed around the transducer, or its
shell magnetized, so that it will adhere to the work.   This is sometimes
convenient, since it helps support the crystal and frees the operator's
hands.   Magnetic wheels, bearings, etc., have been used on special units.

When magnetic holders are used, the crystal button must be sprung,
since otherwise it will not make good contact with the work.

Holders for Angular Propagation.   It is sometimes advisable to transmit energy into a material at an angle, and holders for this purpose can
be constructed.   An angular wedge of material of the same nature as
the medium is fastened to the front of the crystal.   Since the material is
the same and since there is a very thin film of oil between it and the

medium of travel, there will be essentially no refraction at the interface, but the waves will travel directly through into the material in a straight line. There will be no transformation of ultrasonic energy at the interface.

Holders for this purpose have been constructed and used here and in Great Britain and are well known in the art. However, they are not suitable for use with the reflective technique, since there is a great deal of reflection at the interface. If the system is set up to measure the time of travel of a pulse, there will be so much interference because of spurious signals returning from the interface that the real signal cannot be distinguished from them. Ultrasonics have also been transmitted into a material at an angle through a liquid.

When angular transmission is used, it is advisable to have a separate pickup crystal, which also operates at an angle and which receives the energy reflected from the obstacle that it is desired to locate.

Suitable angles for such use are about 30 deg. In the case of liquid couplers, mercury or a liquid of an acoustic impedance matching that of the work should be used; otherwise reverberations, i.e., buildup of reflections within the liquid, will occur. Figure 3-18 shows the placement of angular holders. Complete systems are shown in Chap. 9.

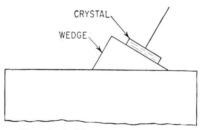

FIG. 3-18. The angular faceplate.

Angles of a material other than the medium may also be used. In that case transformation of waves and refraction both occur. The angles are designed according to the theory of wave transformation, so that only S waves are propagated in the material. Under such conditions there is little reflection at the interface, and accordingly the unit can be used for pulsed reflective applications.

Angles for Beam Conversion. Change of wave types at boundaries have been applied in material testing where it is possible to send an L wave into the material at such an angle that it is wholly changed into S waves in the material (or vice versa). The conversion into only one type of wave is necessary so that false indications do not result from the differing velocities of various wave types when used in pulse equipment. The conversion is carried out by means of a Lucite (or similar) wedge, as shown in Fig. 3-19.[1]

Units of this type may be used to produce surface waves; in that case the wedge angle is chosen so that the refracted angle is 90 deg. The theory of wedge design is considered in Chap. 1. Special shapes of

[1] B. Carlin, U.S. Patent 2,527,986 (1950).

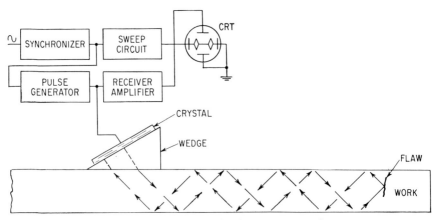

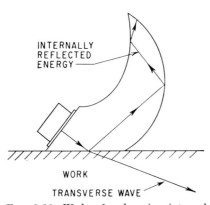

FIG. 3-19. Beam conversion by means of wedges.

wedges to minimize the reflections within the wedge have appeared. One such unit is shown in Fig. 3-20.[1]

Other Means for Controlling Direction. For use in liquids, transducers with various directional characteristics have been developed. Nondirectional magnetostrictive and crystal arrays have been developed for indicating the presence of energy. Laminated ring stacks or circular sections have been used in magnetostriction, and cylinders of barium titanate. However, it is also sometimes desirable to limit the beam to small angles. Transducers or stacks of large size in relation to the wavelength will accomplish this in part, and beam limiting devices (or lobe suppression devices) are discussed elsewhere.

FIG. 3-20. Wedge for damping internal reflections. (*After Sproule and Wells.*) Other shapes have also appeared.

The angles of transmission may also be controlled by using a number of transducer elements and shifting the phase of the signal on each, causing a tilting similar to that caused by a wedge (Fig. 3-21).[2]

Holders for Shear or Surface Waves in Solids. Shear waves can exist only in solids, since there is no shear modulus in liquids or gases. A holder for shear-wave crystals should leave free the two ends of the blank perpendicular to the direction of shear vibration. If those ends are

[1] D. O. Sproule and L. H. Wells, S & T Memo 19/55, *Ministry Supply Gt. Brit.*

[2] L. Batchelder, U.S. Patents 2,408,028 and 2,406,340 (1946).

closely clamped, the vibration of the crystal will be stopped. The buttons are, therefore, constructed in a manner that closely resembles the longitudinal wave button except that the two ends are open. The same button can be used for both surface and shear waves except that in the

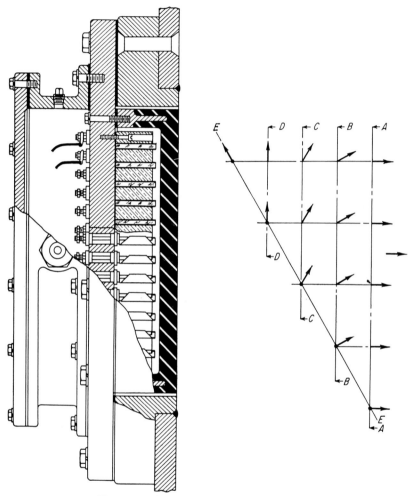

Fig. 3-21. Phase method of beam rotation.

case of surface waves it is usually much longer and thinner than in the case of shear waves.

Surface waves can sometimes be propagated in only one direction by tilting the crystal slightly. The waves will then travel away from the edge that is against the medium. A surface-wave holder is shown in Fig. 3-22.

Rayleigh or surface-wave crystal design criteria already have been discussed. Obviously the button must be designed to fit such crystals. Wedges for producing these types of waves are discussed in Chap. 11.

Beam Interrupter. It is occasionally desirable to interrupt a beam of ultrasonic vibrations that is traveling through a liquid bath. A beam interrupter (Fig. 3-23) can be made that will perform this function. The device consists of a plate that can be interposed in the ultrasonic beam and will not allow the energy to be transmitted through it. Since the reflection from an air-metal interface is practically 100 per cent, the simplest type of interrupter is formed of two sheets of metal or other material between which there is a small air pocket. Sometimes a sheet of material that does not transmit ultrasonics may be included in the air space. Bakelite or a similar plastic can be used. An interrupter should be furnished with a handle by which it can be manipulated.

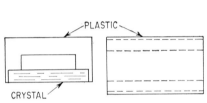

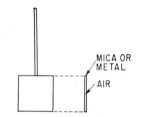

Fig. 3-22. Surface wave-holder.   Fig. 3-23. The beam interrupter.

The design of a beam interrupter is therefore essentially the same as that of the reflecting plate of a torsion balance. The beam interrupter is used as a means of checking indications that occur when working in a liquid. In such a case it is difficult to say whether a specific signal indication results from an ultrasonic wave or not. However, when the interrupter is interposed in the energy stream, the signal disappears when it is an ultrasonic one. If the indication were an electrical one, the placement of the interrupter would not influence it.

Tanks. Most through-transmission systems operate effectively when used in conjunction with a tank containing liquid in which the articles under test are immersed. The liquid acts as the coupling agent and may be oil, water, etc. It also allows the continuous passage of the material between the two transducers. A tank system is shown in Fig. 3-24.

Naturally, some means of moving the material must be provided. This may take the form of rollers or a screw mechanism. Any part of the setup that is to be touched by the operator must be grounded and preferably insulated. The transducers are normally mounted on railings such as those shown in Fig. 3-24 and may be slid back and forth so that their positions can be conveniently adjusted.

The tank should be large enough so that there is very little reflection either from its sides or bottom or from the surface of the liquid. The crystal must, therefore, be deep enough under the surface so that ultrasonic energy, due to spreading or scattering of the beam, does not reach the liquid surface.

Wetting agents, such as Aerosol, will prevent the formation of bubbles on the transducer faces.

Waves or currents in the liquid can be prevented by screens or baffles. Materials such as cellophane will prevent currents without interfering with the passage of ultrasonics.

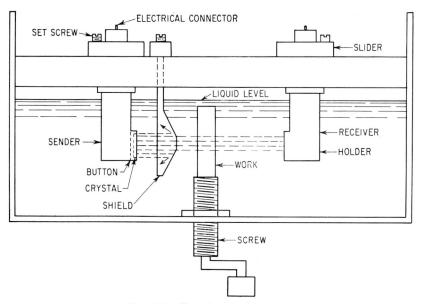

FIG. 3-24. Complete tank system.

Means for filling and emptying the tank easily should be provided. Temperature-control devices and immersion thermometers are also useful. However, close control of experimental factors is not necessary for most applications other than laboratory ones.

An entire system for testing in a tank is shown in Fig. 3-24. Sending and receiving crystals are mounted in the L-shaped holders. The path of the ultrasonic beam is indicated by the dashed lines. A shield is provided for limiting the cross section of the beam. The work is supported in the path of the beam on a turntable on which it can be rotated and concurrently raised or lowered. The entire mechanism operates on a slide on which it can be moved about. This type of system seems to have been originally used by Shraiber. A combination of such systems for testing tires ultrasonically is shown in Fig. 3-25.[1] Various ways of positioning the search units will become obvious from a study of the figure, which illustrates a number of possible combinations.

Tanks the size of large rooms are now in common commercial use for testing materials. Cleaning installations of considerable size have also been made.

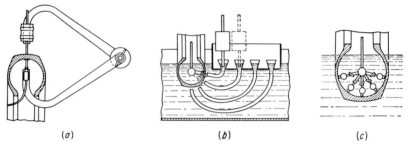

(a)   (b)   (c)

Fig. 3-25. Search unit positions for testing tires in a liquid bath.

Beam-limiting Devices. In certain cases the divergence of the beam may be too great for use. In others waves may be produced that travel in directions other than that desired, and their production may be unavoidable. Such waves cause troublesome reflective effects, which obscure the test or signal results to an appreciable degree. Some of these waves may be produced by the back face of the crystal, and in that case absorptive material may be fastened where it will interrupt them without interfering with the motion of the crystal. Holders of this sort may also

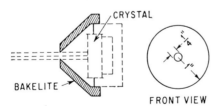

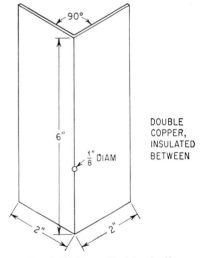

Fig. 3-26. Beam-limiting device.   Fig. 3-27. Beam-limiting baffle.

be used in liquid transmission systems, where the setup is more or less such as that shown in Fig. 3-26. In this case it is desired to test for very small flaws in the work, and the beam is appreciably greater than the size of the flaws. As a result some of the energy will pass around

[1] W. E. Morris, U.S. Patent 2,378,237 (1945).

the flaw and travel through the good material that surrounds it. Since the principle of operation is that the flaw must interrupt the energy in the beam, the whole mechanism is inoperative under such conditions. Therefore use is made of limiting devices (such as Fig. 3-26[1]) in which the aperture is about as large as the smallest flaw being sought. The beam is therefore limited, and the excess portions either absorbed by the baffle or reflected in such a manner that it is not harmful. For this purpose the inside of the baffle may be corrugated to break up the beam or fitted with absorbent material.

The baffle may also take the form of a sheet of ultrasonically non-conductive material held perpendicular or at any angle to the ultrasonic beam or may be formed of two pieces at angles to each other (Fig. 3-27). A number of combinations are possible, but the basic principle is the same. In each case a small hole is drilled to allow energy of the same cross section to pass through. The use of baffles for calibration purposes is now standard.

Coupling the Crystal to the Work. If a crystal is placed on the surface of a dry part, very little energy will be transmitted through the interface into the material because of the great difference in specific acoustic impedance at the interface. It is therefore important that some kind of coupling medium be used. This coupling may be looked upon as a transformer, which matches the impedance of the crystal to that of the work. It therefore preferably takes the form of a liquid whose specific acoustic impedance is somewhere between that of the quartz and that of the material. Probably the most satisfactory material for this purpose would be mercury if this were the only consideration. However, mercury is both expensive and dangerous. Luckily the particular couplant is not critical, and various oils have become popular, the most common of which is a nonconducting transformer oil such as Wenco. Glycerin gets slightly more energy into a metal part but is messy and hard to use. Experiments have been carried out using transformer oil, automotive oil (SAE 20), glycerin, water, benzene, Prestone, chlorine and sugar solution, soapsuds, mercury, and various amalgams. From the point of view of simplicity and economy a thin transformer oil appears ideal. This oil is spread upon the surface of the part, and the crystal pressed upon it. However, the oil must wet the part, and it is sometimes necessary to include wetting agents for this purpose.

When the crystal is used to transmit into water or a similar bath, a wetting agent may be used; otherwise small bubbles will form on the crystal and other solid parts and interfere with the transmission of the ultrasonic energy.

When y-cut crystals are used, a stiffer medium is necessary to couple

[1] B. Carlin, U.S. Patent 2,448,352 (1948).

the transverse vibration into the work.　Liquids will not normally transmit S waves efficiently.　A mixture of rosin and oil will, however, couple them satisfactorily, and a one-half mixture of Texaco Marfak and rosin has proved practical.　The x-cut crystal may, of course, be cemented permanently to the medium by a wax or cement.

In certain cases it is possible to use a thin foil as a couplant between the crystal and the work.　It will be noticed in such a case that the magnitude of energy transmitted depends critically upon the thickness of the coupling.　When a liquid is used, the thickness cannot be maintained constant during work, but the same effect can be accomplished by the use of a foil a few thousandths of an inch thick.　Any material can be used, the principal consideration being the mass per square centimeter.　Aluminum foil is sometimes satisfactory.

Faceplates may also be used in the same manner as coupling devices, and this is very often done in submarine work.　Such a device, as Fig.

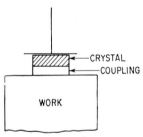

FIG. 3-28. Impedance coupling the crystal.

3-28, for example, shows the addition of a faceplate of an acoustic impedance that is between that of the transducer and the medium into which it is desired to operate.　This plate acts as the transformer to match the acoustic impedances of the work and the medium.　Naturally a plurality of plates to gradually change the impedance is also possible.　In such a case the improvement in loading also has the effect of heavily damping the crystal and shortening the pulse.[1]

For this and other reasons submarine transducers are ordinarily made with a medium between the Rochelle salt crystals and the water itself.　This medium takes the form of a sound transparent window or plate, which is coupled to the sea on one side and to a liquid couplant, such as castor oil, on the other.　The crystal sends waves into the castor oil and through the window into the water.

Matching the Crystal.　Better results may be expected from a crystal when it is properly matched.[2]　This is often done in the holder for reasons of convenience.　The importance of proper matching has been borne out both experimentally and theoretically.　When the transducer is connected directly across the input of an amplifier, the transformation of energy from electrical to mechanical is poor.　However, the addition of an inductance, either in series or in parallel, neutralizes the capacity, and considerably greater efficiency may be expected.

[1] D. H. Howry, U.S. Public Health Service *Grant C*-2423(*C*).

[2] W. P. Mason, "Electromechanical Transducers and Wave Filters," Van Nostrand, 1942.

The value of such a coil can be computed from the formula

$$f = \frac{1}{2\pi \sqrt{LC}}$$

where C = capacity of the crystal and holder
L = inductance of the coil

The capacity of the crystal can be measured (by a Q meter) in its actual operating condition, since it will change with the position of the search unit. Once the inductance of the coil is determined for a given set of conditions, it will remain close enough to the correct value to be fixed at it. The coil can be mounted in any manner but should be placed inside the crystal holder for greater convenience.

For a 5-Mc crystal ½ in. square, about 38 μh is a satisfactory value; for 2¼ Mc 1 in. square, about 340 μh; and for 1 Mc, about 850 μh.

Naturally these coils may be slug tuned if it is more convenient, so that they may be varied in inductance after they are mounted in the crystal holder.

One explanation of the theory involved is as follows. In order to get the greatest amount of energy out, it must be delivered into the radiation resistance. A filter is required to do this and in the ideal case delivers to its output all the power put into it. The addition of a coil in series or parallel to the crystal will accomplish this by counteracting the reactance of the unit capacitance at the frequency at which the crystal vibrates.

The series coil gives a lower input impedance than the shunt type, and several combinations of coils and crystals can accordingly be put in parallel. This is not true of the shunt type of inductance. This is an important factor in submarine work, where groups of transducers are the rule.

The capacitance of the crystal should not be measured at resonance, since it will give misleading results at that point. A frequency far from crystal resonance is preferable; 1,000 cps may be used for submarine units.

Holders for Agitating Liquids. Crystals are widely used in the fields of chemical, metallurgical, and biological research to drive ultrasonic agitation systems. The systems themselves have been the subject of considerable research and are discussed elsewhere.

The simplest form of holder for agitation is to suspend a crystal in a liquid and force it to vibrate. However, in such a case the damping effect of the liquid itself upon the surface of the crystal is appreciable. Moreover, certain liquids do not act as sufficiently good insulators to the voltages applied to the transducer.

Generally, the radiation from one side of the crystal is used. Therefore, only that face need be coupled to the bath. Holders can therefore be used; and since the crystal gets thinner with increasing frequency, the function of such holders is to support the crystal so that the crystal rupture and voltage breakdown will be prevented and the crystal will give maximum ultrasonic output.

Methods and experience with such crystal mounts have been given by Wood[1] and Loomis and others. The first mounting suggestion was simply to lay the crystal on a flat lead plate. A brass ring was then laid over the face of the crystal to bring the voltage to it. The ultrasonic energy streamed out through the hole in the ring. The diameter of this ring was usually somewhat smaller than the cross-sectional dimension of the crystal in order to prevent voltage breakdown. Lead was used for the crystal backing, since it is a nonconductor of ultrasonics.

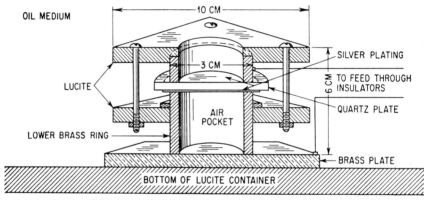

FIG. 3-29. Holder for agitating purposes (quartz).

Gruetzmacher was evidently the first to suggest the use of an air backing. He pointed out that all materials on which the crystal could be laid unavoidably conducted away some ultrasonic energy, and this led to losses in the usable output. He therefore suggested the now well-known expedient of a relieved support of Bakelite or other similar material, which supports the crystal around the edges but leaves a pocket of air behind the main body of the crystal. Ultrasonic output is greater, and damping less.

A more recent arrangement for ultrasonic agitation[2] is shown in Fig. 3-29. The crystal is supported by two electrodes with an air pocket behind it. The entire assembly is held together by Lucite plates, which have great resistance to voltage breakdown. These systems are essentially for quartz which requires high voltages. Barium titanate at low frequencies may be bonded to the outside wall of the treatment chamber.

[1] R. W. Wood, "Supersonics," Brown University, 1939.
[2] F. W. Smith and P. K Stumpf, *Electronics*, **19** (April, 1946) 116.

The bonding is not critical if the thickness of the wall is small with respect to the wavelength.   When the thickness becomes great it is usually preferable to make it resonant as in the design of front faces.   Epoxies, or other cements, are satisfactory as bonding agents.

Submarine Signaling Transducers.   Magnetostrictive systems are commonly used for underwater projection and reception.   However, a crystal unit is sometimes used as the receiver even though the projector is a magnetostrictive one.

In an underwater listening (without range) device, crystal transducers are commonly used.   They are superior to the magnetostrictive type in that the bandpass is much wider, and the sensitivity actually greater. Crystals are therefore somewhat more successful when used to listen for distant noises.

There are many ways of mounting such crystals.   Mosaics are always used to get greater sensitivity, and Rochelle salts or artificial crystals are preferable because they are more efficient than quartz.   These crystals are mounted with their backs fastened to a steel plate.   Metal coatings are evaporated on the crystals in the usual manner and are used as contacts for the electrical connections.

In order to keep out the water, a metal plate is usually mounted in front of the unit.   The crystals themselves do not bear against this window, which is of steel or a similar material, but the energy is transmitted through a liquid to the window.   Castor oil is normally used.   There are various special schemes for coupling into the ocean and for the design of such windows.

The Cable Connection.   The capacity between the crystal and ground must always be kept at a minimum; otherwise a great part of the signal will be lost owing to it.   Low-capacity coaxial conductors are satisfactory with sufficient shielding, since the receivers are necessarily of high gain. The most important factor is, however, the capacity to ground, since the signals are of high frequency.   It is assumed that the crystal is directly connected across the oscillating circuit by means of a cable.

However, various methods of matching the output to the crystal are possible and will be discussed elsewhere.   In those cases capacity effects are of less importance.

The cable may be designed to be part of the oscillating-circuit capacity. However, in that case only one length and type of cable may be used, i.e., a piece of given capacity.   Slight variations will detune the oscillator. It is therefore advisable not to follow this procedure unless it is absolutely unavoidable.

Lenses and Reflectors.   Many attempts have been made to focus ultrasonic beams, and some success has been reported.   Lenses made of glass and of various metals, ground according to the usual optical principles, have been tried without notable success. Metals have also been used as the outside skin of lenses, which were then filled with a liquid that formed the actual body of the lens. Copper is generally used. Carbon tetrachloride is a possible filling material. Plastic lenses may be designed, usually of Plexiglas or polystyrene. Synthetic resins have also been tried.[1,2] Polystyrene has a lower absorption than Lucite and therefore appears superior. The lens material should have a velocity which is different from the material in which it is used, and an acoustic impedance close to that of the medium. It should not scatter, absorb, or otherwise interfere with energy transfer.

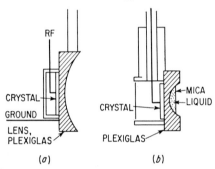

FIG. 3-30. Plastic lens: (a) simple Plexiglas; (b) compound Plexiglas and liquid (for liquids which attack Plexiglas). (After Sette.)

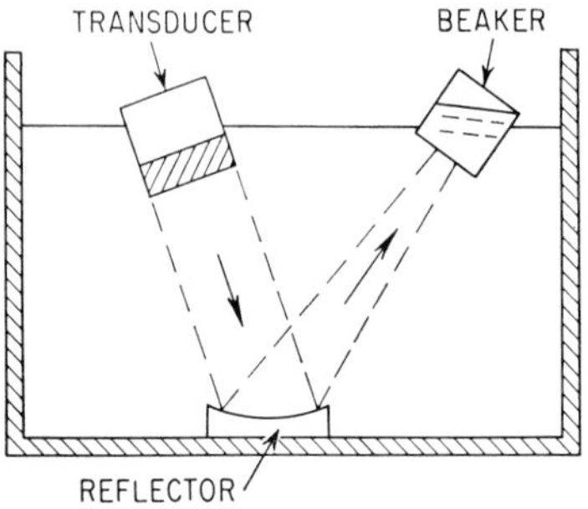

FIG. 3-31. Ultrasonic reflector.

One suggested lens is shown in Fig. 3-30,[2] showing a Plexiglas contact lens used in liquids. A number of other experimenters have suggested such lenses.

The focus of a spherical (planoconvex) lens is

$$f = \frac{r}{1 - V_L/V_S} = \frac{r}{1 - 1/N_{SL}}$$

where r = lens radius

f = focal length

$V_S/V_L = N_{SL}$ = index of refraction, solid to liquid

V_S = velocity in solid

V_L = velocity in liquid

Curved crystals may also be used to focus beams and are considered in Chap. 2. They should be mounted in holders that are matched to their contours. The radius of curvature of the button and blank should be approximately the same. If the curvatures of the two elements are not accurately matched, the motion of the crystal may be interfered with. In order to keep accurate alignment, indexing pins or keys may be used.

[1] D. Sette, *JASA*, **21** (1949) 375.

[2] P. J. Ernst, *J. Sci. Instr.*, **22** (1945) 238; *JASA*, **19** (1947) 474.

When the crystal is small, the button or holder should be made considerably larger in order to give greater surface to follow the curvature.

Two suggested lenses are shown in Fig. 3-30. They were used at about 1 Mc. Lenses may be either in direct contact with the crystal or isolated from it but in the direct path of the ultrasonic beam.

Shaped lenses may also be used as reflectors and will form the beam in a similar manner. The design of the reflector is similar to that of the lens and follows usual optical procedures (Fig. 3-31).

Holders for Resonance Testing. Holders for resonance should be the same as those used in other types of work except that damping must be held to an absolute minimum or it will obscure the points of resonance. Resonance crystals are ordinarily spring mounted; otherwise the pressure of the operator's hand may affect the readings.

Best results are obtained with crystals $\frac{1}{2}$ in. in diameter when the frequency is more than about 1 Mc and crystals at least 1 in. in diameter when it is under 1 Mc. Naturally, the entire face of the crystal must be seated on the work and when the work is small, the crystal must also be small.

When crystals are designed for resonance work using longitudinal waves, as they have always been to date, it is particularly important that the crystal does not also produce shear waves, which travel in the work at a different velocity and obscure the results by spurious peaks. This can be avoided by making certain that the crystal button fits about the edges of the crystal extremely tightly and constrains it from vibrating in the y dimension.

Interferometry. Special ultrasonic crystal mountings are necessary when they are used in an interferometer system. In such work the experimenter requires great purity of waveshape. He must also closely estimate the amount of radiation, etc. An ultrasonic interferometer works on the reflection of waves from a plane reflector back to their source. Resonances are then noted as either the reflector or source is moved (usually the reflector). This can be done by noting the dips in the current flowing in the electrical parts of the system, usually the plate current of the oscillator that drives the crystal.

In order to make these dips as sharp as possible, the damping must be a minimum. The crystal is therefore carefully plated and mounted for optimum vibration and minimum damping. The general idea is apparently to get a perfectly pistonlike vibration of the quartz (see Chap. 6).[1]

Holders for Microscope Use. In biological or similar work the worker sometimes wants to observe the action of ultrasonics on microscopic bodies or particles. In order to do this, a special holder must be made which will agitate the substance under observation while it is in the microscope.

[1] F. E. Fox and G. D. Rock, *Rev. Sci. Instr.*, **9** (1938) 341.

Such a holder may be in the form shown in Fig. 3-32. The crystal drives a bath in which the object is suspended. The microscope is so arranged that the observer can look directly down into the holder, which is of suitable physical dimensions to fit on its stage.

Glues. One of the problems in designing transducers using crystals is the question of fastening the crystal to a backing or faceplate.[1] These plates may be of steel or other materials. In some cases when the crystal is Rochelle salt, a porous ceramic wafer, 1 or 2 mm thick, is placed between the crystal and the steel plate to cut down distributed capacity. In order to do this, a glue must be used which will (1) not dissolve or dehydrate the crystal, (2) dry at reasonable temperatures, (3) have good electrical properties, and (4) have good mechanical properties.

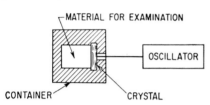

Fig. 3-32. Holder for microscope.

Studies have been carried out by gluing crystals of known sizes and frequencies to other materials and measuring the change in frequency and resistance at resonance which is caused by the glue. The equivalent electrical properties of the glue depends upon its layer thickness, drying characteristics, and the surfaces involved. With a perfect glue, resonant frequency and resistance will be determined by the crystal and bar which are cemented together and will not be affected by the glue. A decrease in frequency and increase in resistance are an indication of the glue effect. The following factors will influence the quality of the joint:

1. Drying temperatures and time
2. Humidity, ventilation, and pressure
3. Amount and method of applying cement
4. Type of cement

It is obvious that the cement must cover the entire surface and when dry should occupy as small a thickness as possible. In some cases, drying is aided by raising the temperature. When forcing the two cemented parts together, pressure must be maintained at a low enough value not to expel all of the cement and high enough to hold the two parts together. Among cements satisfactory for Rochelle salt are Bakelite cement, Vulcalock, and various acryloids.

Among cements satisfactory for quartz crystals and barium titanate are the various epoxy resins.

[1] "Mechanical and Acoustic Attachments for Piezoelectric Crystals Used in Transducers," *Contract OEMsr-346.*

CHAPTER 4

MAGNETOSTRICTION

History. The discovery of the magnetostrictive effect is usually credited to Joule.[1] However, the effect that bears his name, though one of the most famous and also the one of which the greatest number of applications have been made, is far from the only magnetostrictive effect. To explain certain results that occur in practice, it is desirable to discuss the entire phenomenon more completely.

The most general statement of magnetostriction may be made in the following manner. When a material is in a particular magnetic state, apparently only one combination of physical or chemical characteristics can exist within it. In a like manner, once the particular chemical or physical characteristics of a material have been determined, the magnetic state has also been defined. The progress of magnetostriction in its most general sense is therefore the definition of a set of physical characteristics by controlling the magnetic ones, and vice versa. This effect appears most strongly in the ferromagnetic metals, iron, nickel, cobalt, and their alloys.

There are many possible physical changes a material may undergo; and, as might be expected, a large number of magnetostriction effects are accordingly mentioned in the literature. Those mechanical changes due to a change in the magnetic field are referred to as *direct effects.* They may be in the linear dimensions, in the circular ones, or in the volume. The Joule and the inverse-Joule effects are among the first of these. Both of these are changes in the length of a rod or bar due to the magnetic field.

Other linear effects are the Guillemin, a bending of the rod caused by the field, and a change in Young's modulus. Any of these reactions may theoretically occur separately, or they may all occur simultaneously. In practice, the effects are more likely to occur as a combination of several than alone. The Joule is the most famous of the direct effects and is the most extensively considered in this context for that reason.

The circular changes take the form of a twisting, which is referred to as the *Wiedemann effect,* and of a change in the coefficient of rigidity. The former is rather well established in the experimental laboratory, but the exact order of the latter is still subject to question.

[1] J. P. Joule, *Phil. Mag.,* **30** (1847) 46.

A change in volume with the field is known as the *Barrett effect*. It also appears likely that a change in the bulk modulus takes place.

All these direct effects are physical changes caused by the action of the magnetic field. Most of them are extremely slight and are therefore not considered at all in ordinary work with magnetostriction units. Special methods must actually be resorted to in order to investigate even the best known and largest, i.e., the Joule effect. A brief mention of such apparatus may therefore be of interest.

However, before attempting to observe the Joule effect, certain precautions must be taken. The samples must be carefully magnetized in such a way that they are kept free of extraneous fields. The magnetic fields must be very uniform, and the sample placed in them symmetrically. The temperature must be exactly controlled, and the part supported in such a manner that the effect is not physically interfered with in any way.

The apparatus used in the theoretical laboratory for the investigation of this effect is known as an *extensometer*. It consists of a set of rods connected so that the total movement at one end is much greater than the activating motion applied at the other.

The most commonly used arrangement is a modification or variation of the Michelson interferometer used for the investigation of light. By means of this apparatus, a mirror fastened to the end of the extensometer bar is made to shift the interference fringes that the instrument projects on a screen. The change must then be interpreted in terms of the change in length of the magnetostriction bar. The unit is extremely sensitive, and the minute changes in dimensions associated with the Joule effect may accordingly be easily examined with it.

The statement seems to have been originally made by Le Chatelier that once a body of material was placed in a state of chemical and physical equilibrium, it would resist any attempt on the part of an outside agency to change that equilibrium. This may be taken as the reason for the inverse magnetostriction effects.

The inverse effects may be subdivided in the same manner as the direct ones. The most well known, because they are the most easily investigated, are the Villari and the transverse-Villari effects, both of which are linear. These may be examined by applying the proper linear mechanical forces to a bar in which they can occur and using any of the known ways of investigation of the magnetic properties during this application.

The circular effects are known as the *second Wiedemann* and the *Wertheim* effects; the first is a change in the longitudinal component of magnetism due to a twisting of the rod; the "Wertheim" bears a close resemblance to the "Wiedemann," except that the sample is initially a longitudinally magnetized bar.

The changes in volume are known as the *Nagaoka-Honda effect* after the men who did extensive work in the field in Japan.[1] This is usually demonstrated in the form of a change n the magnetic induction caused by hydrostatic pressure.

Miscellaneous Effects. Besides the listed actions, which can be classified in a more or less regular manner, there are a number of other effects that have been often observed but never entirely satisfactorily explained.

Among these are a change in the material resistivity, a change in the thermoelectromotive force, a change in the frequency of a vibrating body, and the production of the so-called "magnetic ticks" or clicks that occur when a body is undergoing magnetization.

The Joule and Villari effects are the only ones of any interest in design work of longitudinal oscillating bars, which are by far the most commonly used. However, other effects may in time be more extensively applied as more and more is known about them.

General. The magnetostriction effect has been widely investigated by Pierce[2] and his students, who first applied it to many practical problems. It was they who first conceived of the idea of using it to control and maintain oscillations in a bar of metal, which is then used as a device to control the frequency of electronic oscillators, as a filter, as a time standard, and as a device for the production of ultrasonic vibrations in various media. In short, the effect may be applied to many uses just as the piezoelectric effect may.

Magnetostriction units have also been used as the driving elements in agitation systems and have been proposed for the resonance testing of materials. They have not been extensively used in testing materials. However, the use of magnetostriction as the basis for ultrasonic signaling systems is widespread, especially in the lower frequencies and in applications such as submarine signaling, where considerable amounts of power are necessary. In such systems one magnetostriction rod can be used in an oscillator and form the transmitting transducer, while another rod is attached to a receiver and indicator and acts to transform the ultrasonic signals to electrical ones. Rods have been used as transducers in all types of ultrasonic equipment, as well as frequency-control devices and filters.

The output of the average magnetostriction unit is much less than a crystal when both are being used to receive mechanical oscillations and transform them into electrical signals. As a transmitter, the magnetostriction rod is also less efficient than the crystal but has the great advantage that almost any amount of driving power can be applied to it.

Controlling Device for Oscillators. As already indicated, the magnetostriction bar may perform the same function as a crystal in stabilizing the

[1] H. Nagaoka, On Magnetostriction, *Intern. Elec. Cong.*, 1904.
[2] G. W. Pierce, *Proc. Am. Acad.*, **63** (1928) 1.

frequency of an oscillator, and in such use it maintains the frequency
with a constancy that compares favorably with the latter.

The action is based upon the fact that the coil and rod act as a variable
inductance fluctuating in such a manner that it opposes any change in the
oscillator frequency and moreover changes very sharply for only a minor
variation in the frequency. The range of voltage, etc., over which such
units act suitably is wide and also compares favorably with that in crystal
work.

Materials. The ordinary metals used in the production and reception
of ultrasonic waves are the alloys of nickel, chromium, iron, and cobalt.
Others are Invar, stoic metal (36 per cent nickel and 64 per cent iron),
and Monel (68 per cent nickel, 28 per cent copper, and small amounts of

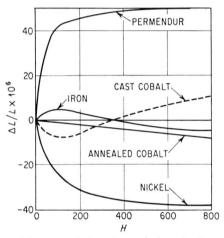

FIG. 4-1. Magnetostrictive change in length of materials.

other metals). The most common are nickel and permalloy (45 per cent
nickel, 55 per cent iron). These last two materials produce magnetostriction effects that are mutually reversed; i.e., in a particular polarity
of field one material will shorten while the other will lengthen. However,
the total absolute dimensional change is about the same. The amount
of length change of the various common materials is shown in Fig. 4-1.

It has been experimentally discovered that annealing adds to the magnetostrictive properties of such bars, of whatever metal they are made.

The only materials that show regular behavior characteristics as regards
the amount of change in length caused by a particular magnetic field
strength are rods of nickel and annealed cobalt. Almost all other materials will exhibit these regular length variations until the field becomes
stronger than a limiting value, at which point the length change exhibits
a change in sign, i.e., goes in the opposite direction.

Combinations of materials may also be used for vibrating bars. For example, tubes of nickel can be made hollow and filled with lead or type metal to bring down the velocity of wave propagation and thus produce very-low-frequency waves. Again, materials of different temperature coefficients can be combined to get a desired characteristic. Thus, one material with a negative temperature coefficient may form one part of a bar, while a piece with a positive coefficient may form the other part. In this way the temperature coefficients balance out and the bar is more stable to temperature changes. These bars may be either longitudinally composite or concentrically composite, depending on how they are joined.

In simple materials the magnetostriction effect decreases as the temperature rises, and vanishes at the Curie point.

When a steady field is applied to the bar in this manner, the change in length is minute; e.g., in nickel it is about $1 \times 10^{-6}L$ per gauss. However,

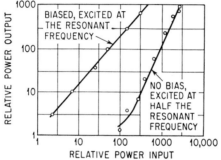

Fig. 4-2. Power relationships in units with and without bias. (*From International Nickel Co., Design of Nickel Magnetostriction Transducers, NDRC Tech. Rept., div. 6, V13, PB 77669.*)

when the field is oscillating (at resonance), the effect is much greater, since the elastic forces of the bar no longer oppose the changes in length, and the only force that must be overcome is the viscosity of the material.

The change in length in the bar due to the magnetostrictive effect will usually be very small unless the length of the bar is resonant at the vibrating frequency, in which case the greatest change will be about $10^{-4}L$, where L is the length of the bar. The change under nonresonant conditions is about ± 25 ppm. It may be either positive or negative depending on the material and the temperature. However, the force associated with the small change in length is the entire elastic force of the bar, and as a result large ratios of force to applied current are common. When the bar is resonant, this change becomes greater. If the flux intensity is low, the change in length is proportional to its square. Ordinarily, polarizing units must be used with magnetostriction bars. The power output with and without bias is shown in Fig. 4-2.

In a solid part there is usually some loss due to eddy currents, which flow in the material. Because of this, magnetostriction oscillators are usually constructed of thin tubes, or laminations, or fine wires, fastened together to form a single solid part. There are also losses due to hysteresis. The use of laminations cuts down these losses and provides fairly wide-band elements.

The mechanical impedance of the system tends to be large, and magnetostriction driving systems can therefore be used to drive high-imped-

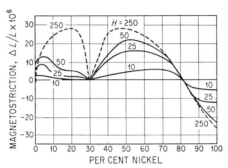

FIG. 4-3. Relationship between activity and percentage of nickel in nickel-iron alloys. (*Schulze; from International Nickel Co., "Magnetostriction."*)

ance systems, such as solids and liquids. Moreover, units have recently been developed which operate well in air.[1]

Nickel, which is most often used for ultrasonic work, is not completely satisfactory for stabilizing frequency, since it does not maintain so consistent a frequency as other materials.

Nickel iron, 45 per cent Ni, is the peak of positive magnetostriction; nickel iron, 63 per cent Ni, is most strain sensitive; and pure nickel is the peak of negative magnetostriction. Figure 4-3 gives the variation between magnetostriction and percentage of nickel. Iron cobalt has not been widely used because of cost and lack of availability.

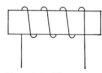

FIG. 4-4. Magnetostriction rod.

Systems. *The Magnetostriction Oscillator.* If a rod is magnetized and a coil wrapped around it and the rod is lengthened or shortened by compression or tension, voltage will be induced in the surrounding coil (Fig. 4-4). When the rod is allowed to return to its original position, another voltage will be induced but of opposite polarity. If then the rod is vibrated continuously at some a-c frequency, it is obvious that an a-c voltage of the same frequency will be induced in the coil, and the magnitude of that voltage will be proportional to the amplitude of vibration. This roughly describes the action of a magnetostriction receiver when

[1] S. M. Bagno, U.S. Patent 2,832,952 (1957).

struck by sound waves. At some particular frequency the rod will resonate, and therefore maximum voltage will be induced. However, the
tuning may be fairly broad, and the receiver will respond to a wide range
of frequencies.

In a similar manner the reverse effect will take place; i.e., a voltage
may be impressed upon the coil of wire, and the rod will then vibrate at
the frequency of the applied voltage and with an amplitude roughly proportional to the voltage magnitude. If this is done, ultrasonic waves
will be radiated from the ends of the rod. At the resonant frequency the
effect will be greatest and waves of the greatest amplitude will therefore
be produced.

In both cases, if the rod is supported in the center, as on a knife edge,
it will have a secondary resonance point at every odd multiple of the
fundamental.

If the rod were totally unmagnetized, every time a flux were set up it
would shorten, without regard to the flux direction. The rod will therefore vibrate at twice the frequency of the exciting a-c voltage. It is more
usual to work with magnetized
rods, and therefore some means is
normally included for maintaining
the magnetization. This may be a
superimposed constant current, or
a permanent magnet may be used
(Fig. 4-5).

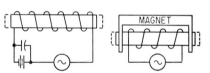

FIG. 4-5. Methods of magnetizing the rod.

When a material does not retain magnetism efficiently, a small permanent magnet may be placed somewhere in its vicinity, within 6 in. or so
of the bar, and it will maintain its polarity by induction. In some cases
the rod is flashed by discharging a current through the coil, thus providing enough permanent magnetism to operate on.

Because the bar is polarized when it is magnetized in any such manner,
it will vibrate at the same frequency as the frequency of excitation.

Dimensions and Frequency. In any ordinary case the magnetostriction rod is designed to oscillate at its fundamental mode, although in
some cases harmonic modes may also be used. These modes are almost
always longitudinal. The critical dimension accordingly is the length.
Harmonic modes are used only in those cases where it is impossible to
get the required frequency by means of the fundamental ones. Torsional
modes are practically the only other ones used besides the longitudinal.

The theoretical formula for the velocity of ultrasonics in such a longitudinal bar is

$$c = \sqrt{\frac{\text{Young's modulus}}{\text{density}}}$$

It may be noted that this is not the formula given for velocity in a bulk medium, but it is rather what is sometimes referred to as the *velocity of the compressional wave*, or as *bar velocity*, because it exists only in a medium where the ultrasonic energy extends to the limits of the part through which it is traveling in a direction parallel to the main motion. Accordingly, the effect of the sides of the part must be taken into consideration when the velocity is being computed. The waves in the magnetostriction bar are ordinarily of this type because of the small cross-sectional area of the bar.

The ordinary fundamental bar would be one-half of the wavelength. The length of the bar can accordingly be calculated when the velocity or wavelength in a particular material is known and would be

$$L = \frac{K}{2f}\sqrt{\frac{E}{\rho}}$$

where K = order of harmonic
L = length
E = modulus of elasticity
ρ = density

Using this formula, it can be seen that at about 20,000 cps, which may be considered as the boundary point between sonic and ultrasonic waves, a nickel bar would be about 5 in. long. Since the bar becomes shorter as the frequency becomes higher, this is the very longest that it is likely to be (except for sonic frequencies).

Naturally, the length would change with the materials used and vary in each one according to the frequency desired and the velocity of the ultrasonics in the rod. For example, in Nichrome, where the velocity is about 1.96×10^5 in.,

$$L = \frac{1.96 \times 10^5}{2f}$$

where L is the length. The cross-sectional dimensions of a bar of this nature would vary from $\frac{1}{8}$ to $\frac{1}{4}$ in. in diameter.

Incidentally, one of the advantages of the magnetostriction bar is that it can be made with a smaller cross-sectional area than the quartz crystal and can therefore be inserted into ultrasonic fields where the interference produced by a transducer of a larger cross section would destroy the action under investigation.

The ordinary range of magnetostriction bars is from 5,000 to about 60,000 cps. After that point, the rods become so short that they cannot be conveniently handled.

The magnetostriction rod is almost the only device used for the production of ultrasonics or the stabilization of oscillators under a frequency of about 25,000 cps. It has been used in laboratories to produce oscillations up to a maximum of about 2 Mc, but at the higher frequencies its output is so small as to be negligible. At the present time, the maximum usable frequency of a simple bar is about 60,000 cps, where a bar about 1½ in. long may be used. Such bars can be designed from the nomograph (Fig. 4-6).[1] However, more detailed design data will be discussed hereafter.

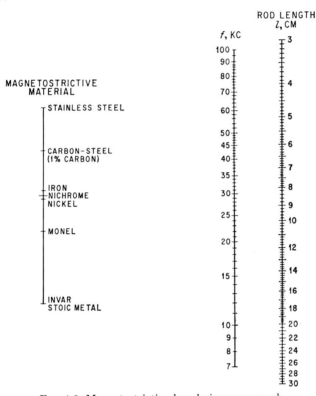

FIG. 4-6. Magnetostrictive-bar-design nomograph.

Shapes. Magnetostriction bars have been made in many types and shapes. These variations have been dictated mainly by these two considerations: (1) the elimination of losses in the bar and (2) the desire to control the shape or field pattern of the transmitted beam. When a long rod or bar (of the type discussed so far) is excited so that it sends out ultrasonic vibrations, those beams are transmitted out from its ends only. The pattern of such a beam may be seen from Fig. 4-7.

In order to control the shape of the beam, some transducers have been designed that are highly directional. Others are so proportioned that

[1] R. C. Coile, *Electronics,* **20** (1947) 130.

they produce a beam that spreads out evenly in all directions. To accomplish this latter objective, circular rings may be set into oscillation in such a way that the radius of the ring is continually changing with the excitation (Fig. 4-8). In this case the ultrasonic energy will spread out evenly from the center of the ring in the same manner that light spreads out from a point source. Marconi constructed special ring transducers in which the magnetostriction rod, which was nickel, was fixed and the

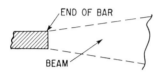

Fig. 4-7. Beam from end of bar.

Fig. 4-8. Simple ring oscillator.

windings were allowed to move. If the outside edge of such a ring is serrated or has teeth attached to it, the frequency of oscillation will be lowered. The frequency of such a ring is

$$f = \frac{c}{2\pi r} \sqrt{1 + (1 - K^2)}$$

where K is the order of harmonic and the other letters have the usual meanings. Magnetostriction units can also be formed of a number of rods fastened at one end to a large mass from which they point radially outward, so that the ultrasonic waves are sent out from their free ends.[1] Each spoke is then separately excited longitudinally. However, each rod has a separate winding, and those windings are so arranged that the flux in each one is of the opposite sign from that of either of its neighbors. This is done so that there will be a closed magnetic circuit.

For high frequencies, other special rods have been suggested. These may be very short cylinders or types such as beaded rods (Fig. 4-9).[2] These are bars which have grooves cut in them to raise the frequency.

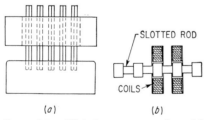

Fig. 4-9. High-frequency rods: (a) cylinders; (b) beaded rods.

The production of higher-frequency oscillations is particularly important, since frequency is one of the main limitations to the use of magnetostriction.

All these units are usually constructed of some form of laminated

[1] W. Kallmeyer, German Patent 607,048 (1934).
[2] G. W. Pierce, U.S. Patent 1,882,397 (1932).

material in order to cut down losses from eddy currents. They may be of strip construction; or else rolled sheets or stamped rings may be used, depending upon the size and type of unit. The magnetostriction rod may also be in the form of a tube, usually of metal; in this case the coil is placed inside instead of being wrapped around it. This is of interest in those cases where the unit needs to be waterproofed for submersion or in those instances where a very large cluster of transducers are to be operated side by side and space is a consideration. Rods have also been constructed in small vacuum chambers so that they are less affected by their surroundings. Movable weights have been used to change the frequency of oscillation, giving a sort of tunable rod.

Still another design used with agitating systems is the combination of the rod and the cup in which the material is placed for exposure to the ultrasonic energy. The rod is firmly fastened to or integrated with the base of the cup, so that it is vibrated directly. The unit may be cooled by a water jacket or by a jet of water directed against it at a convenient point. It will operate over any range from the middle-audio up to the low-ultrasonic range. The rod would normally be from 5 to 10 in. long and about ½ in. in diameter.

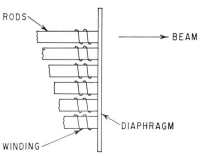

FIG. 4-10. Rods and diaphragms.

When placed in a bath or other medium where there is danger of stray pickup, all ultrasonic units must be suitably shielded to eliminate extraneous signals. This can be done by placing the entire unit in some form of holder or placing a braided shield about it. Naturally, this shield must not interfere with the ultrasonic beam.

When simple rods are cut to a given frequency, first the frequency is calculated from one of the formulas already given, and the rod is cut slightly oversize. It is then tried out in an actual oscillator and ground down to calibrate with an exact standard, which may take the form of another bar. Calibration may also be made against any exact source of frequency by beating the magnetostriction oscillator with it. Exact frequency is only rarely required, and on other occasions the bars may merely be cut to size and will be exact enough for ordinary use. Many bar designs have been used in specialized apparatus over a period of time and are recorded in the literature.

Diaphragms. The ends of the rods, whatever shape they may be, are usually coupled into a diaphragm (Fig. 4-10) that actually acts to send the ultrasonic waves into the medium. The diaphragm takes the form of a large sheet (with respect to wavelength in it) driven by one or more rods. One of the problems is the tendency of the plate to vibrate with some sections out of phase with the others. To overcome this, the diaphragm can be broken up and a number of smaller diaphragms used, each so connected that it is in phase with the others. An alternative method is to place the vibrating rods so that the entire face of the diaphragm is in phase.

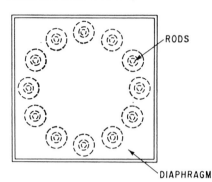

The use of a plurality of rods driving a single diaphragm seems to have been originally attributable to Pierce. In this case all the rods must have approximately the same period. One end of the core is at-

FIG. 4-11. Connection of rods.

tached to the diaphragm (Fig. 4-11).[1] The activating coils may be either in series or in parallel. The units have greater power capabilities than

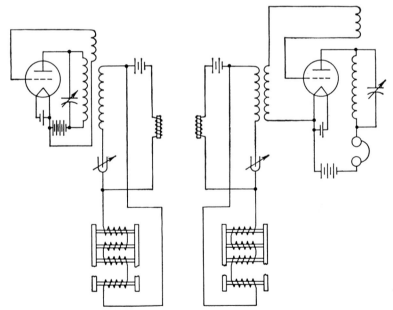

FIG. 4-12. Magnetostrictive diaphragms in transmitters and receivers.

single units of the same size and have less eddy current and other losses. The complete system from the patent is disclosed in Fig. 4-12.

[1] G. W. Pierce, U.S. Patent 2,014,411 (1935).

A more complicated modern device of the same sort is illustrated in Fig. 4-13.[1] This consists of 600 nickel tubes in coils which are connected in series-parallel. A diaphragm 16 in. in diameter and about 1 in. thick is fastened to one end of these rods. The diaphragm is made of steel. The rods are polarized by direct current. The length of the steel-diaphragm-nickel rod is a half wavelength, for resonance. The method of mounting the unit on a ship is shown in Fig. 4-14. The frequency response is also indicated.

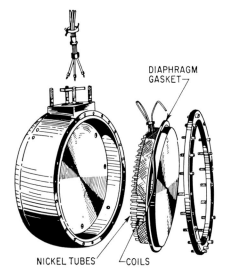

Temperature Coefficient. Using Nichrome, Pierce found that frequency was independent of circuit variations and that the temperature coefficient was

$$\frac{1}{f} = \frac{\Delta f}{\Delta \theta} = -(1.07 \times 10^{-4})°C$$

where f = frequency
Δf = frequency change
$\Delta \theta$ = change, °C

Temperature coefficients are usually large in magnetostriction bars but can be compensated for by methods already described. The concentric type appears to have some power advantages.

The change in frequency with temperature is caused by its effect upon elasticity and not upon other characteristics. Drift which takes place in magnetostrictive systems is due to the transducers' sensitivity to temperature, which must accordingly be guarded against by cooling or other means.

Drift. Another apparent effect of the temperature rise is a change

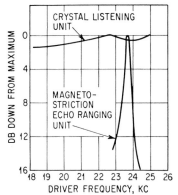

Fig. 4-13. Modern rod and diaphragm transducer.

in frequency of the transducer due to a change in velocity of sound in the material. This is usually attacked by having some sort of afc system in which the transducer itself is the controlling element (see Chap. 11). Some materials have been described in the literature in which the tem-

[1] R. J. Evans, *Electronics*, **19** (1946) 88.

perature characteristics have been so combined that the net drift is negligible. However, these materials are not in common use.

Curie Temperature. A magnetostrictive material loses its activity as the temperature is increased, gradually to a point, and then very rapidly. The temperature at which the speed-up takes place is known as the *Curie temperature*. The way in which the activity falls off is shown in Fig. 4-15.

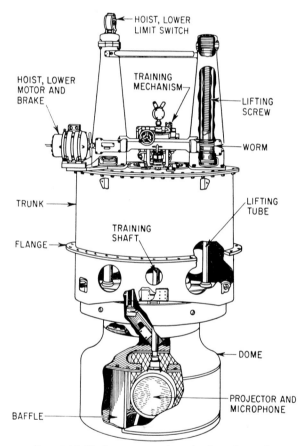

FIG. 4-14. Underwater section of submarine unit.

Limits. The performance of a transducer is a function of (1) the material, (2) the strain level which can exist, (3) the heat which can be dissipated, and (4) the design, i.e., geometry.

The strain level is a function of the fatigue strength of the material and the physical design of the core (sharp edges, etc). The heat generated within the core is also a major factor. Ninety per cent of the heat loss is in the core; the remainder, in the coil. The cooling of the core is accordingly very important. About 10 to 25 watts/in.[1] can be dissipated without cooling.[1]

Power Available. The amount of power which can be generated by a half-wavelength transducer depends on the Q and is about

$$\text{Power} \simeq 90QS \text{ (nickel)}$$
$$\simeq 150QS \text{ (Permendur)}$$

where S is the cross-sectional area in inches. This is shown in Fig. 4-16 for nickel.

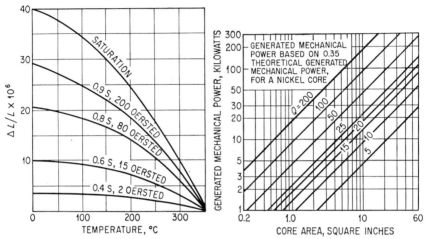

FIG. 4-15. Temperature vs. magnetostriction, nickel.

FIG. 4-16. Core area vs. power (maximum) for various Q's for nickel half-wavelength bar.

Designing the Magnetostrictive Unit. The magnetostrictive transducer is constructed of two sections:

1. The core, which is made of magnetostrictive material
2. The coil, which surrounds the core and through which the electrical energy is impressed on it

Cores. The core is the heart of the transducer and may be made in many convenient shapes, but, in general, common cores are in one of the following forms:

1. Solid rod
2. Hollow rod or tube with or without the wall slitted
3. Laminated bar
4. Laminated bar or sheet with slots in it

[1] "Design of Nickel Magnetostriction Transducers," The International Nickel Company.

5. Laminated bar whose cross section is not uniform (usually with larger ends than centers)

6. A ring or cylindrical stack

7. A cylindrical scroll

Each of these types is shown in Fig. 4-17.

ROD. One of the simplest forms of transducers and the one commonly used where very low powers are required is a rod of magnetostrictive material. The fundamental resonant frequency of this rod is

$$f = \frac{c}{2L}$$

where f = resonant frequency
c = velocity of sound
L = length of rod

This rod is usually supported at the center in a solenoid which does not touch the rod so that it does not restrict the motion. The attachment to

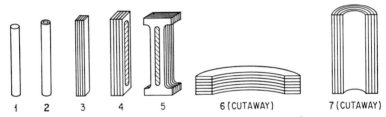

1   2   3   4   5   6 (CUTAWAY)   7 (CUTAWAY)

FIG. 4-17. Common configurations of transducer cores.

the rod is made at the center, where minimum interference to the vibration will take place. The coil should be located symmetrically about the center, where maximum electromechanical coupling (and strain) is possible. The experimentally determined resonant frequency vs. the length of a $\frac{1}{4}$-in. rod is shown in Table 4-1. It must be emphasized that size, shape, diameter, etc., affect frequency, and therefore the formula may not give exact results, but modification may then be made to get these results. Small adjustments in frequency may be made by grinding material from the end of the bar, or from its body, usually in the center.

TUBE AND SLIT TUBE. One of the limiting factors in magnetostrictive cores is the existence of eddy currents which become greater with frequency. This current has two effects:

1. The loss of power due to I^2R losses

2. The shielding of the interior of the material from the field produced by the coil

Thus the interior does not contribute to the magnetostrictive output. It therefore appears reasonable to eliminate the interior and to cut down on the losses by using tubes instead of solid rods. The slitting of the tube has a further effect in eliminating currents. It also has the effect of allowing wall thickness to be about five times greater than without slitting. The length of the tube is calculated in the same way as the length of the bar. However, practically, there are slight variations in frequency. For example, Table 4-1 shows actual measured frequencies vs. length of tubes of various diameters, and that of a solid rod of ¼-in. OD.

TABLE 4-1. DEPENDENCE OF FREQUENCY UPON LENGTH AND MASS OF SEVERAL NICKEL ELEMENTS—NO LOAD

(Each of the following nickel elements was cut to the given length and the frequency noted at the maximum activity)

Length, in.	Frequency, kc (nickel, ½-in. OD, 0.028-in. wall)	Tube-wall mass, g	Frequency, kc (nickel, ¼-in. OD, 0.017-in. wall)	Tube-wall mass, g	Frequency, kc (nickel, 0.830-in. ID, 0.010-in. wall)	Tube-wall mass, g	Frequency, kc (nickel, ¼-in. OD, solid)	Rod mass, g
12	8.25							
11½	8.60							
11	9.00							
10	9.85							
9½	10.35				10.30	36.4		
9	10.95	56.5			10.75	34.6		
8½	11.50	....	11.30	...	11.40	32.5	11.90	
8	12.20	....	12.0	...	12.10	30.6	12.55	
7½	13.00	....	12.80	...	12.85	28.8	13.40	
7	13.95	....	13.75	...	13.85	26.9	14.40	49.7
6½	14.99	....	14.75	...	14.75	25.2	15.50	46.0
6	16.25	33.9	16.25	...	15.99	23.2	16.75	42.5
5½	17.75	....	17.45	...	17.49	21.1	18.25	39.2
5¼	18.50	....	18.30	...	18.25	20.2	18.90	37.4
5	19.50	....	19.20	...	19.20	19.3	19.80	35.6
4½	22.75	....	21.35	...	21.40	17.4	22.50	31.85
4	24.25	....	24.00	...	24.00	15.7	25.00	28.40
3½	27.99	....	27.50	...	27.50	13.9	28.80	23.50
3¼	29.95	....	29.50	...	29.25	13.0	31.00	23.00
3	32.50	....	32.00	...	32.00	12.1	33.50	21.3
2½	38.50	....	38.10	4.5	38.00	10.1	40.00	17.8
2¼	43.00	14.5						
4 31/32	.....	....	.....	...	.....	....	19.95	
4 29/32 = 4 15/16	.....	....	.....	...	.....	....	20.25	35

LAMINATED BAR. The disadvantage of the tube is that the cross-sectional area of its face (wall) becomes very small. By making a laminated bar fabricated of thin sections electrically insulated from each other, the advantage of the tube plus a large cross-sectional area is possible. Each lamination acts as though it were exposed independently to the exciting field.

The laminations are insulated from one another by a suitable covering on their surfaces. They are then bonded together by riveting, welding,

or soldering.   If the bonded areas are a small part of the total area, the
bonding will have little effect.   With a simple shape as shown in case 4
of Fig. 4-17, and a length-to-diameter ratio which is large, these units
will give adequate operation.   The thickness of the laminations may
affect the frequency response.   Thickness may be taken from Fig. 4-18;
usually about 0.015 in. thick may be used below about 30 kc; above this,
about 0.005 in. may be used.

More complicated bar shapes represent more complicated design problems.   If it is desirable to use these types the design becomes difficult
and sometimes requires considerable trial and error.   However, some of
the basic ideas may be of interest; first, the bar will always be smaller
than a half wavelength when loaded, so every loaded bar is shorter than

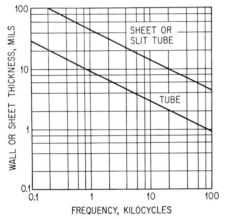

FIG. 4-18. Sheet thickness vs. frequency for   FIG. 4-19. Typical 25-kc lamination.
low loss and good flux penetration.

case 4 in Fig. 4-17.   In these cases the calculation of resonant frequency
must be done by considering the bar as a transmission line with standing
waves.

SLOTTED BAR.   Slotted bars may come in many shapes, depending upon
the area to be activated.   They are satisfactory for operation at higher
frequencies and where the ratio between length and diameter is small.
The slotting improves the magnetic circuit and renders the unit more
independent of external objects.   Generally speaking, an equal number
of turns is placed on each leg.   The magnetic field is closed by the ends
of the laminations and leakage flux eliminated.   Since this is the function
of the ends, the cross section of the end should always be greater than a
cross section of any leg.   It has been experimentally determined that an
area ratio of 2:1 is adequate.

A typical slotted bar for 25 kc is shown in Fig. 4-19.   The type shown
represents a simple transducer.   However, it is possible, by adding sec-

tions, to build up transducers similar to those in Fig. 4-20d, f, and g, etc. These combinations may be made depending upon the power and area requirements. However, it will be noted that the frequency will change slightly in such units. Figure 4-20 shows typical laminations manufactured by Atlas-Werke, Germany.

RING OR CYLINDRICAL TRANSDUCERS. Ring transducers are made by stacking circular punched sections. A toroidal winding is then placed around the stack. The fundamental frequency is

$$f = \frac{c}{\pi D}$$

where c = velocity
D = diameter
f = frequency

The unit is usually used to produce radial vibration. However, it may also be energized in the same way as a tube is energized, and then the unit will radiate from the ends, like a tube. In such a case, the length would also be computed in the same way as a tube.

Rings may also be formed by stacking thin sections longitudinally. Such a unit is made of ½-in.-wide sections, slightly crimped in the length dimension, and stacked to give about a ¼-in. wall with a diameter of about 3 in. and (at 20 kc) a length of about 5 in.

Lamination Cutting. Rough treatment of the laminated material may effect magnetostrictive characteristics. It is generally preferable to punch laminations from hard rolled stock. After punching, they must be annealed to give the proper magnetostrictive characteristic (usually dead soft). It is possible to cut laminations in many other ways, but in all cases a treatment for annealing should be carried out after deburring.

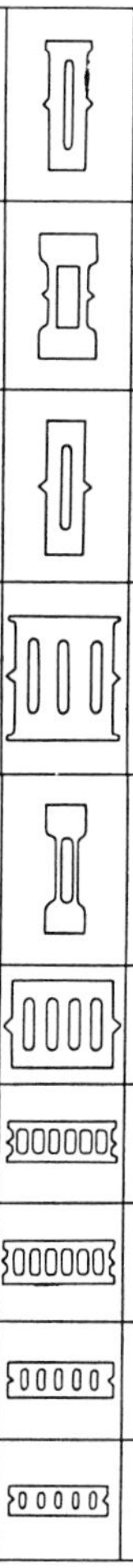

	FREQUENCY	FORM	WIDTH, CM	LENGTH, CM	OVERALL DIMENSIONS
(a)	15		58	152	58 × 58 × 152
(b)	15		46	98	46 × 46 × 98
(c)	20		30	112	30 × 30 × 112
(d)	22		85	98	85 × 85 × 98
(e)	23		23	69	23 × 23 × 69
(f)	30		82	68	82 × 82 × 68
(g)	30		140	50	140 × 140 × 50
(h)	38		112	40.5	112 × 112 × 40.5
(i)	80		85	25	85 × 85 × 25
(j)	175		40	11	40 × 40 × 11

FIG. 4-20. Typical laminations. (*Atlas-Werke.*)

In cases where annealing must be done before bonding, since the bonding is carried out by plastic means, there should be a minimum of working of the material so as to retain its magnetostrictive properties.   When the stack is machined as a unit, it may be necessary to remove burrs by means of etching in a dip of 187 cm^3 concentrated nitric acid, 150 cm^3 sulfuric acid, 138 cm^3 water, and 3 g sodium chloride under a ventilating hood for several minutes.

Bonding.   Materials may be bonded in many ways.   It is possible to rivet or bolt laminations together.   There are also a number of epoxy resins satisfactory for fastening them.   These resins will also act as an insulator.   However, in general, they are only suitable for comparatively low temperature use.   In cases where it is necessary to fasten the stack to a diaphragm or other metal, silver soldering or welding is called for. This must be done before annealing, since the uneven heat may cause undesirable local conditions in the metal.   In the case of laminations the end may be nickel, welded together forming a solid mass, which may then be soldered or welded to the tool.

Annealing.   The magnetostrictive properties of a material depend upon the internal structure, and the internal structure depends upon the composition, included impurities, crystal structure, and orientation, etc. There are several ways in which these characteristics can be controlled:

1. By the selection of the material itself
2. By the mechanical treatment to which the material is subjected
3. By the heat treatment

These characteristics may have as much effect on the operation of a transducer as its actual operating conditions.   The magnetostrictive alloys which are available are largely materials which are made for other uses, since magnetostriction is not a sufficiently large market to dictate the property of materials.   There is, therefore, no great choice of materials for cores and pure (A) nickel is commonly used together with certain types of Permendur and nickel-iron combinations.   These materials may be obtained in a heat treatment which is satisfactory for magnetostrictive transducers but since they must always be punched or otherwise worked, a further treatment to restore the magnetic properties is advantageous.

Moreover, it is sometimes easier to punch a hard metal than a soft one but, in the case of nickel, soft anneals are preferable from the point of view of magnetostriction.   It is therefore always advisable to anneal the transducers at some point in their fabrication, usually at a point where further work will be the minimum.

Nickel Anneal.   Annealing nickel in the air for one hour at 800°C and cooling at a rate less than 100°C/hr will produce both a soft anneal and an insulated oxide coating.   The stacks, while being annealed, should be supported so that they are exposed to the air and should be cleaned before treatment. Electric furnaces of the common laboratory type are satisfactory for carrying out annealing.

A more complicated type of anneal may be necessary for Permendur and other alloys by heating in hydrogen for one hour at 1000°C and cooling at 70°C/hr in hydrogen. This would probably have to be carried out by special equipment. It is also possible to carry out the same procedure under vacuum and get most of the advantages of hydrogen annealing. It may be noted that materials which are annealed as described above will be difficult to magnetically treat for remanent operation, and in cases where the latter is desirable annealing for less softness may be necessary. In the case of nickel, annealing for one hour at 600°C will give a half-hard condition suitable for this type of operation.

Permendur Anneal. Permendur must be annealed before stamping. The procedure is as follows: After assembly, the stack is heated to 550°C for 3 hr in a hydrogen-nitrogen atmosphere. It is then cooled at a rate of 10°C/min. The individual laminations are insulated by placing mica between them, since Permendur does not form an insulating coating on heating. Laminations are about 0.004 in. thick. Assembly techniques are then similar to those using nickel.

Oxides (Ferrites). Ceramic-based oxides are now being used as magnetostrictive elements. Since they are made of sintered materials initially, there is no need to laminate the materials. The resonant frequency of such a bar is

$$f_1 = \frac{N}{2L} \left(\frac{E}{\rho}\right)^{1/2}$$

where f = frequency
E = Young's modulus
ρ = density
N = order (harmonics)
The velocity is

$$v = \left(\frac{E}{\rho}\right)^{1/2}$$

The length of typical ferrites is about the same as that of nickel; mechanical characteristics are inferior.

Coils. The second part of a transducer is the coil structure. In the case of a rod, a simple solenoid may be used. The number of turns is optional. The magnetic field strength necessary for operating with nickel and other common materials is between 50 and 200 oersteds. The winding should be such that

$$H = 50\text{--}200 = \frac{0.4\pi NI}{L} \quad \text{oersteds}$$

where H = magnetic field, oersteds

    N = number of turns in solenoid

    I = current

    L = approximate length of solenoid

In many cases, it is simpler to merely wind a large number of turns on the solenoid and remove turns until optimum operation is arrived at. However, in many practical transducers, the d-c bias is also impressed by the same coil. In that case, the wire size must be sufficiently large to allow both the a-c and d-c currents to flow without excessive heating. Moreover, the value of d-c voltage across the coil will have to be independently adjusted for optimum bias operation after the alternating current has been determined. It may be noticed, by looking at Fig. 7-12, which shows alternating and direct current being impressed on the same coil, that this may be done by a variable resistor in a d-c circuit.

The coil for a slit-tube transducer can be designed by a method similar to the rod-type transducer, and this is also true in the case of a laminated bar. For example, with a transducer of this type operating at about 20 kc or a little less, that is, with a length of about 6 in., a suitable coil would have about 700 turns and about 1 amp of direct current would be required.

In the case of slotted bars, the number of turns which may be placed through the slot is limited by the slot size and by the difficulty in winding. It is therefore common to have a small number of turns (between 15 and 50) on each leg of such a unit. This naturally means that the output impedance of the driving generators will be lower. For example, in the case of the unit described above, an output impedance of several hundred ohms would be satisfactory while in the case of laminated transducers, an output impedance of 100 ohms or less would be common. It is usually simpler to pick the output transformer to match the transducers than design the transducers to match the output transformer.

Transducers are usually operated at resonance since this is the point at which they will undergo maximum vibration together with maximum stress and strain in the material. The output mechanical power will be found to be directly proportional to the dynamic strain level and the higher the strain in the core, the higher the mechanical energy produced. In other words, the output of a transducer is proportional to its Q.

$$Q = \frac{\omega M}{R}$$

where ω = $2\pi f$

    f = resonant frequency

    M = mass

    R = mechanical resistance

Effect of Load.   One of the major problems in the design of transducers is to get energy out of the transducer.   Coupling a load to the transducer has a tendency to damp out the transducer itself, and no energy can be obtained from it.   This is particularly true where the transducer is fastened to a solid body.   It is generally advisable to mount the transducer so that a minimum damping takes place.   Theoretically, it may be shown that the maximum useful power may be obtained under conditions where half the power is dissipated at the load and the other half in the transducer.   However, the mechanical problems are so great that it is very difficult to satisfactorily compute such conditions and the common approach is to mount the transducer so that minimum damping takes place.

Effect of Loading One or Both Ends.[1]   If a bar is used as a longitudinal wave generator with zero mechanical loss and unit cross-sectional area and is uniformly excited over its length it may be shown that the maximum output is

$$E_1 \text{ (end velocity)} = \frac{2f(H)}{Z_1 + Z_2}$$

where $Z_1 + Z_2$ = load impedances
$\quad\quad f(H)$ = stress set up by exciting field

$$\text{Total output } w = \frac{[2f(H)^2]}{Z_1 + Z_2}$$

It may therefore be shown that with one end unloaded, the total output is double that with both ends loaded.   This is the reason for using backing material which only allows radiation from one face.

Tool Design.   It is very often necessary to design tools for use with magnetostrictive stacks.   These tools may also be used with crystal drivers but are more common in the case of magnetostriction.   They are actually horns, and the theory of horns may be applied to them.   As such, they essentially transform the impedance and motion at their ends to match the desired conditions.   Several types of tools are shown in Fig. 4-21.   The tools take the form of extensions bonded to the transducer proper.   The following general considerations may be of interest.

Resonance.   In order to obtain maximum output from the transducer, it is necessary to operate at a resonant frequency determined by the transducer itself in combination with the tool.   In most cases, the addition of the tool to the stack will cause a change in the resonant frequency, but if the tool is properly designed, this change will be slight.   Frequency may go either up or down when the tool is added.   The bonding will also affect this.   As the tool and stack approach each other in frequency, they will

[1] T. M. Leslie, *JASA*, **22** (1950) 4.

resonate at the stack frequency. The tendency is, however, for the total assembly to operate at this tool frequency rather than at the stack frequency when not on frequency.

Use. The design of the tool is required in order to transmit the vibration to its end in such a way as to amplify the motion or to provide a shape which is not easily obtained with the laminations. It may also be desirable to have a tool interchangeable by means of a threaded portion. It also provides support means (particularly in the case of cutting units).

It appears that the rate of cutting by ultrasonics is a function of the amplitude of vibration. The tool should therefore be designed to give a large motion. This may be accomplished by means of a tool whose cross-sectional area changes sharply. A number of such tools have been

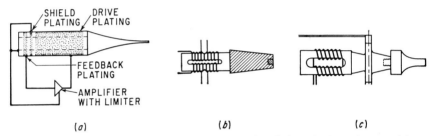

FIG. 4-21. Typical tool configurations: (a) tool bonded to barium titanate driver; (b) tool bonded to a magnetostrictive stack; (c) multiple tools bonded to a magnetostrictive stack.

designed and the gain in motion appears to be proportional to the change in the cross section. This cross-sectional change may be either a straight taper, a sharp step change, or an exponential taper (or multiples or combinations thereof).[1]

Generally, the area at the top of the tool is determined by the size of the transducer stack and should, of course, not be any larger than it. This is normally about 1 to 3 in. in diameter. The bottom diameter of the tool may be anything from approximately $\frac{1}{8}$ in. up.

The tool itself is usually designed to be at a frequency which is the same as the transducer's resonance and its length may therefore be designed as

$$L = \frac{cK}{2\pi f}$$

where L = length

c = velocity

f = frequency

K is a constant which has been experimentally or theoretically determined for various types of tools, and which is determined by the shape and

[1] W. P. Mason and S. D. White, *Bell System Tech. J.*, **31** (1952) 469.

mass. This is the same formula as for the stack itself. The velocity may be found in tables for the particular material being used and the frequency is the operating frequency of the transducer. It will become clear that it is almost impossible to completely calculate exact lengths owing to the complications added by boundary conditions. However, close approximations may be made.

Rod Tools. The simplest type of tool is a straight rod. The only thing that has to be determined is its length, which can be calculated from the equation above (with minor adjustments which are a function of the mass and must be made experimentally). The diameter is arbitrary except that it must be smaller than a suitable mounting area. The factor K is 1 (or can be omitted). A suitable material is R Monel, which has a high Q and is therefore a good material for vibration. Cold-rolled steel or brass may also be used. The velocity in this material is about 1.8×10^5 in./sec. A tool for use at about 25 kc would therefore come out to be about $3\frac{1}{2}$ in. long. The basic use for such a tool would merely be as an extension of the transducer since the motion at both ends would be the same. In cases where the tool was to be used for cutting, a further extension, about $\frac{1}{4}$ in. long with a diameter something less than that of the tool, could be added to the end; or another tapered tool similar to the first may be added.

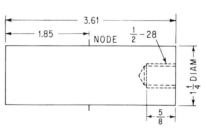

FIG. 4-22. Straight rod tool, 25 kc.

The point of maximum strain and the motion node of a straight bar is in the center, and supporting rings may be attached at this point. Figure 4-22 shows a typical straight rod tool for 25 kc, a convenient frequency for use.

Cones with Straight Tapers. Tools may also be designed with a gradual straight taper from top to bottom (conical horn). Table 4-2

TABLE 4-2. COMPARISON OF CONICAL AND EXPONENTIAL HORNS

D_2/D_1	Kl	Gain (conical)	Gain (exponential)
1		1	1
2	3.29	1.92	2
3	3.48	2.55	3
4	3.63	3.15	4

compares conical and exponential horns. The bottom of the tool is chosen arbitrarily and is usually about $\frac{1}{2}$ in. in diameter or less. The top size will therefore fall at some diameter which will be satisfactory so long as it is less than the size of the stack to which it is being fastened. This might be about 2 in. Once these two dimensions are known, the length of the rod can be determined from the following formulas:[1]

$$\text{Resonance condition} = \frac{Kl}{\tan Kl} = 1 + (Kl)^2 \frac{D_2 D_1}{(D_1 - 1)^2}$$

where D_2 = larger diameter
D_1 = one smaller diameter
$K = \omega/c$
l = tool length

$$\text{Gain} = \frac{\varepsilon_1}{\varepsilon_2}$$

$$= \frac{D_2}{D_1} = \frac{1}{\cos Kl \text{ (radians)}} \frac{1}{1 + (\tan Kl)/Kl\{[1 - (D_1/D_2)]/(D_1/D_2)\}}$$

The node (motion) is displaced toward the thick end and the strain maximum toward the thin edge. The node of such a tool is essentially

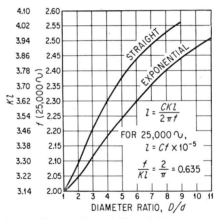

Fig. 4-23. Tool design chart, values of Kl and f for various diameter ratios.

its center of mass and it is therefore supported nearer the thick end. The distance from this end may be computed from the relationship below, which is derived from the formula for center of mass of a tapered cone.

Values of Kl have been worked out and are shown in Fig. 4-23 (which considerably simplifies the design of the tool). The top and bottom diameters are chosen according to the requirements of use. For 25,000 cps, the value of f shown is read off. Then

$$L = 10^{-5} cf$$

[1] R. H. Quint, private communication.

For any other frequency the value of Kl is read off. Then

$$L = \frac{cKl}{2\pi f}$$

Step Tools. A large gain in motion may be accomplished by means of step tools (two connected cylinders). Again the bottom diameter and top diameter are chosen. The top diameter is usually twice the bottom. The distance which the step falls from the top of the tool is approximately

$$D = \frac{L}{2} \quad \text{in.}$$

where D = distance from top

L = total length, in. (i.e., the step is about halfway up the tool)

The ratio of gain (motion) is the ratio of diameters or of masses of the two sections. The nodal plane (motion) and stress are the same (at the center).

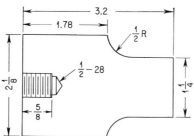

Fig. 4-24. Typical 25-kc step tool.

In cases where the two sections are the same length, the nodal points are moved to one of the sections. However, amplification becomes less than in the equal situation.

The support of such a tool is at the center of the mass, which can be easily computed from the diameters of the two sections. Figure 4-24 is a typical step tool at 25 kc.

Exponential Cones. The exponential cone has a length which is also dependent upon the ratio of the top and bottom diameters. When the tool is tapered exponentially, the radius changes as

$$r = r_0 e^{-\alpha x}$$

where r = radius at tool end (or section)

α = taper factor

r_0 = radius at top of tool

The length may be solved for, and becomes

$$L = \frac{V_0}{2f} \sqrt{1 + \left[\frac{\ln (r_0/r)}{\pi} \right]^2}$$

Thus, the tapered tool is always longer than a straight one. For example, if r_0/r is 10, at 25,000 cps the tool is 4.46 in. long and exponentially tapered.[1] The curve (Fig. 4-23) gives a relationship between D_2/D_1, f, and Kl, and the procedure is the same as for the conical tools.

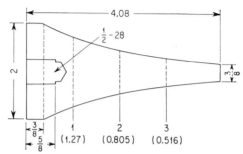

FIG. 4-25. Typical exponential tool, 25 kc.

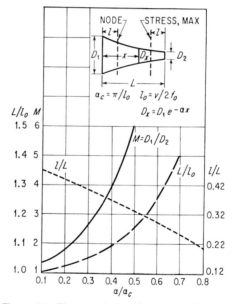

FIG. 4-26. Characteristics of exponential cone.

l_o = length of cylinder
L = length of exponential cone
M = magnification
l = length from thick end to node

The nodal point (motion) is also not in the center but nearer the larger end. The stress node, however, is displaced toward the smaller end. The nodal point of mass and of motion are close enough to be the same

[1] N. Clark, *IRE P. G. Ultrasonic Eng.*, **2** (1954) 10.

for design purposes.   The support may accordingly be found by finding the center of mass.

A typical exponential tool for 25 kc is shown in Fig. 4-25.   The center of mass of the exponential cone may be found from the graph relating the various characteristics of the exponential cone.[1]

Choice of Tool.   The type of tool used is a function of its use and the complication of machine work necessary to fabricate it.   The maximum top diameter of most of these units to date is about $2\frac{1}{2}$ in.   Ranges of these are indicated in Table 4-3.

TABLE 4-3. COMPARISON OF VARIOUS TYPES OF TOOLS

(Dimensions in inches)

Type	$D_{\max}$	$D_{\min}$	Maximum ratio	Gain	Tool length, in.
Rod.................	$2\frac{1}{2}$	...	1	1	$\frac{3}{8}$
Straight taper........	$2\frac{1}{2}$	$\frac{1}{2}$	4	D/d	$\frac{3}{8}$
Step................	$2\frac{1}{2}$	1	2	$(D/d)^2$	$\frac{3}{8}$
Exponential..........	$2\frac{1}{2}$	$\frac{1}{8}$	20	D/d	$\frac{3}{8}$

Materials.   Among other satisfactory materials for fabricating tools are Monel, cold-rolled steel, and brass.   Monel has a high Q and is therefore preferable.   Velocities in some of these materials are all very similar and are given in Table 4-4.

TABLE 4-4. VELOCITY IN TOOL MATERIALS

Material	$V \times 10^5$, in.
R Monel	1.804
K Monel	1.847
Monel	1.795
Steel	1.99
Brass	1.407

Several materials may be used with very high frequencies or where large motions (or large tools) are required.   Such a material, for example, would be beryllium aluminum.

Tips.   It may sometimes be necessary to add supplementary tips to the ends of tools.   When these tips are less than $\frac{3}{8}$ in. long, no adjustment is necessary to the tool itself.   When longer, the tool must be shortened by an amount equivalent to the weight of the tip.   The cross-sectional area of the end of the tool is always greater than that of the tip.   Since nomenclature is still developing, some experimenters refer to the tip as the *tool*, and the tool as the *cone*.

Determining the Center of Mass.   Mountings for tools are usually at the point of minimum motion, i.e., the center of mass.   For a cylindrical

[1] L. Balamuth, *IRE P.G. Ultrasonic Eng.*, **2** (1954) 23.

tool the center of mass is, of course, the center of the linear dimension of
the tool.

For a homogeneous right circular cone (straight taper tool) it may be
derived from any standard text on solid geometry and becomes

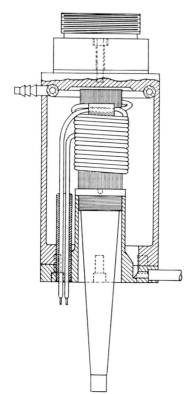

$$w = \frac{L}{4} \frac{R^2 + 2Rr + 3r^2}{R^2 + Rr + r^2}$$

where L = length

R = larger radius

r = smaller radius

However, other types of mountings are
possible.[1] For example, a rigid support
of low impedance can be connected at
an antinode. This support is a quarter
wavelength and therefore moves at the

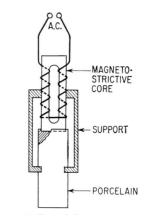

Fig. 4-27. Tool support.

Fig. 4-28. Porcelain tool for high heat.

point of attachment to the tool and is rigid at the point of attachment
to the support (Fig. 4-27).

Insulating Tools.   It is sometimes necessary to contact materials which
are at very high temperatures, or which react with metals in such a way
that direct contact is impossible.   In such cases ceramic tools have found
use (Fig. 4-28).[2]   Porcelains of low thermal conductivity have been suggested.   These tools are, of course, designed similarly to the tools already
described.

Diaphragms.   One of the basic problems in ultrasonic work is the
means of getting energy from the transducer into the medium in which it
is desired.   One such means of coupling is a diaphragm, the dimensions

[1] C. E. Calosi, U.S. Patent 2,632,858 (1953).

[2] H. Thiede, *Akustische Z.*, **8** (1943) 20.

of whose face are large in relation to the wavelength of the sound which is being radiated. It is furthermore usually assumed that all points on the diaphragm face are vibrating in phase and with equal amplitude.

Unfortunately, for practical reasons, it is important that the diaphragm be clamped around its edge to make it liquid tight. This has a tendency to cause different parts of the diaphragm to be out of phase with one another.

It is obvious that merely taking an arbitrary plate of thin material and using it as a diaphragm will produce an untuned member which is extremely inefficient. Such a unit should be tuned to the frequency of the ultrasonic energy with which it is being used.

One form of diaphragm would therefore be a tuned tool (such as those described in the section under tools) which has a ring fitted around its node which is fastened to the part through which it protrudes. Since the entire tool is resonant, it is supported at a point of no vibration which has the effect of passing the energy through the wall as a diaphragm. The disadvantage of such a unit is, of course, that at the frequency at which one can operate with magnetostrictive materials, the diaphragm will be 4 or 5 in. thick, and this is sometimes awkward.

In designing very thin diaphragms, it must be realized that the waves progressing from the center to the edge of the diaphragm (in center mounting) are transverse. Their velocity is accordingly that of this type of wave in a thin plate (close to the velocity of compressional waves in air).

This velocity may be stated as

$$c = \frac{K}{L} \sqrt{\frac{E}{d}}$$

The diaphragm should be supported at a node, and be flexible enough not to damp the tool.

Thick plates may also be designed as diaphragms. These are normally clamped about the edge to seal them into the tank or part being agitated. They may then be designed from

$$c = \frac{(3.2)^2 c^2}{2\pi a^2} = \frac{(3.2)^2 \sqrt{Q}\, h}{2\pi a^2 \sqrt{3\rho(1-\mu^2)}}$$

which simplifies to (ignoring μ^2)

$$f = \frac{2.4 \times 10^5 \times 2h}{a^2}$$

where $h = \frac{1}{2}$ thickness, cm
    a = radius, cm
    ρ = density
    Q = Young's modulus

Backing. Since it was shown that radiation from the back face cuts the usable output to about one-fourth, it is advisable to back all transducers with a material, such as Coprene, which does not allow back radiation, especially when water-cooled, since radiation into the water may be considerable.

Cooling. Magnetostrictive units are usually mounted in a water- or oil-cooling jacket so that the transducer is kept at a usable temperature. A complete transducer, complete with tool and jacket, is shown in Fig. 11-1. The cooling jacket also acts as the support. The design of such jackets is obvious, and the only major problem lies in the support of the tool within it.

Bending Transducers. It is possible to secure several sections of magnetostrictive material side by side, excited out of phase, so one lengthens while the other shortens, causing sideways motion.[1] Such transducers may be used, for example, in drilling teeth, where sideways motion is desirable.

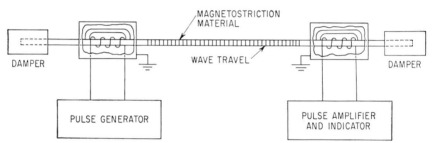

Fig. 4-29. Magnetostrictive delay line.

Magnetostrictive Delay Lines. The use of magnetostrictive delay lines is not so common as that of crystal types (described in Chap. 9). However, this application of magnetostriction appears to be a promising one. The basic idea is shown in Fig. 4-29.[2] A sending coil is placed about one end of a magnetostrictive bar, and a receiving one is spaced at a convenient distance from it, according to the delay desired. The ends of the bar are damped so that energy is not reflected back and forth in the bar. Suitable electronic apparatus for sending and receiving pulses are also included. The pulse from the sending coil is propagated down the bar and after a delay is picked up by the receiving coil.

Distributed Amplifiers. Long magnetostrictive rods may have traveling waves set up in them. This phenomenon has been applied to ultrasonic delay lines, and also for generating power. Figure 4-30 shows the principle of such a unit.[3] A pulse is impressed on the first coil and starts

[1] British Patent 2623/52 (1952).
[2] A. M. Nicholson, U.S. Patent 2,401,094 (1946).
[3] M. Apstein, U.S. Patent 2,717,981 (1956).

to travel down the bar.   It is also sent down an electrical delay line of
such a character that it is impressed on the second coil at the same time
that the ultrasonic pulse traveling in the bar reaches that section of the
bar under the coil.   Thus the electrical signal in the coil reinforces the

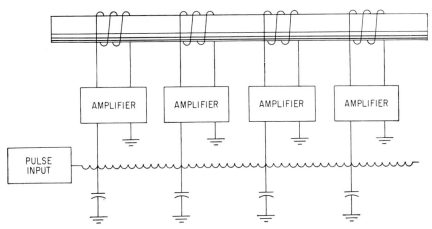

Fig. 4-30. Distributed magnetostrictive amplifier.

pulse in the bar.   This action is repeated any convenient number of
times, causing a more powerful signal to be generated than by conventional means, and with less losses, since they are also distributed throughout the bar.

CHAPTER 5

MISCELLANEOUS TRANSDUCERS FOR
GENERATING ULTRASONICS

General. Although the bulk of attention has been given to the more popular types of transducers (such as magnetostriction and piezoelectric), there are other means of generating ultrasound, some of which exhibit great promise. It may be expected that when these or other units are developed to a further extent they will play a large part in industrial applications. These may be divided into the following:

1. Whistles
   a. Galton whistle
   b. Hartmann whistle
   c. Jet-edge systems
   d. Miscellaneous
2. Sirens
3. Electromagnetic systems
4. Mechanical
5. Miscellaneous

Whistles. Sounds may be generated by passing a gas or liquid through an orifice or over an edge. Such devices are known as *whistles* and are satisfactory for generation of energy in suitable materials. The passage of the gas generates vortices, spaced periodically, which propagate as a sound wave. While a simple circular hole may be used for this purpose, more stable results may be obtained in various ways. These devices may be used in either gases or liquids, but are especially suited to gases or liquids where their low impedance allows better coupling.

As indicated, the ultrasonic energy produced by the liquid or gas flowing through an orifice or over a blade is caused by vortices which are produced by it and which move through the gas or liquid. These vortices are periodic and the frequency of their occurrence is also the frequency of the sound wave which is produced.

Galton Whistle. One of the first types of whistles is attributable to Galton.[1] It basically consists of a jet which sends out a stream of gas

[1] F. Galton, *Nature*, **27** (1883) 491.

against a small cavity. Figure 5-1 shows the inlet (A), the orifice (C), and an adjustment (B) which varies spacing. D is the cavity. The depth of the cavity may be varied by the micrometer E. The frequency produced by such a whistle is

$$f = c \frac{1 + t/273}{(4d + K)^{1/2}}$$

where c = velocity of sound, mm/sec
t = temperature, °C
d = depth of the cavity
K = pressure constant (about 6)

A number of frequencies are produced by the gas stream, and the resonant cavity activated at its natural frequency, if it is one of those produced. Units of this sort are used today for control and signaling purposes.[1]

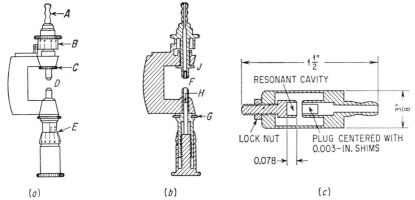

(a) (b) (c)

Fig. 5-1. (a) Classical type of Galton whistle; (b) cutaway view; (c) used with atomizer bulb.

A whistle designed for use in controlling a lantern-slide mechanism[1] is shown as an adaptation of the principle. This unit operates at 25 kc, by pressure from a rubber bulb. This is about the upper limit easily attainable in frequency. Higher ones may be reached by substituting other gases, such as hydrogen, for air, to actuate the device.

Hartmann Whistle. The Hartmann generator consists of a nozzle from which a jet of compressed air emerges. It is directed against the ring-shaped edge of a hole, as shown in Fig. 5-2b. Shock waves are set up in the gas and are reflected to form zones of reflection. The basic difference between the Hartmann and the Galton whistle is that the velocity in the gas in the former is much greater; and therefore higher frequencies are attainable. The shape of the jets has also been modified to conical.

[1] S. G. Lutz and G. Rand, *Electronics*, **22** (1949) 96.

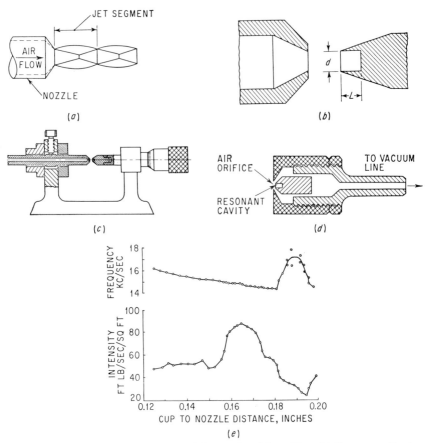

Fig. 5-2. The Hartmann generator: (a) jet produced by orifice; (b) diagrammatic view of unit; (c) classical whistle for laboratory use; (d) automobile vacuum-operated device; (e) cup-to-nozzle distance vs. intensity and frequency.

This has a tendency to introduce a side injection of gas. The air in the resonant hole will oscillate with a frequency

$$f = \frac{c}{\lambda} = \frac{c}{4(L + 0.3d)}$$

where L = depth of hole
d = diameter
c = velocity of sound in gas

The nozzle alone produces a structure similar to that shown in Fig. 5-2a.[1] When a cup is placed before the orifice and on the same axis, the output varies with distance for any size cup, as shown in Fig. 5-2e.[1] Vari-

[1] H. O. Monson and R. C. Binder, *JASA*, **25** (1953) 1001; J. Hartmann and B. Trolle, *J. Sci. Instr.*, **4** (1947) 101.

ations with output are also apparent for different sized cups.   Hartmann originally used a cup with a diameter-to-depth ratio of 1:1 and a cup diameter the same as the nozzle diameter.   This does not produce maximum results; slight variations in sizes may raise the output.

Instabilities in operation occur at points where the output frequency falls at positions of the cup for which slight movements cause large changes.

The Hartmann generator has been suggested as a precipitator of dust or fog.   It has also been used for signaling.   One application is an ultrasonic garage-door opener[1] (Fig. 5-2d).   Such a device may generate about

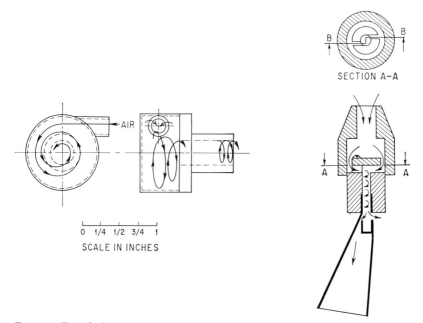

FIG. 5-3. Two designs for vortex whistles.   [B. Vonnegut, JASA, 26 (1954) 18.]

50 to 100 watts in air at about 10 kc.   However, efficiencies are low, about 5 per cent.   This is offset by the ease of generating air pressure.

A number of modifications have appeared in the literature from time to time to improve operation and adapt the unit to present requirements. By using gases other than air, frequencies of up to 0.5 Mc may be attained.

Vortex Whistles.[2]   Whistles for use in gases or liquids have been designed to produce a vortex in the gas.   The frequency is a function of the pressure or rate of flow.   A number of designs have been suggested (see Fig. 5-3).   The air is introduced in such a way that it rotates rapidly.

[1] B. A. Andrews, *Electronics*, **20** (1947) 116.
[2] B. Vonnegut, *JASA*, **26** (1954) 18.

The frequency of operation is

$$f = \alpha \left(\frac{c}{\pi D}\right)\left(\frac{P_1 - P_2}{P_2}\right)^{\frac{1}{2}}$$

where f = frequency

D = tube diameter

c = velocity of sound

P_1 = pressure at entrance

P_2 = pressure at exit

Jet-edge Systems (Pohlmann Whistle). A jet-edge system is a device which produces a jet of gas or liquid and projects it against the edge of a rigid blade,[1] as shown in Fig. 5-4. It may be used with either gases or

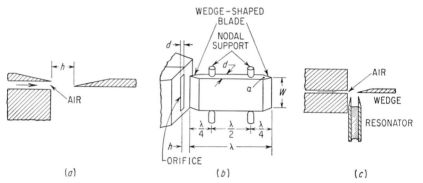

Fig. 5-4. The jet-edge whistle (Pohlmann): (*a*) basic system; (*b*) diagrammatic view; (*c*) unit with resonator. [W. L. Nyborg, M. D. Burkhard, and H. K. Schilling, *JASA* **24** (1952) 293.]

liquids. In the latter case it is particularly suited to emulsification applications. The operation seems to be a function of flow velocity, size of the orifice, edge distance, etc. The frequencies produced occur in steps or stages, which are a function of air velocity. The orifice is usually a rectangular slit in front of which a tapered plate is positioned, vibrating in flexure, and pinned at its nodes. The stream is divided by the blade, whose thickness is of the same order as the orifice. The blade is about twice as long as it is wide, about a wavelength long. The ends are tapered at about 30 deg. The frequency is

$$f = \frac{22 \times 4d}{4\pi\lambda^2 \sqrt{3}} \sqrt{\frac{E}{\rho}} = 2.8 \frac{d}{\lambda^2} C_b$$

where λ = length of plate

d = thickness

E = Young's modulus

ρ = density

C_b = bar velocity

[1] G. B. Brown, *Proc. Phys. Soc. London,* **49** (1937) 493.

Brown[1] gave an empirical formula for frequency:

$$f = 0.466 \frac{ju}{h}$$

where f = frequency
    j = stage of operation
    u = air velocity
    h = distance between orifice and blade edge
The relationship of these factors is shown in Fig. 5-4.

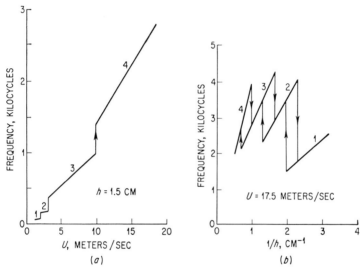

FIG. 5-5. Relationships in the jet-edge system: (a) frequency vs. stream velocity; (b) frequency vs. reciprocal 1/h of wedge distance. (After G. B. Brown.)

Jet-edge devices may be modified by having resonators set near them (see Fig. 5-4c). A resonance occurs when the frequency of the jet-edge system nears that of the resonator. It is proportional to the dimension between the edge of the blade and the nozzle. Low ultrasonic frequencies and high sonic ones are possible (up to 200 kc). Powers to 10 dynes/cm² have been observed in air. Various other gases, particularly helium, have also been used to drive the whistle.

The theory of operation indicates that the oscillating jet produced by the orifice causes sound to be produced by the blade. Transverse forces are produced which influence the stream, producing oscillations. A considerable literature on the theory has grown up and is listed in Nyborg's article.[2]

The design of the wedge may be approached as follows.[3] Consider

[1] *Ibid.*
[2] W. L. Nyborg, *JASA*, **26** (1954) 174.
[3] A. Leitner and E. A. Heidemann, *JASA*, **26** (1954) 509.

Fig. 5-7a, where the length of the bar is $2L$, and the thickness $2r$.   The uniform bar would be one wavelength long.   As the wedge is elongated, the frequency initially is increased owing to the loss of mass.   As the amount of material becomes great enough to lower the stiffness the frequency again goes down.   For design purposes r is the ratio of tapered section to uniform section (both ends are the same).   The change in frequency with respect to a uniform bar is shown in Fig. 5-7b.

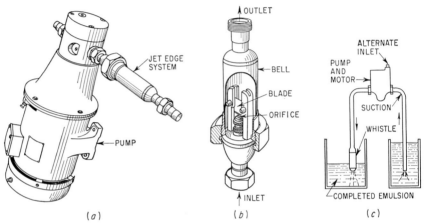

FIG. 5-6. Commercial jet-edge system: (a) pump and whistle; (b) cutaway whistle; (c) setup.

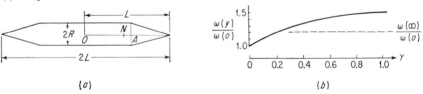

FIG. 5-7. Resonant wedge: (a) wedge; (b) ratio of frequency of tapered reed to uniform one, frequency-vs.-taper ratio. [*A. Leitner and E. A. Hiedemann, JASA*, **26** (1954) 509.]

The jet-edge system has had industrial applications to emulsification and mixing of liquids where it has proved practical and economical.

Sirens.   Most of the standard types of ultrasonic transducers are not satisfactory for producing high-amplitude waves in air or gases.   One method of doing so which shows great promise is the siren.[1]

A cutaway view of a typical siren is shown in Fig. 5-9.[2]   It basically consists of a source of air such as a compressor, a ported stator, and a rotor which interrupts the air through the ports.   A rotor-drive motor of $\frac{1}{2}$ to 1 hp at about 133 rps will drive a unit producing 300 to 1,200 watts

[1] C. H. Allen and I. Rudnick, *JASA*, **19** (1947) 857; R. C. Jones, *JASA*, **18** (1946) 371.

[2] Allen and Rudnick, *loc. cit.*

at from 3 to 30 kc/sec.   An air supply of about 60 ft³/min is required and is led to the ports by baffles giving equal distribution.

At the high-frequency end (30 kc) the ports radiate well, but at the low-frequency end a horn (Fig. 5-9b)[1] may be added.   The equivalent circuit of such a siren is shown in Fig. 5-8, where

E = air pressure

R and L = acoustic impedance of throat of horn or atmosphere

H and M = acoustic impedance into pressure chamber

G = resistance to airflow from pressure chamber to throat of horn

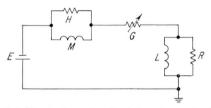

FIG. 5-8. Equivalent circuit of the ultrasonic siren.

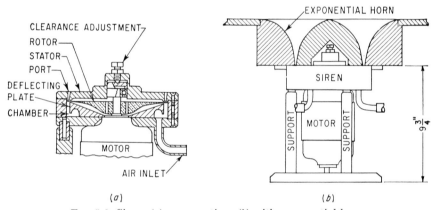

(a)   (b)

FIG. 5-9. Siren: (a) cross section; (b) with exponential horn.

For high efficiency and power M, L, and R should be high, so L and R must be large compared with the other resistive elements in the circuit when the ports are open.   This leads to requirements for rapid opening and closing of the ports, an exponential matching horn, and other design details.

Sirens of this type have a theoretical maximum efficiency of 50 per cent and produce an essentially pure fundamental frequency.   With sirens which contain other frequencies, i.e., have ports open about half time and closed half time, the efficiency is much greater (from 81 to 100 per cent possible).   A usual efficiency figure varies between 17 and 32 per cent.

The application of this type of transducer to agglomeration of particles

[1] *Ibid.*

in gas, i.e., smoke, etc., is still somewhat controversial, although pilot applications have been made.   The mechanical construction of the unit is critical, requiring a high-strength rotor, carefully placed holes and teeth, etc.

Electromagnetic Transducers.   The motion of a coil carrying current in a magnetic field may be used to generate ultrasonics.   Devices of this type are well known at low frequencies (loudspeakers) and the problem is to get high frequencies at high powers.

Moving-coil Systems.   The dynamic loudspeaker is a device in which a coil moves in a magnetic field.   Such a device has been built at ultrasonic frequencies[1] using a resonant bar instead of the paper cone (Fig. 5-10).   The vibrating bar is a solid section of Duraluminum, supported

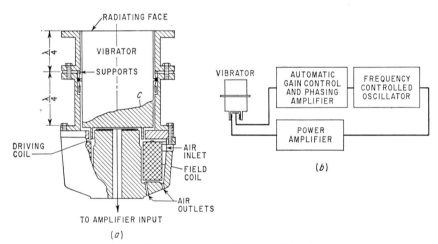

Fig. 5-10. (a) Electromagnetic vibrator; (b) driving element.

in the center and free to vibrate longitudinally.   The bottom of the bar has a thinner section fastened to it (or integral with it) which projects into the gap of a magnet and acts as a secondary winding magnetically coupled to an exciting coil wound on the magnet.   The current in the secondary then drives the vibrator without any mechanical connection being necessary.   In this case the magnet is electrically energized by a field coil.   A capacitive pickup is used to stabilize the frequency since the bar is sharply tuned and a small amount of drift cannot be tolerated.   A driving unit[2] is shown in Fig. 5-10b incorporating the capacitive frequency control and feedback system.

The bar is supported at the center, which is a node for longitudinal vibration.   Since the bar diameter is great with respect to wavelength,

[1] H. W. St. Clair, *Rev. Sci. Instr.*, **12** (1941) 250.
[2] E. Potter, *Rev. Sci. Instr.*, **14** (1943) 207.

radial vibrations will also exist and tight clamping would cause heavy losses in output. The support is therefore a soft one.

The frequency of a bar of this type has been given by Rayleigh[1] as

$$f = \left(\frac{1 - \sigma^2\pi^2r^2}{4L^2}\right)\frac{1}{2L}\left(\frac{E}{\rho}\right)^{1/2}$$

where σ = Poisson's ratio

r = radius

L = length

As would be expected with this order of radius, plane waves in sharply defined beams are produced. Typical design data given by St. Clair are as follows:

> Diameter = 15.2 cm
> Length = 13 cm
> Frequency = 17 kc
> Exciting coil = 54 turns
> Efficiency = 30 per cent

Miscellaneous Mechanical Vibrators. At first glance it appears that mechanical means of generating ultrasonic waves would be simple. Unfortunately, difficulties of coupling, etc., make most of these approaches

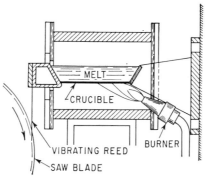

FIG. 5-11. Mechanical setup used by Muhlhauser.

almost impossible. One such apparatus has been described[2] and consists of a vibrating reed driven from a circular saw. This was used by Muhlhauser in early experiments and is shown in Fig. 5-11. A reed is made to vibrate by resting it on a rotating wheel with teeth. The frequency was about 10 kc. The operation is obvious. Apparatus of this sort actually dates to the seventeenth century (Hooke).

Other types of vibrators have also been tried. Shafts carrying eccentrics have been used for low frequencies (Fig. 5-12).[3] This was also for

[1] Lord Rayleigh, "Theory of Sound," Dover Publications, 1945.

[2] E. A. Heidemann, *JASA*, **26** (1954) 831.

[3] H. J. Seeman and H. Menzel, *Metall*, **1** (1947) 39.

a metallographic application. In the same frequency range, pneumatic devices driving a piston have been used to rap on the end of a chamber. Other extensions of this type of reasoning are readily apparent. In general, this type of approach has not been successful because of the difficulty in getting the energy in usable form.

Another type of mechanical generator is the Holtzmann generator in which a solid rod is supported in its center and is driven by leather belts. At present this has only historical interest.

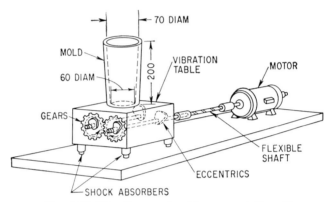

FIG. 5-12. Vibrating mold. (*Seeman and Menzel.*)

Hydrodynamic Valve Transducers. Liquid flowing through a pipe may be modulated by means of a valve. The effect is not new, but means of feeding energy back to the valve for stable operation have not been known. More recently such devices operating at low frequencies have been experimentally produced.[1]

Thermal. When the temperature of the closed end of a gas-filled pipe is suddenly raised, the gas near that end expands and pushes toward the open end, producing a wave which travels down the pipe.[2] This produces a sound wave.

Singing Flames.[3] It has been known for some time that placing a tube containing air over a flame will produce sound waves in the air of the tube. Standing waves may be set up in the tube; but this is not necessary, and the phenomenon appears to be a function of the time of travel of the gas in the flame, the size of the flame, the gas viscosity, and the various parameters of the physical setup.

It is also known that a flame may be used as a rough indicator of the presence of sonic waves, since the sound pressure will cause the flame to be displaced.

[1] J. V. Bouyocos, *Harvard Univ. Acoustic Research Lab. Rept.* 122969 (July, 1955).
[2] L. Trilling, *JASA*, **27** (1955) 424.
[3] A. T. Jones, *JASA*, **16** (1945) 254.

CHAPTER 6

MEASUREMENT

A major aspect of ultrasonic work is the measurement of ultrasonic energy in a medium. A number of different approaches have been made to this problem, depending upon different effects of ultrasound. The measurements themselves may be of level (or intensity), frequency, focusing, or any other characteristic.

In the case of level measurements, the following types of detectors may be used:

1. Mechanical devices. This category includes one of the first measuring devices suggested, i.e., the Rayleigh disk or radiometer, as well as such indicators as drops of water, moving flames, smoke, dust, etc. With the possible exception of the radiometer, it is difficult to measure differences between ultrasonic fields of closely similar power levels by these means, especially after the power becomes fairly great.

2. Optical devices such as Schlieren or diffraction-pattern devices, shadow projectors, etc. These units are mainly used in getting pictures of waveforms or standing waves but are not of much help at present in measuring intensities.

3. Microphones of various types. These may include transducers made by any method for the production or reception of ultrasonic waves.

4. Electrical devices such as hot wires, resistors, etc.

5. Interferometers.

6. Thermal devices: devices for measuring thermal effects.

7. Miscellaneous: shadowgraph, etc.

Reliable measurements can only be made at levels where cavitation does not occur, or is prevented by pressurizing the bath or other techniques. The visualization or exploration of the ultrasonic field is complicated by the difficulties of transforming the results into meaningful quantitative ones, rather than merely qualitative indications.

Detection of Ultrasonic Waves—Pressure. *Theory.* When ultrasonic waves are projected against a boundary, they exercise on it two different effects: One is the alternating pressure at the frequency of the wave propagation, and the other is a direct pressure due to the radiation. The alternating pressure is determined by the formula

$$P = \frac{2J}{u} = \frac{dc}{2}\,(\omega A^2)$$

where J = intensity/cm², in unit time
    d = density
    A = maximum amplitude of vibration particles
    P = sound pressure
    u = velocity of individual particle
    $\omega = 2\pi f$

A quartz crystal will actually respond to and follow these variations, but most mechanical systems, because of their inertia and mass, cannot vibrate at the frequency necessary to reproduce such fluctuations. However, besides the high-frequency vibration there is also the unidirectional effect, which is expressed by the formula

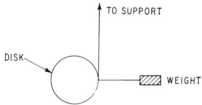

FIG. 6-1. Ultrasonic radiometer.

$$S = \tfrac{1}{2}(K - 1)\,\frac{J}{c}$$

where K is the ratio of the specific heats.

A measurement of the unidirectional pressure gives an indication of the intensity of the ultrasonic field and is the basis of much of the practical work done in such measurement.

Mechanical Devices. If a plate or disk is inserted in an ultrasonic field and if the waves in the field hit the disk at a normal incidence, they exert pressure upon the disk. If the material from which the disk is made has a specific acoustic impedance which is very different from the fluid in which it is inserted, it will reflect a large amount of the energy, and when the disk is hung on a torsion balance, the force of the ultrasound pressing upon the disk will cause it to rotate (or move), since the force at the face of the disk is equivalent to the sum of the energy arriving at that point and the energy being reflected from it. A number of ways may be used for measuring this energy and have been suggested in the past. In one case (Fig. 6-1) the torsion head is twisted to bring the disk back to its original position, and this indicates the amount of power produced by the ultrasound. In general, devices of this sort have been classified as to whether they are large or small in comparison to the wavelength and are referred to as *Rayleigh disks* if small, and *radiometers* if large. A number of experiments have been made to determine the effects of standing waves, and in some cases, specially shaped disks have been designed to reflect the energy in a direction which will not affect the source. This principle has been used as the basis for a number of commercial instruments, and in these cases, the radiometer may take the form of two thin metal parts separated by an ultrasonic insulator and bent at right angles. The energy which hits the face of this device is split and reflected at a 90-deg angle. It is then absorbed by an absorbing medium (Fig. 6-2a). Some sort of mechanical coupling is then used to measure the ultrasonic force and move a needle to indicate it. These devices, of course, must be calibrated against some absolute measurement of power, since the reading they give is comparative rather than absolute. In some cases the acoustic power may be computed on an absolute basis.

The radiation torsion device suffers from the basic problem that it must be comparatively large if it is to be at all sensitive. On the other hand, inserting a large device in the ultrasonic field produces distortion of the

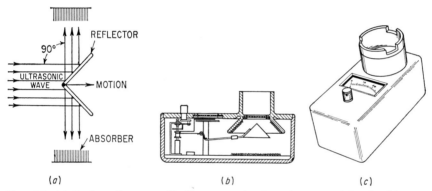

(a)   (b)   (c)

Fig. 6-2. (a) Basic radiometer; (b) diagrammatic view of commercial unit; (c) commercial unit. (*Atlas Werke.*)

field, which makes accurate measurements difficult. Moreover, these units are only independent of frequency when small in comparison to a half wavelength. The net result is an instrument which has certain advantages for measuring gross powers, but is not of very much use in exploring the details of sound fields.

Figure 6-2b and c shows the application of the radiation disk to a commercial instrument. Figure 6-2b includes the use of a right-angle reflector to eliminate the effects of standing waves. The reflector itself is made of thin metal sheets isolated by fish paper and sealed. The sound beam is split into two sections and then absorbed. The action of the split beam in any direction other than desired is eliminated by its symmetry, and the net force is against the face of the disk, and in the direction of the beam. This force can then be measured by a scale. Another form of this device is shown in Fig. 6-3 (this is a side view).[1] The balance hangs

[1] G. W. Willard, *JASA*, **21** (1949) 360.

from an axle which turns on bearings. The sound absorber or reflector hangs from it. In addition two arms are provided for a counterweight and a balance weight. In operation, the balance weight is removed, and the counterweight adjusted for zero reading. With sound input, the balance weight is then adjusted to give the original reading.

The radiation force is then equal to the balance weight times the ratio between the distance to the axle of the balance weight and the center of the sound beam.

This type of device may take many forms. By suspending a sensitive balance in the ultrasonic field it is possible to measure the power generated. If the source is below the balance pan, the pressure of the ultrasonic waves is indicated by the pointer in the same way that weight is indicated on a scale. One such system is shown in Fig. 6-4.

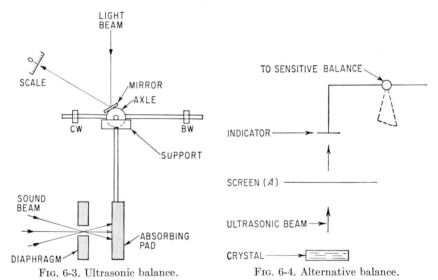

FIG. 6-3. Ultrasonic balance.   FIG. 6-4. Alternative balance.

A similar method of measuring power was described by Wood.[1] A glass disk about 8 cm in diameter was fastened by a rod by which it could be raised and lowered in a bath. A mound of oil was then excited by ultrasonic means until it reached its maximum height. The glass disk was lowered onto the oil, on which it rested, supported by the power of the ultrasonic waves. Weights were then placed on the top of a pan positioned so that its weight was supported by the disk, and additional weights added until the disk sank into the liquid (see Fig. 6-5). The point at which the glass disk sank was an indication of the power output. This apparatus allowed an excellent demonstration of the way ultrasonic waves are built up in a liquid.

This procedure showed that maximum weight could be supported when

[1] R. W. Wood, "Supersonics," Brown University, 1939.

the distance traveled by the ultrasonic waves was a multiple of a half wavelength. Under such conditions very great amplitudes of vibration result. The glass disk may be forced down through the ultrasonic waves, but in so doing the resistance encountered seems to take place in steps, concentrated at points of half-wavelength distance.

Wood concluded from this that the way to get maximum energy into a bath is to adjust the depth in this manner so that the energy builds up by means of standing waves.

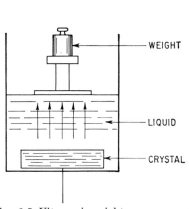

FIG. 6-5. Ultrasonic weight measurement.

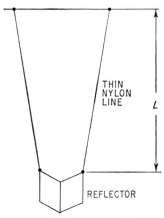

FIG. 6-6. Laboratory reflector.

One of the simplest and most practical forms which the deflection device takes is shown in Fig. 6-6. The unit itself is a right-angle reflector, hung from nylon line attached to a support giving a 3- or 4-ft length of line, or any convenient length. The energy to be measured is completely reflected. Usual measurements are made in water. With this apparatus, wattage computations may be easily made as follows:

$$\text{Power (watts)} = \text{radiation force (dynes)} \times \frac{\text{velocity}}{\text{erg-sec/watt}}$$

$$\text{ergs/sec} = \text{force (dynes)} \times \text{velocity}$$
$$\text{watts} = \text{ergs/sec} \times 10^{-7}$$
$$\text{Force (g)} \times 980 = \text{dynes}$$
$$\text{Velocity} = 1.44 \times 10^5$$

Then
$$\text{Force (g)} = \text{weight in water (g)} \times \frac{\text{deflection}}{\text{length}}$$

$$\text{Power (watts)} = \text{force (g)} \times \frac{980 \times 1.44 \times 10^5}{10^7} \qquad \text{(for small length)}$$

For example, if the weight is 100 g and the length is 40 in., then

$$\text{Power (watts)} = \frac{\text{deflection} \times 100 \times 980 \times 1.44}{40 \times 100}$$
$$= \text{deflection} \times 38.16$$

The simplicity and accuracy of this method recommend it highly when occasional measurements are to be made.

It is generally considered that hydrodynamic flow of the liquid must not be allowed, since it produces extraneous variations in the readings. Screens of cellophane or similar material can be used to prevent this. Such a screen (shown in Fig. 6-4) allows the ultrasonic waves to pass freely but stops the formation of currents in the liquid. However, with reflecting devices, results agreeing closely with theory have been obtained without such screens.

Other Mechanical Means. Scattering particles of lycopodium or similar material to indicate standing waves is a well-known method. Experiments have been carried out with particles that exist in tobacco smoke or water to indicate ultrasonic output. For example, the fountain produced by an ultrasonic transducer resting on the bottom of a container of liquid may be used as an indication of the output. In some cases such methods can produce fairly accurate approximations when employed by an experienced experimenter. However, quantitative data is difficult to obtain by these means.

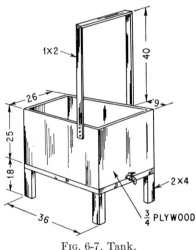

FIG. 6-7. Tank.

In the early nineteenth century, Kundt described a means of making ultrasonic waves visible by powdering the object in which they were traveling with a very fine dust (such as lycopodium). This dust arranged itself on the surface of the piece in a configuration which was determined by the dimensions and shape of the waves in it. Similar methods were also used in liquids, where a fine suspension of dust such as powdered coal or coke was used. Any form of mist, dust, or smoke, or even small bubbles can be used to indicate the passage of ultrasonic waves in the various media. There has been a good deal of discussion of these means in the classical literature, but they are mainly interesting in a historical connotation or for laboratory use.

Tanks. Since many measurements are made in water or other liquid, it is apparent that some form of tank is necessary to hold it. The general criterion for such a tank is that it be sufficiently large to prevent great reflections at the walls. Tanks made of plywood (Fig. 6-7) are quite satisfactory for this purpose. While absorbing linings further damp out extraneous reflections, this is not absolutely necessary.

Diffraction of Light. The original application of ultrasonics to the diffraction of light in the testing of materials seems to have been made by Sokolov.[1] In his apparatus diffraction patterns were used as an indication of the presence or absence of ultrasonic energy.

The actual phenomenon was first noted by Debye and Sears[2] and is therefore usually referred to as the *Debye-Sears ultrasonic diffraction action.* The action makes possible the production of actual diffraction gratings and was concurrently demonstrated by Lucas and Bequard. The original theory was due to Brillouin.

The phenomenon depends upon the fact that the ultrasonic waves actually consist of alternating compressions and expansions, which alter the density of the medium through which they pass. If a monochromatic beam of light is used in the form of a slit, there will be a central image and various lines. The index of refraction depends on the density, and

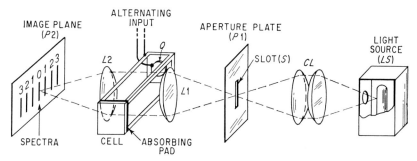

FIG. 6-8. Ultrasonic light-diffraction system.

changes in the index cause the light to be diffracted. The central image and the various lines are separated from each other by a distance that depends on the frequency; and as the frequency becomes greater, this distance increases. Many different frequencies can be impressed on the system at the same time, and each will produce its own diffraction lines. The lines can therefore be used as an actual indication of frequency and also of velocity and wavelength.

This field of investigation has been widely examined and exhaustive surveys of the work have already been published.[3] The application is extremely useful in tracing the passage of ultrasonic waves and in examining the action of lenses, crystals, etc.

Diffraction Systems. The action of a typical light-diffraction system is shown in Fig. 6-8.[4] Light from a lamp is focused on a narrow slit. It

[1] S. J. Sokolov, *Physik. Z.*, **36** (1935) 142.

[2] P. Debye and F. W. Sears, *Proc. Natl. Acad. Sci. U.S.*, **18** (1932) 410.

[3] L. Bergmann, "Der Ultraschall," Berlin, 1942.

[4] G. W. Willard, *Bell Lab. Record*, **25** (1947) 194.

passes through the slit, then through another lens, which again makes it parallel. The light is then sent through an ultrasonic cell, which consists of a quartz crystal transmitting through a liquid. An absorbing medium is placed in the beam so that there are no reflections. When ultrasonic waves are generated in this cell, the sections of compression and rarefaction cause the light to produce a diffraction pattern. The system works on the principle of the optical grating.

Patterns from optical cells appear very similar to those produced by gratings. One such pattern is shown in Fig. 6-9.[1] As the ultrasonic beam becomes narrower, the pattern becomes sharper.

If one frequency of vibration is sent through the liquid, one pattern results; if another is sent, a second pattern appears; if both frequencies are sent, both patterns appear as a combination of the two original ones.

Since standing or stationary waves are due to two waves, one transmitted and one received, such a wave should produce a pattern similar to the superposition of those separately produced by each wave. Several investigators have shown that such is actually the case. When the waves are not stationary but traveling, the Doppler effect can be shown experimentally.

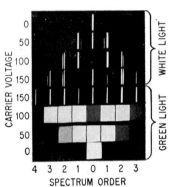

Fig. 6-9. Ultrasonic grating pattern.

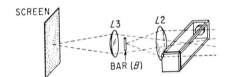

Fig. 6-10. Image system.

It is further possible to make the entire shape and path of the ultrasonic beam visible by a change in the apparatus (Fig. 6-10).[1] This is accomplished by so placing an opaque bar that it blocks out the zero-order light produced by the ultrasonic beam. This has the effect of causing the amount of light transmitted to vary with voltage. Adding a lens after the bar focuses an actual picture of the beam on the screen.

Another method, attributable to Bar and Meyer, produces a similar picture by means of a screen full of small holes positioned before the ultrasonic cell. This apparatus produces a picture that looks as if it were made up of a large number of small dots. However, the unit has been successfully applied several times in obtaining pictures of ultrasonic waves.

The pictures of ultrasonic action obtained optically are extremely

[1] *Ibid.*

interesting and useful in making visible the passage of ultrasonic waves in a liquid or transparent solid. All kinds of phenomena such as focusing, diffraction, and reflection can be examined. In many cases there is no other way to get this information.

The actual shadow picture of a part can be made visible by passing an ultrasonic wave through such a part and projecting the transmitted portion of the beam onto a screen. The piece is usually immersed in a liquid bath, which acts to couple the ultrasonic energy to it. That part of the beam which has been interrupted by flaws in the material will be blocked out. Unfortunately, other characteristics of a material may also interrupt such beams.

In order to make the images more brilliant, experiments have been carried out with various types of particles that are suspended in the liquid and orient themselves in the beam,[1] arranging themselves according to the amount of ultrasonic energy that passes through the object under test.

The action of ultrasonics on light has also been suggested as a source of light for observing other rapidly recurring phenomena. This ultrasonic effect causes the light passing through the cell to become stroboscopic. A number of papers on the phenomenon have been

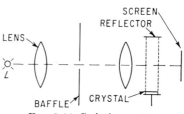

FIG. 6-11. Striation system.

published in Germany.[2] An elaborate optical system is used to isolate suitable orders of the diffraction pattern so that they can be used to view a rapidly repeating action stroboscopically.

The diffraction of light has been extensively examined in specific applications in the literature by many investigators. Up to the present it has not been widely applied to any but laboratory uses in this country, but elsewhere it has been used as the basis for television and testing systems.

Striation. Another optical method of making ultrasonic waves visible is referred to as *striation* and is attributable to A. Toepler.[3] The optical system necessary is somewhat different from the diffraction type and is illustrated in Fig. 6-11. The arrangement shown is for making stationary waves visible. The parts under compression appear as dark lines, and the others as light ones.

The system operates on the principle that the refraction between compression and rarefactions bends the light away from a blocking screen. The same system can be applied to traveling waves if stroboscopic or very

[1] E. Czerlinsky, Non-destructive Material Testing by Supersonic Methods, *Deut. Versuchsanstalt Luftfahrt PB* 23946, **1** (1942) 723.

[2] P. Cermak and H. Schoeneck, *Ann. phys.*, **26** (1936) 465.

[3] A. Toepler, *Ostwalds Klassiker*, **158** (1866) 103.

short pulses of illumination are used. A number of investigators have examined waves by such means.

Wavefront Effects. Divergent light may be directly used to make standing waves visible.[1] The setup is shown in Fig. 6-12. Light is passed through an aperture and goes into the ultrasonic cell in which the standing waves exist. A screen is placed behind the cell. A picture of the sonic waves appears if the light rays are approximately normal to the screen. Only standing waves may be seen.

Bragg Reflection. It appears that Bragg reflection occurs from ultrasonic waves.[2] Light would therefore be reflected from the wavefronts at an angle equal to the angle of incidence when the ultrasonic wavelength and light wavelength were proper (Fig. 6-13). This would therefore be another means of making the ultrasonic wavefront visible.

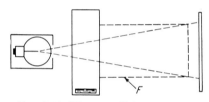

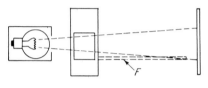

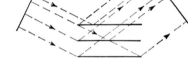

FIG. 6-12. Divergent-light system.   FIG. 6-13. Bragg reflection.

Light Diffraction in Solids. It is also possible to apply light-diffraction methods to translucent materials such as fused quartz. This material becomes birefringent when stressed (as by the passage of ultrasonic waves). This will then cause diffraction. The photoelastic material may be chosen to have resonant dimensions. Certain high polymers (such as gelatin) exhibit photoelasticity to a high degree. These materials exhibit the phenomenon both in the solid state and in solution. Other materials such as clear catalin and castor oil may also be used.

Microphones. Among the most useful devices for exploring sound fields are microphones. The terms *microphone* and *transducer* are sometimes used interchangeably. Various types of transducers (especially small crystals of ADP or barium titanate) have been used as the active parts of pickups. Microphones have also been constructed as capacitor assemblies. A number of units of quartz and other materials have also been used for plotting the field of quartz transducers or the travel of ultrasonics in liquids. The output of such a unit may be amplified and indicated by any suitable means.

[1] L. Bergmann and H. J. Goehlich, *Kultur*, **108** (1936) 47.
[2] G. W. Willard, *JASA*, **21** (1949) 103.

Small magnetostrictive transducers have also been built using very small cylindrical pieces of magnetostrictive material wound with a coil. These units may then be calibrated and their output amplified in the usual manner.

An example of each of the following types of transducers will therefore be given: (1) barium titanate, (2) magnetostrictive, (3) *x*-cut Rochelle salt, (4) quartz, and (5) capacitive. Electrical devices such as those described operate by measuring the alternating pressure. These devices have minimum mass and maximum stiffness at ultrasonic frequencies. Condenser microphones have been used to 80 kc, quartz crystals up to 1 Mc, barium titanate up to about 0.5 Mc. Particle velocity may be measured by electrokinetic probes.

Barium Titanate. Probes have been constructed using barium titanate as the active element (Fig. 6-14).[1] A tube of material $\frac{1}{16}$ in. OD,

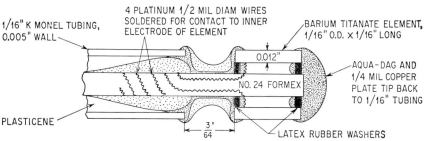

FIG. 6-14. Barium titanate probe.

$\frac{1}{16}$ in. long, and with an 0.012-in. wall was used. The mounting is shown in the figure. Silver electrodes were fired on the cylinder, which was supported on rubber washers. Leads were then cemented on the silver faces. The details of the construction are shown in Fig. 6-14; in general the probe is designed to minimize stray acoustic coupling. It is also sensitive to radial fields.

Magnetostriction. Magnetostrictive probes may also be used. Such units may be made as shown in Fig. 6-15.[2] The core is a piece of nickel tubing $\frac{1}{16}$ in. long and $\frac{1}{16}$ in. OD, 0.040 in. ID. One hundred turns of No. 48 wire were wound toroidally on it. The ring is operated on magnetic remanence. Its sensitivity is of the order of 180 db *re* 1 volt/(dyne) (cm²), and its impedance of about 15 ohms.

Another type of probe,[3] used at high frequencies (570 kc), is shown in Fig. 6-16. Bias is supplied by a dry cell in series with one coil.

[1] Atmospheric Physics and Sound Propagation, *Penn. State Coll. Acoustics Lab. Final Rept.* (1950).

[2] *Ibid.*

[3] A. W. Smith and D. K. Weiner, *Rev. Sci. Instr.,* **18** (1947) 188.

Magnetostrictive probes produce a voltage proportional to the rate of change of pressure in the field. Maximum voltage produced by this probe was about 9.3×10^{-3} volt.

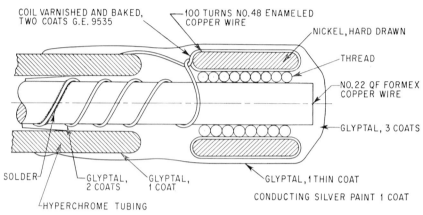

FIG. 6-15. Magnetostrictive probe.

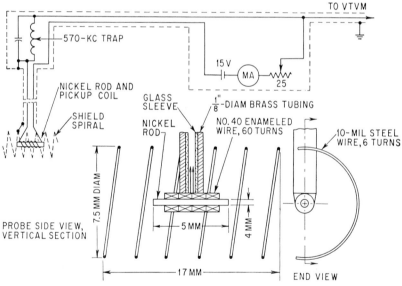

FIG. 6-16. Probe and associated circuit.

Devices of this sort have the very great advantage that their size is small, and therefore the amount of distortion introduced into the sound field is also small.

x-cut **Rochelle Salt.** Microphones of this material have been used to investigate high-intensity air-borne ultrasonic waves at frequencies of about 15 kc. They have also been used in water and water-solid mixtures.

Figure 6-17 shows the configuration of a microphone which is made of four small Rochelle salt crystals in parallel.[1] These units give comparatively large output but are rather delicate in comparison with other materials.

Another type of Rochelle salt probe may be used to explore the surface of the crystal or other ultrasonic field to determine how the deformation is distributed and what the frequency characteristics are. This can be done with a quartz crystal connected to an amplifier. In most cases, however, the area of the face of the exploring crystal is so great that it

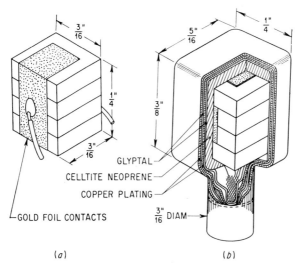

GLYPTAL

CELLTITE NEOPRENE

COPPER PLATING

GOLD FOIL CONTACTS

$\frac{3}{16}$" DIAM

(a)   (b)

Fig. 6-17. Rochelle-salt transducer.

tends to integrate a large amount of the ultrasonic field. An instrument for such exploration may therefore be designed as follows:

A plate is cut from a Rochelle salt piece, polished, and placed between two brass electrodes. These electrode surfaces are also optically polished, and a pointed glass rod is firmly fixed with shellac to one of the plate surfaces. Both the Rochelle salt and the electrodes are wet with transformer oil so that ultrasonic energy will easily pass through them. One electrode is then grounded, and the sharpened tip of the glass rod is placed vertically on the surface of the field or crystal to be explored. This tip covers a very small area, and detailed readings are therefore possible. The movement of the glass rod is coupled into the Rochelle salt crystal, which is connected to an amplifier. Rochelle salts used for this purpose should have the largest possible area, and all parts must be very well polished. The output of the unit is calibrated suitably.

The system is supported in a metal box from which only the end of the

[1] Atmospheric Physics and Sound Propagation, *op. cit.*

glass rod protrudes. Glass is used for the pickup because it does not conduct electricity. A device for such use is shown in Fig. 6-18.

Capacitive Probes. A number of capacitive probes or microphones have appeared in the literature. They generally consist of a movable diaphragm close to an electrode. The motion of the diaphragm changes

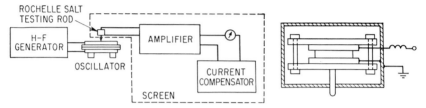

FIG. 6-18. Probe for exploring transducer faces.

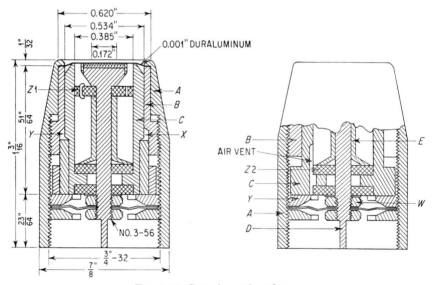

FIG. 6-19. Capacitor microphone.

the capacitance, which is proportional to the average displacement. The displacement in an ultrasonic field is caused by the unidirectional pressure already described. Figure 6-19 shows one such microphone.[1] The output is amplified electronically. The resonant frequency is limited by the diaphragm strength. Diaphragms with a thickness of a few thousandths of an inch have been used.

Hot-wire Instruments. It has been shown[2] that the resistance of a thin, electrically heated wire is proportional to the air velocity going past

---

[1] T. H. Bonn, *JASA*, **18** (1946) 496.

[2] L. V. King, *Trans. Roy. Soc. London*, **A214** (1914) 273; W. S. Tucker and E. T. Paris, *Trans. Roy. Soc. London*, **A221** (1931) 319.

it—for both steady and oscillatory streams of air. At high frequencies, the oscillatory changes disappear. The wire may therefore be used as an indicator, giving minima resistances at the nodes and maxima at the antinodes. The effect is due to cooling of the wire by the particle motion caused by the ultrasonic waves. Such wires may be used as indicators in air and other vapors or as the indicator for a fixed-path interferometer.[1]

Platinum wires forming one side of a Wheatstone bridge can be used. The resistance of the wire fluctuates directly with the amplitude of the ultrasonic waves. This change usually takes the form of a drop in the resistance and is linear enough so that the ultrasonic amplitude can be directly calibrated with it. Units of this type have been used up to about 200 kc. The output of such a device may be shown in Fig. 6-20.

Interferometers. One of the most accurate ways of measuring ultrasonic constants in fluids or gases is to set up stationary-wave resonances.

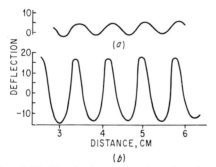

FIG. 6-20. Signals from hot-wire microphone.

This is usually done in a column at one end of which the source is located and at the other end of which is placed a reflector. This is known as an *interferometer* and was originally proposed by Pierce.[2] As presently used, interferometers may be either (1) fixed path or (2) variable path.

A large number of interferometers for special purposes have been described in the literature. Basically they are as accurate as their mechanical construction allows. Any means of indication may be used. Usually the change in impedance due to the resonances causes variations in current drawn by the energy source.

Fixed Path. Stationary waves are set up by a source and reflector, and the wave pattern explored with a probe, usually a hot wire in gases.[3] The frequency is varied to get resonances. In addition, units have been constructed in which the frequency of the source was varied while the

[1] K. Matta and E. G. Richardson, *JASA*, **23** (1951) 58.
[2] G. W. Pierce, *Proc. Am. Acad. Arts*, **60** (1925) 271.
[3] E. G. Richardson, *Proc. Roy. Soc.*, **A146** (1934) 56.

path remained fixed. One such unit, attributable to Matta and Richardson, is shown in Fig. 6-21a. Such a unit is suitable for gas measurements.

Variable Path. In the variable-path interferometer either the source or reflector is moved (usually the latter), and the plate current of the

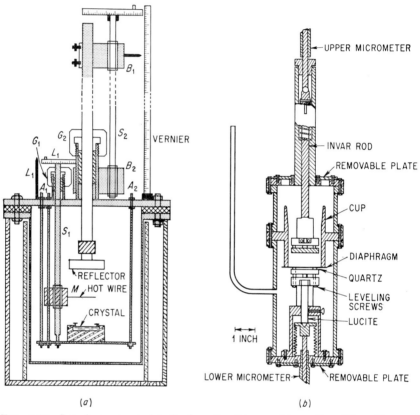

FIG. 6-21. Interferometers: (*a*) fixed path; (*b*) movable path. (*Macmillan and Lagemann.*)

driving oscillator monitored. The frequency remains constant. A variable-path interferometer is shown in Fig. 6-21b. This unit is suitable for liquid measurements.

Thermocouple Probes. Ultrasonic waves produce heat when they are absorbed, and this heat may be used as an indication of the amount of energy in the original waves.

One type of probe which has been suggested is a thermocouple embedded in a sound-absorbing material which is similar in density and velocity to the liquid in which the measurement is to be made.[1]

[1] W. J. Fry and R. B. Fry, *JASA*, **26** (1954) 294.

The probe will indicate the initial temperature rise, which is then used as a measure of the level. It must be first calibrated in a known sound field, and may then be used to measure unknown ones.

A second approach[1] is to measure the initial time rate of change of temperature when the sending transducer is turned on. In addition, the acoustic absorption of the material and its heat capacity must be known to calculate the absolute sound intensity. An outline drawing of such a unit is shown in Fig. 6-22.[2] The acoustic material is castor oil. Acoustic pulses lasting one second were used. A number of other thermal units have appeared from time to time and may be found in the literature.

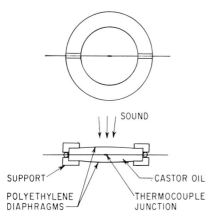

FIG. 6-22. Thermocouple probe.

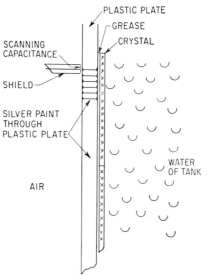

FIG. 6-23. Crystal mosaic shadowgraph.

Shadowgraphs. A number of techniques have been used to make ultrasonic waves produce a rough analogy of the X-ray picture, and several of these have been referred to as *shadowgraphs*.[3] One such system has been described elsewhere (the ultrasonic telescope). A second is shown in Fig. 6-23.[4] This is based on scanning a crystal having on its surface a multiplicity of small conducting areas, each isolated from all others, so that essentially a mosaic of active crystals has been formed. Scanning the crystals gives a picture, limited in resolution to the crystal size.

Another device uses small aluminum particles suspended in a liquid (xylene) between two plates. These are orientated in one direction by a prepolarizing voltage. The ultrasonic energy then causes them to turn,

[1] S. Moritz, *J. Phys. Soc. Japan*, **7** (1952) 214.

[2] Fry and Fry, *loc. cit.*

[3] E. E. Suckling and W. R. Maclean, *JASA*, **27** (1955) 297.

[4] *Ibid.*

producing a picture, since the areas under agitation appear bright against a dark background.[1] The aluminum particles should be between 5 and 25 μ (microns) in effective diameter and, when this size, will not settle out if occasionally agitated by an air tube. The diaphragm may be aluminum sheet or plastic coated with graphite to make it conductive. The window should be conducting glass. The voltage will keep the particle plane horizontal and allow a 90-deg turn when an ultrasonic field appears. Small particles seem to migrate toward the negative pole (usually the diaphragm).

Electrokinetic Effect. The electrokinetic effect has been suggested as the basis for a transducer (Fig.

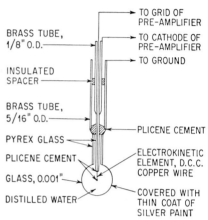

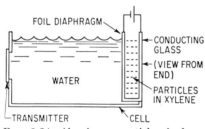

Fig. 6-24. Aluminum particle shadowgraph.

Fig. 6-25. Electrokinetic microphone.

6-25). This effect is the production of a voltage on a wire covered with a porous coating when subjected to an ultrasonic field in an electrolyte. Responses of as much as -135 db re 1 volt/(dyne) (cm^2) seem possible. In some cases the glass bulb may be dispensed with.[2]

Bleach-out. Methods have been suggested from time to time to make films on plates directly sensitive to ultrasonic waves. One such method is known as *bleach-out*.[3] In essence, a spectrographic plate is dyed and exposed to ultrasound in the presence of a bleach. The ultrasound is more intense at some points and mixes the bleach at those points, causing more rapid bleaching and thus producing a picture.

One procedure is as follows: The plate is dyed with a simple purple dye (Rit). The bleach is Clorox diluted with water. Figure 6-26 shows a typical picture made in this manner.

Starch Plate. A method similar to bleach-out is the starch-plate technique.[4] A glass plate is coated with starch (10 g dry, 10 ml liquid,

[1] R. Pohlmann, *Z. Physik*, **107** (1937) 497.

[2] H. Dietrik, E. Yager, J. Bogosh, and F. Hovolka, *JASA*, **25** (1953) 461.

[3] T. P. Schilb, Classical Diffraction Patterns in Sound by the Bleach-out Method, University of Louisville thesis.

[4] G. S. Bennett, *JASA*, **24** (1952) 470.

200 ml water). Iodine is dissolved in alcohol and water. This is added to the water tank. During ultrasonic action the part being irradiated does not darken as rapidly as the rest, thus producing evidence of the ultrasonic beam. The plate is then washed, leaving the picture.

Direct Photographic Effects. The effect of ultrasonics on photographic plates was first described by Marinesco.[1] There seems to be some question as to the effect and its order of magnitude. However, it has recently been established that the effect exists.[2] Other than this further work is still to be done.

A number of phenomena involving ultrasonic waves have been noticed which have been produced in the laboratory. Some of these may be applicable to use in devices. They may be classified as (1) luminescence, (2) chromotropism, (3) labile compounds, and (4) reaction measurements.

FIG. 6-26. Indication by bleach-out.

Luminescence. Luminescence has been observed in materials in which intense ultrasonics exist. In all cases it appears to be accompanied by cavitation. Within the medium it is known as *triboluminescence*[3] caused by crystal planes, separated by a small distance, on which a high voltage gradient appears. Discharge occurs, producing luminescence in certain phosphors. The same effect may be produced in water, presumably due to gaseous discharge when cavitation produces electric charges. The variety of conditions under which luminescence appears has led to varying interpretations—some investigators believing chemical luminescence occurred, others believing it was gas incandescence, etc.[4]

Certain phosphors, when treated by ultrasound, store up energy which may be released by heat as luminescence. This effect is only known qualitatively.

Luminescence may also be produced by a quartz transducer driven at

[1] N. Marinesco and J. J. Trillab, *Compt. rend.*, **196** (1933) 858.
[2] P. J. Ernst, *JASA*, **23** (1951) 80.
[3] H. W. Levereng, Luminescence of Solids, Wiley, 1950.
[4] E. Giebe and A. Scheibe, *ETZ*, **47** (1926) 380; E. A. Neppiris and B. E. Nøltingk, *Mullard Research Lab. Rept.* 135 (1951).

resonance.   This may be due to a discharge in the vicinity of the crystal,[1]
or between the vibrating crystal and the plate on which the electric drive
is applied.   The plate may be mounted in air or in a gas such as neon.
The glow may therefore be used to indicate the pressure of the frequency
at which the crystal is resonant.

Chromotropism.   This term refers to the change in color in certain
materials when irradiated by ultrasound.   Some materials have a revers-
ible effect.   Leucobases are materials which are ordinarily colorless
but become colored when irradiated.   Such effects so far remain
questionable.[2]

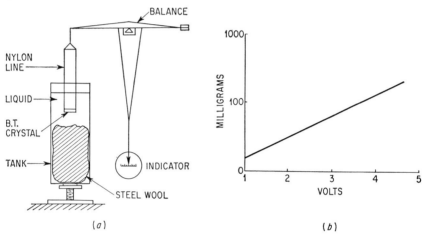

FIG. 6-27. (*a*) Reaction apparatus; (*b*) results with barium titanate disk at 1 Mc.

Labile Compounds.   These are materials which detonate in an ultrasonic field.   Experimentation in this field is scarce and indecisive.[3]

Reaction.   The measurement of power by the reaction on the sender
has been suggested by several writers.[4]   Apparatus for making such
measurements (i.e., applied voltage vs. grams) is shown in Fig. 6-27.
Energy is transmitted from the crystal through the liquid and dispersed
in the steel wool, which eliminates standing waves.   The motion of the
energy for various power inputs is calibrated on the indicator.   Results,
as shown in Fig. 6-27*b*, are quite linear.

Photographing Cathode-ray Screens.   Many ultrasonic devices utilize
the cathode-ray tube as an indicator.   It is accordingly useful to maintain records of results by photographing the screen during or after test.
A simple mechanism can be used to take such pictures (see Fig. 6-28 and

[1] *Ibid.*
[2] P. J. Ernst and C. W. Hoffman, *JASA*, **24** (1952) 207.
[3] W. T. Richards and A. L. Loomis, *J. Am. Chem. Soc.*, **49** (1927) 3086.
[4] E. F. Kiernan, *JASA*, **26** (1954) 451.

Table 6-1).   The camera is positioned over the screen and held in a jig, which fixes its focus on the fluorescent screen of the tube.   A cone of black material is added to keep out light, and a peephole placed in it so

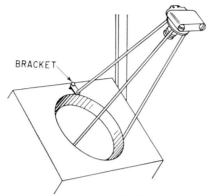

BRACKET

Fig. 6-28. Apparatus for photographing CRT screen and typical exposures.

TABLE 6-1. APPARATUS FOR PHOTOGRAPHING CRT SCREEN AND
TYPICAL EXPOSURES

Kind of film, 35 mm	Weston rating	Grain	Speed	Number of exposures	Lens setting	Average exposure and aperture openings
Super XX	100	Fine	Fast	20 or 36	Infinity or prescribed setting when using adapter lens	5 sec at $f/2$ 10 sec at $f/4.5$
Photoflure	600	Medium fine	Extremely sensitive to green	36		2 sec at $f/2$
Plus X . . .	50	Fine	Slow	20 or 36		15 sec at $f/4.5$

that the operator can watch the pattern while taking a picture.   Naturally, many alternative methods may be used.   A set of exposures for the PI screen using ordinary film in the 35-mm camera is also given.

With this method, successful pictures may be taken for future reference and can be interpreted at any time, since a permanent record exists.

CHAPTER 7

ULTRASONIC POWER EQUIPMENT

High-power Ultrasonics. Agitation by sonic or ultrasonic means is well known in certain fields, especially in cleaning, soldering, welding, drilling, and chemistry. Generally, ultrasonics is more readily usable than audible sound because it is more easily generated at suitable intensities and because the order of wavelength is smaller. High frequencies are more readily absorbed in the agitated systems while low frequencies produce cavitation more readily. Therefore, in most cases frequencies of 10 to 50 kc are used.

The field of ultrasonic agitation is one of the most promising ones commercially. Many theoretical investigations have been carried out in the laboratory, and work has been done toward applying the phenomenon to problems of industrial scope. A number of ultrasonic agitators have been presented commercially from time to time. All are essentially similar and, as far as known, perform more or less in the same fashion. The division of these apparatus into cleaners, drills, etc., is therefore only functional; the apparatus is actually the same.

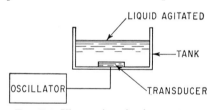

Fig. 7-1. Ultrasonic agitation system.

The basic form of the electronic ultrasonic agitator is shown in the block diagram (Fig. 7-1). Mechanical devices will be considered elsewhere. A high-power oscillator produces radio-frequency energy, which is impressed upon a suitable transducer that sends very powerful ultrasonic waves through the material, usually a liquid held in a tank or container. The waves then react upon the liquid, causing cavitation (see Chap. 10). When a solid is to be agitated, it is immersed in the liquid and treated.

Another common method is to place the liquid or liquids to be agitated in a test tube, or other separate container. This is then immersed in the liquid, which actually carries the ultrasonic waves and which is kept entirely separate. Glass, stainless steel, and polyethylene are suitable materials for containers.

General.   Ultrasonic vibrations of great intensity bring about astounding changes in various forms of matter.   Work has been carried out in the biological, physical, and chemical fields with such effects; and although the application is in its infancy, it appears to offer great possibilities to the experimenter.

The function of this discussion will be to indicate briefly the typical apparatus; more emphasis will be placed upon the apparatus necessary for production of the ultrasonic waves than upon specific effects.   The effects are discussed in Chap. 10.

Ultrasonic oscillations for the purposes of agitation are generally produced by electronic oscillators, which drive individual quartz or other crystals (usually barium titanate) or mosaics of them into strong vibration and couple this vibration into a liquid.   Special crystal holders must be used for such applications and have already been described.   Other types of transducers such as magnetostrictive may also be used.

Frequencies that have been used in the past in this type of work have been in the lower ultrasonic order and have ranged from 10,000 to 1,500,000 cps.   Frequencies as great as 5 Mc have been used.   As the voltage that is impressed on the crystal becomes greater and greater, flashover is more likely to occur unless the crystals are sufficiently thick, i.e., of low frequency.   Moreover, the thinner and therefore higher-frequency crystals are much more likely to fracture.

Ultrasonic waves have been found to cause pressures so large that the resulting mechanical stresses may be as great as 15,000 times the hydrostatic pressure.   The acceleration of a crystal driving such a bath is extremely great and may reach 20,000 km/sec,[1] but the motion associated with such action is extremely small (a very small fraction of 1 mm).   The crystal will build up to maximum velocity in a fraction of a microsecond.

The energy generated reaches a maximum when the distance between the face of the transducer and the top of the liquid is a whole number of half wavelengths.   This can be seen physically, since in that case the phase relation is such that the successive reflections of the energy are additive.   Under such conditions large values of amplitude may occur. For any one tank of liquid there are a great many depths that will give this condition; any one of them can be used, and more rapid ultrasonic effects can be achieved than when the relation does not obtain.

Wood reported a pressure of 150 g against a glass disk 8 cm in diameter and the projection of oil drops 30 or 40 cm above the surface of the liquid. Generally he worked with as much as 50,000 volts and at frequencies between 200,000 and 500,000 cps.

History.   The first experiments with modern high-power generators seem to have been carried out by Langevin, in his work already referred

[1] R. W. Wood, "Supersonics," Brown University, 1939.

to in the development of an efficient means of locating submarines. His compound oscillators gave a method of generating high-intensity beams of ultrasonics, and during his experiments with the Poulsen arc he apparently noticed the lethal effect of the ultrasonic waves upon small marine life. Moreover, the heating as well as the cavitation effects of the waves were mentioned.

Langevin also originally noticed the fact that much greater powers were available for use under conditions of resonance, and he emphasized the necessity for tuning his oscillators to that point.

Various experiments followed the Langevin ones, but the greatest contribution next made seems to have resulted from the collaboration of Wood and Loomis;[1] these men carried out extensive experiments with a specially designed vacuum-tube generator (the Poulsen generator then being obsolete).

The conditions of frequency and voltage under which they worked have already been mentioned. Langevin had been interested only in long-distance propagation in liquids, which had limited the frequencies he used to a maximum of about 40,000 cps because of the great absorption at higher frequencies. In agitation work, of course, this is no problem, since there is very little liquid to travel through, and therefore little absorption. The oscillator was one designed for 2,000-watt output, operating through step-up transformers for greater voltage. Figure 7-2 shows the schematic of the unit. The crystals were disks and rested on a piece of lead placed at the bottom of a container of oil. A second electrode was placed on top of the crystal in the form of a circular sheet of very thin brass. This work was also the basis for the ultrasonic interferometer discussed in Chap. 8 (under resonance).

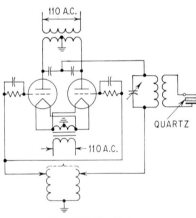

Fig. 7-2. Oscillator.

The action of the ultrasonics upon the liquid in a tank or beaker has been extensively described in the literature. At the interface between the liquid (usually oil) and air, the waves fling the liquid up into the air in the form of fine drops.

This is usually demonstrated with benzoil, which produces a white fog. However, this only occurs at high powers (about 1 watt/cm²). Generally very low power produces an irregular mound or group of mounds over the

[1] R. W. Wood and A. L. Loomis, *Phys. Rev., Abstract,* **29** (1927) 373.

crystal. The mounds gradually become higher and higher as power is added and resolve into a single large (i.e., high) mound. The resultant mound then becomes narrower as the frequency increases. The size of the drops flung up is a function of frequency to an extent; at low frequency they are large and irregular; and as the frequency rises, they gradually resolve into a fine mist. This occurs at about 1 Mc. At that frequency, a fountain approximately 7 cm high should exist when action such as emulsification is taking place within a liquid. Jets 10 to 15 cm high are common and occasional drops may be flung up 30 or 40 cm. If such a mound or fountain does not exist, probably not enough power is being sent into the system to bring about the desired effects. The growth of these mounds is also connected with resonance in the proper dimension of the liquid, as already mentioned, and they are maximum at that point. At low frequencies sharp mounds do not appear as the energy is spread more evenly throughout the material being treated. However, drops may be flung into the air. In addition, mounds may occur if the energy is concentrated by focusing or other means.

The container holding the liquid to be agitated is then introduced into the fountain at the point where maximum effect seems to exist and allowed to remain there while being treated.

As already mentioned, Sokolov investigated the various oscillators and frequencies from 10^4 to 1.3×10^8 cps, with special reference to the use in the metal industry for vibrating materials in their molten state. Work by this investigator is considered in Chap. 3.

Crystal Generators. Ultrasonic generators are essentially high-power oscillators such as are commonly used in radio work. The schematics for two such systems are shown (Figs. 7-3[1] and 7-4). There is nothing special about such oscillators. The refinements necessary for radio-frequency generation for radio work can be discarded, while frequency stability, etc., is necessary for laboratory work only. Both of these units are for high (radio) frequencies. A simple unit for low-frequency operation, using barium titanate transducers, is shown in Fig. 7-5. Note that the transducer is tapped down on the output coil, thus having two effects: it matches the impedance and tunes out the reactance.

The primary purpose of such a generator is to produce sufficient high-frequency oscillations at a high radio-frequency voltage. Langevin used a high-frequency arc (Poulsen) for his generator, but on the whole such methods have been superseded by the oscillator (vacuum-tube type). Some work has also been done on applying motor generators at audio frequencies.

For application in air or gases, a Pierce-type oscillator may be used. That is, the crystal may be used both as a generator of ultrasonic waves

[1] F. W. Smith and P. K. Stumpf, *Electronics*, **19** (1946) 116.

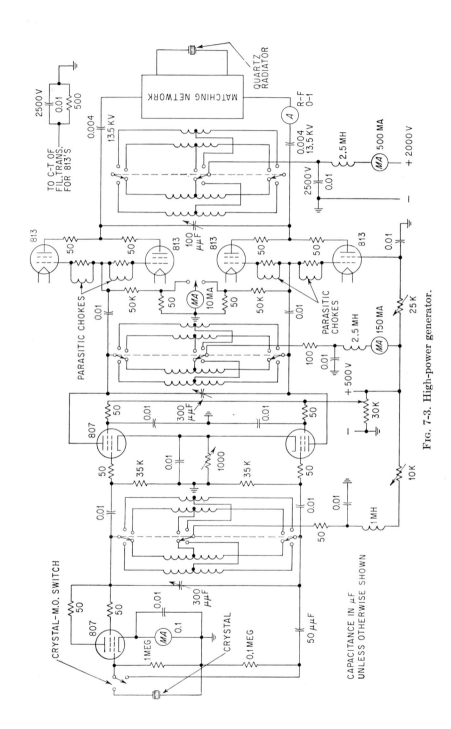

FIG. 7-3. High-power generator.

and as a frequency-controlling device.   When the crystal is used with liquids or solids, the damping effect is too great to allow this; i.e., the oscillating quartz cannot maintain its own oscillations and control frequency at the same time.   In air or gas, whistles or sirens can be used as well as magnetostriction units.

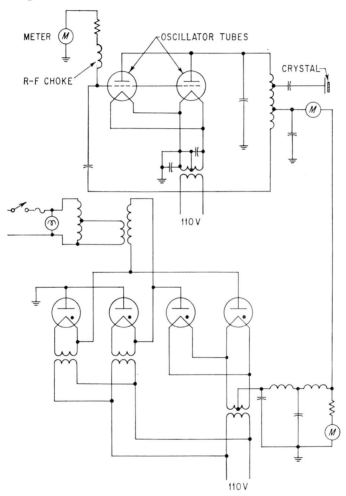

FIG. 7-4. Ultrasonic generator.

Generators may be made to work from 10,000 cps to almost any required frequency, but the amount of power available from a high-frequency generator is less because the transducer becomes very thin.   For this reason, up to the present time most experiments have been performed at frequencies under 1 Mc.   Sonic frequencies are also occasionally utilized.

The frequency of generation can be controlled by a crystal or produced by any of the tuned types of oscillators.

Frequency sometimes causes a difference in the ultrasonic action. A particular effect may take place at a high frequency and not at a low one,

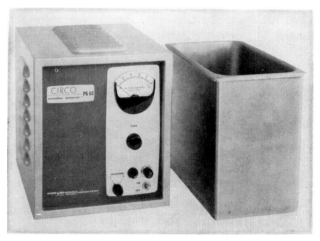

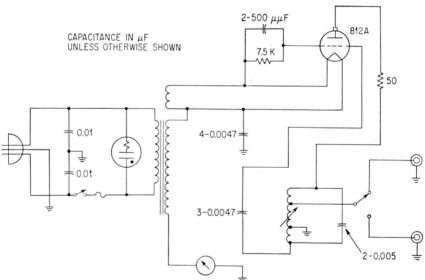

FIG. 7-5. Low-frequency generator for barium titanate.   (*Circo.*)

etc.   The consensus is that frequencies from 15 to 40 kc are best for most industrial uses.

Figure 7-6 illustrates another typical quartz generator (Japanese). A_1 is a d-c ammeter; A_2 is a thermoammeter; Q is the crystal, and V the voltmeter.

An x-cut crystal with the following dimensions was used: the diameter was 3.5 cm, the thickness 6 mm, and the frequency 450 kc.   The crystal surface was copper plated over silver.   The lower electrode was a brass disk, which acted as the high-voltage contact and also was the support. The output of the system was made greater by setting the brass disk at a thickness of an odd multiple of $\frac{1}{4}$ λ, causing it to reflect energy in phase and build up the oscillations.   The experimenter inserted tinfoil between the crystal and disk to tune it, i.e., to build up the correct thickness.

The author measured his output both by a balance measure and by calorimetric measurement of the amount of energy absorbed by a piece of Bakelite 3 cm long.

Figure 7-7 shows the crystal and tank details for this apparatus.[1]   All apparatus of this nature has a strong family resemblance, and the one

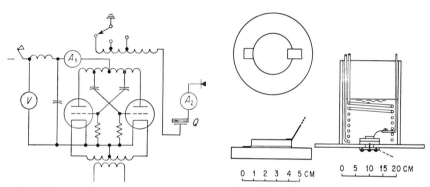

FIG. 7-6. Another form of generator.   FIG.   7-7.   Typical   quartz   transducer arrangement.

shown is accordingly very similar to apparatus produced in this country and in others.   Coils can be used for coupling the crystal to the oscillator in order to raise the voltage to a sufficiently high value.

Piezoelectric transducers are most commonly used today, especially for frequencies between 0.1 and 1 Mc.   Magnetostrictive systems are usually constructed for any range below this (up to about 50,000 cps) where the size of the transducer becomes too small to handle conveniently. The quartz crystals for this purpose are about 75 mm in diameter and between 7 and 14 mm thick (for frequencies between about 0.1 and 0.3 Mc).   Compound oscillators constructed to produce the same frequencies can also be used.

Barium titanate is being used more commonly than quartz.   It may be applied at frequencies from about 20 kc to about 1 Mc.   Since the voltage necessary for equivalent power is much less for this material than for quartz, many of the precautions against flashover need not be used. The configuration of a barium titanate transducer is shown in Fig. 7-8.

[1] H. Oyama, *Rept. Radio Research Japan*, **4** (1934) 41.

The transducer is normally coupled to the oscillator by a transformer, or tapped down on the oscillator coil. The output of the oscillator should be as great as possible and is usually a few hundred watts. A common size of a barium titanate block is 1 by 2 by 2 in. at 40 kc, and 20 watts or so may be applied to it.

If the power output is too small, the desired effect will not be produced at all. The consensus of investigators seems to be that a minimum of several hundred watts is necessary with quartz and a crystal plate of more than about 50-mm minimum diameter (or about twelve 2- by 1-in. barium titanate blocks) should be used. For quartz, the voltage on the secondary should be variable from about 30,000 to 60,000 radio-frequency volts. For barium titanate, 50 watts will drive three blocks to satisfactory levels for cleaning and some chemical reactions.

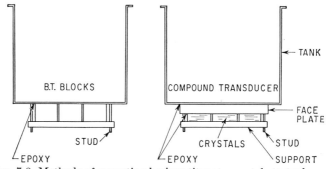

Fig. 7-8. Methods of mounting barium titanate crystals to tanks.

Holders and Containers. Probably the chief difficulty in intense ultrasonic generation is the design of the transducer and associated containers. The problems in the mounting of the quartz crystal are (1) the possibility of electrical breakdown and (2) the support of the holder and container in such a way as to permit the entry of maximum power into the media. With barium titanate mechanical strength and maximum power transfer are the problems.

Another critical element is the possibility of mechanical breakdown. As indicated, the simplest type of support for quartz is to lay the crystal on a block of lead and place a plate of brass or other electrically conducting material on its face. This is essentially what was done by Wood and Loomis.[1] The upper electrode may also be a brass ring, so that the waves can progress through the open center. The upper plate is held down by hooks or clips made of nonconducting material such as glass. The electrode should be as thin as possible for the greatest output. Magnetostrictive units may be welded directly to the tank, and barium titanate coupled by epoxy or similar material.

[1] *Loc. cit.*

When a test tube is dipped into the vibrating bath, it must be constructed of strong thin glass.   However, the container's wall thickness is not critical, since the waves do not progress through the glass as L types only but more commonly as S types.

Chemicals are treated in separate containers in this way, since they might damage the system electrically or mechanically if they were brought into direct contact with it.

Although the wave type is S during the transmission through the glass walls of the containers, only L waves exist in the liquids being agitated, since S types cannot exist in them.

The transformation of the ultrasonic waves takes place because of the angle at which the L waves strike the walls of the container.   The theory pertaining to this action will be found elsewhere.   However, although S waves will be produced in tall, thin test tubes because the energy strikes the walls at the proper angles, there will be no transformation in short flat containers, where the energy hits the bottom at normal angle. This may or may not be an advantage depending on the particular desires of the investigator.   However, wall thickness may be critical with respect to L waves.   Figure 7-9 is a diagrammatic representation of this situation.

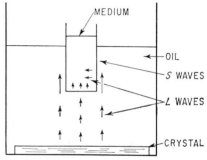

FIG. 7-9. Wave progression through a test tube.

The use of focusing crystals and of air-backed ones has been suggested for agitation work, as well as that of compound oscillators.   Naturally the damping of the crystal is as low as possible, and its faces are polished for greater output.

Barium titanate blocks in the form of compound oscillators are commonly used, i.e., with a faceplate of high-Q material such as aluminum, or in a sandwich of such material.   This arrangement has the advantage of high strength and economy.

Both sides of the barium titanate are plated and the front face grounded to the tank.   Floating systems lead to flashover and burning of the transducer face.

The epoxy used for bonding should have desirable mechanical and temperature characteristics.   Mechanical supports should also be provided for the crystal.

Power Output.   Authorities in the past have disagreed about the maximum power output it was possible to get from a quartz crystal, and figures from 10 to 37 watts/cm^2 have been advanced as the maximum that is possible without shattering. However, it appears likely that greater powers are now possible and are a function of the mounting, medium, frequency, and unit design. The limit at which the crystal is destroyed can be minimized by matching the crystal impedance so that the voltage gradient is made a minimum and by holder design. Claims have been made for 43 watts/cm^2.

Breakdown appears to be an electrical phenomenon.[1] Calculation of the power-production capabilities of x-cut crystals operating in transformer oil appears to offer possibilities as high as 10^4 watts/cm^2. On the other hand, the limit to the power output due to the lack of dielectric strength of the surrounding medium is fairly low; and once breakdown occurs, as in oil, the heat from the arc that results produces strains and resultant crystal failure. These arcs appear to occur in the oil alone, which has a dielectric strength of 100 or 200 kv/cm, while quartz has one of about 5,700 kv/cm for 0.05 mm.

As indicated, many experimenters have used air backings to minimize oil breakdown and also because there is much greater reflection at the back surface of the transducer, and therefore the energy projected into the liquid is greater. In addition to making the medium one that will not support breakdown, it is advisable to make the path of rupture as long as possible.

Barium titanate blocks presently available can take about 10 watts/in.^{2} maximum. Breakdown appears due to heat buildup within the crystal, and appears as loss of drive or fracture of the crystal.

Coupling to the Crystal. The coupling of the generator to the crystal is the only critical part of the system and has to be done with care to prevent high-voltage breakdown and also to provide a maximum transfer of power. The simplest system is merely to connect the crystal across the oscillator output, and such a system works fairly well. Other methods for coupling are shown in Fig. 7-10 and are fairly straightforward in their application. These are all designed to give maximum energy transfer from the oscillator to the crystal.

The transducer should naturally be matched to the generator. Quartz transducers are of very high impedance, while barium titanate is rather low (about 3,000 ohms per crystal). Both are reactive (capacitors) and coils may be used to tune out the reactive elements for greater output. Magnetostrictive units, on the other hand, are inductive, and the coupling capacitor may be varied to tune out the reactance.

Magnetostrictive Transducers. The basic requirements for driving magnetostrictive transducers is the source of a-c voltage which usually takes the form of a vacuum-tube oscillator, amplifier, or of a motor generator of some sort. A source of direct current for bias is also required

[1] L. F. Epstein, M. A. Anderson, and L. R. Harden, *JASA*, **19** (1947) 248.

where permanent or remanent magnetization is not used. When used for receiving or low-power use, a short pulse of direct current sent through the coil will give enough remanent bias for operation.

A typical system utilizing the magnetostrictive principle is indicated in Fig. 7-11. Such systems are useful where lower frequencies (or greater

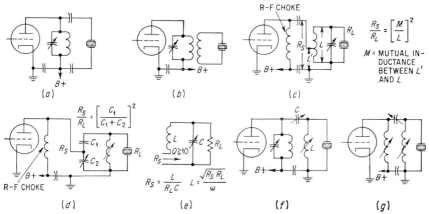

FIG. 7-10. Methods of coupling the output: (a) direct connection; (b) inductive coupling; (c) and (d) tapped tank circuit; (e) impedance transformer; (f) L matching network; (g) Π matching network.

concentrations of power) are satisfactory. The design of the unit itself is considered elsewhere. The transducer may be coupled through a diaphragm or mounted at its node, projecting through the tank wall.

Magnetostriction systems can be cooled by a jet of cold water thrown against the vibrating system or be completely water-cooled, and greater outputs can be obtained in that manner. In some cases the vibrator is directly in the material to be agitated; in others a separate vessel is used in the same manner as with crystals.

These units have the additional advantage that they can be used in gases as well as liquids. Unfortunately, the wavelengths obtainable

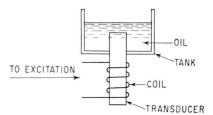

FIG. 7-11. Magnetostrictive agitation system.

are not entirely satisfactory for all liquid work. A further advantage is that the vibrators can be sterilized for medical or chemical work. They can easily be used in the low-audio as well as the ultrasonic range.

The circuit most commonly used is shown in Fig. 7-12 and is basically a parallel circuit with a means for keeping each source isolated, that is, the oscillator source is in series with a capacitor C through which direct current cannot flow while the d-c source is in series with inductor L, which keeps alternating current from flowing through it. The output of both circuits is combined to flow through the transducer winding. For matching purposes it is usually considered as a resistive load of one impedance.

The capacitor C may be selected to have a very low impedance so that it will not block any alternating current to the inductor. It may also be chosen so that it is tuned with the reactance of the transducer so that the transducer itself appears as a receptive load to the generator. This is the method commonly used today and is usually done empirically by varying C with a given transducer until the output is maximum. In this condition, the maximum output for exciting power is obtained. Of course, if the transducer is going to be constantly changed, new values of C will have to be inserted.

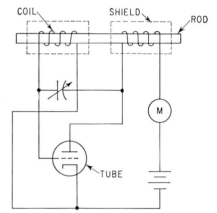

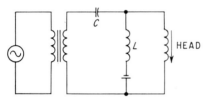

FIG. 7-12. Method of supplying bias to a magnetostrictive transducer.

FIG. 7-13. Simple magnetostrictive oscillator. (*Pierce.*)

The inductor L is commonly chosen so that its impedance to alternating current is much greater than the impedance of the head. This will ensure that the maximum amount of alternating current will flow through the head. In addition, it must be able to carry the direct current without losing inductance and without dropping the d-c voltage too much.

Electronic Generators for Magnetostrictive Use. The electronic generators used with magnetostriction are basically two types:

1. A power oscillator operating class C.

2. An oscillator–power amplifier with the power amplifier operating class AB2.

The first type of magnetostrictive oscillator in its most elementary form is shown in Fig. 7-13 and was originated by Pierce. The coil is loosely placed around the circumference of the rod. Oscillations are self-excited. The movement of the bar produces a voltage in the feedback coil that sustains the oscillation and without which the oscillator cannot operate.

The coils are connected in a degenerative direction and are shielded from each other; i.e., they are connected in a direction opposite to the usual manner for an electronic oscillator. The rod, however, provides feedback in the proper polarity.

When the rod is removed, the oscillator either may or may not continue to operate. If it does, it may be at a different frequency, since the frequency is controlled by the rod. Once the rod is inserted, the tuning capacitor is not necessary, and the oscillator will actually continue to operate at the same frequency for various different settings of the capacitor.

Generally the rod is inserted, and the capacitor is tuned until a large jump in plate current (two to three tunes) occurs. At that point the capacitor loses control and may be varied further without much effect.

Pierce stated that at 500 to 3,000 cps it was preferable for the oscillator not to operate when the rod was out of its place, and at 3,000 to 300,000 cps it was desirable to have the oscillator run independently and merely be stabilized by the rod. In these cases, however, the usual degenerative connections were used. The conditions are valid for frequency-controlled

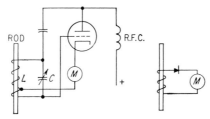

Fig. 7-14. Oscillator for driving rod, showing method of coupling meter.

oscillators. The danger in using this circuit is that the system may be unable to maintain its oscillations when the rod loading is great.

An alternative scheme is to use an ordinary oscillator connected in the usual regenerative manner to drive the rod for producing the ultrasonic energy. There are various circuits applicable to this use. One of the simpler circuits is shown in Fig. 7-14. The rod is inserted and supported in the coil that constitutes the resonant circuit. It also shows one method of connecting a meter for indicating the presence and amplitude of a signal. Either the rod is permanently magnetized, or the magnetization current is applied through an independent coil. In both cases the magnetostriction rod is used in the same manner as a crystal; it may either excite itself or be merely a driven element.

The action of the oscillator is described in greater detail, since it is characteristic of the entire class of units. The two coils are connected in the plate and grid leads, respectively, while the magnetostriction rod is clamped in its center. The meter in the plate circuit merely indicates the presence or absence of oscillations. The part of the rod in the plate side is driven by the output, while the other section in the grid side couples part of the energy back into the tube.   The sections of coil are shielded from each other so that only the rod controls the feedback, and they are moreover connected degeneratively.

The frequency of oscillation is determined by L and C, but especially by L.

The same effect can be produced in a two-stage unit in which the input coil is coupled into the first tube, amplified, and fed into a second tube. The output is then taken from the second tube.   This is, of course, for control purposes.   A second magnetostriction unit must be coupled into the output if ultrasonic power is required.

Two tube units may also be used as magnetostriction units after the fashion of the multivibrator.   The second tube feeds back to the first one through the magnetostriction system.   This arrangement is not commonly used.

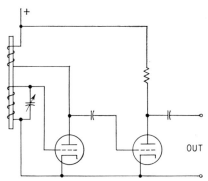

FIG. 7-15. Two-tube oscillator.

The torsional type of magnetostriction transducer is also important. Torsion bars may be designed to operate in high temperatures and humidities without variation in their characteristics.   The action is based on the change in reluctance when the bar is twisted torsionally in a field. In the same manner as the magnetostriction longitudinal type, torsion bars must be polarized if a linear output is desired.

One method of utilizing the effect is to pass a wire of magnetostrictive material between the poles of a horseshoe magnet.   These units may be used as phonograph pickups.   The stylus is fixed to the center of the wire, and pickup coils wound around it.   The device gives excellent frequency response.[1]

A practical type of magnetostrictive oscillator is shown in Fig. 7-16 which may be used as a driving unit for either cutting or mixing.   In this unit, two power tubes are used as a push-pull oscillator.   The grid-cathode circuit comprises the oscillator proper while the output trans-

[1] Stanley R. Rich, *Electronics*, **19** (1946) 107.

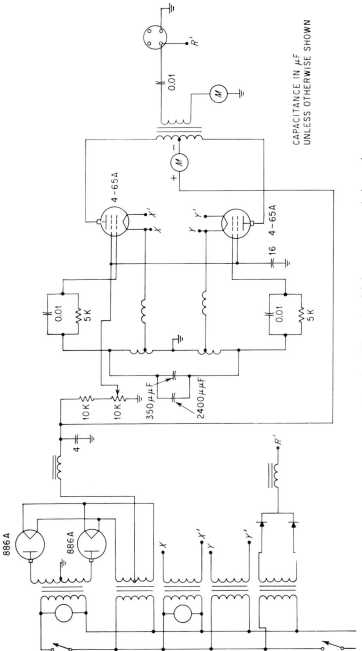

CAPACITANCE IN μF
UNLESS OTHERWISE SHOWN

Fig. 7-16. Typical push-pull oscillator for driving magnetostrictive units.

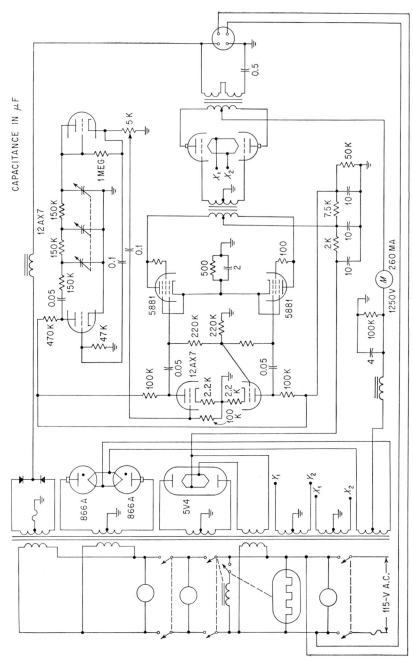

CAPACITANCE IN μF

FIG. 7-17. Typical oscillator–power amplifier for driving any type of transducer when properly matched.

174

former is in the plate circuit. The frequency may be controlled by moving the two coils in the grid circuit with respect to one another and also by changing the value of the tuning capacitors. The unit shown is designed to operate at about 20 kc. However, it will cover the entire range to be used by magnetostrictive units by changing the value of L and C. The output impedance is set by the number of turns on the output transformer, and a separate source of direct current is fed in parallel to the transducer itself.

A unit comprised of an oscillator and power amplifier is shown in Fig. 7-17. This unit is conventional and the only difference is that the oscillating circuit is isolated from the transducer by means of the intermediate power amplifier. Either type may be designed for any desired power output.

Pulsed or Continuous Generators. Generators have been constructed with 60-cycle power (self-rectified), 120-cycle power (self-rectified), and direct current. A 500-watt unit (measured by average power into a resistor load) of the first type would be rated as 500 watts average, 2,000 watts peak; a unit of the second type would be rated as 500 watts average, 1,000 watts peak; and a unit of the third type as simply 500 watts. The consensus is that all three would do the same as far as operation is concerned.

CHAPTER 8

NONDESTRUCTIVE TESTING OF MATERIALS:
CONTINUOUS-WAVE AND RESONANCE

Continuous Wave

The original experiments with the use of ultrasound for testing materials seem to have been carried out by Muhlhauser;[1] his experiments and extensions and variations on them have been repeated by various other investigators.

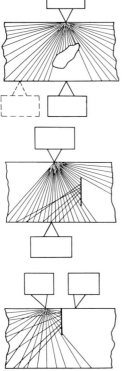

History. The publication of the Muhlhauser patent in 1933 disclosed the use of ultrasonic energy for the location of various types of defects within solid media. The basic disclosure of the patent is the transmission of ultrasonic energy into a part at one point and the reception of the energy at another point after it has traveled into the part. The interpretation of the differences in energy level at various points on the material therefore indicates the presence or absence of included flaws.

Figure 8-1 is the drawing of the patent disclosure and represents several possible positions of the ultrasonic transducers. In the first case they are directly opposite each other, and the presence of a flaw in the material between them entirely interrupts the flow of ultrasonic energy from one to the other. In the second case, although there is no flaw directly between them, a crack normal to their faces and to one side reflects a sufficient amount of the otherwise divergent waves to cause an indication. Third and last, the presence or absence of reflected energy is noted. In every case except the first there is obviously some energy transmission at all times. The function of the system is

FIG. 8-1. Muhlhauser's method of testing materials.

[1] O. Muhlhauser, German Patent 569,598 (1933).

therefore to discriminate among different energy levels and on this basis indicate whether the material is flawed or not.

Experiments carried out with these types of transmission indicate very strongly that the most promising method of test is the first, and as a matter of fact the change in energy level transmitted in either of the other setups is indistinguishable because it is so slight compared with the

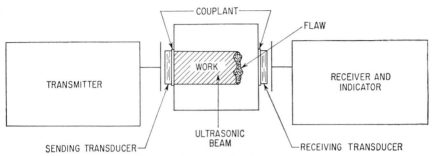

FIG. 8-2. Testing, direct contact.

amplitude of the over-all signal. These arrangements are therefore rarely used in practice.

The general conception revealed in this patent is basic to all similar methods of testing materials and has had some use in medical diagnosis and other fields. In each of these systems a transmitter and receiver for ultrasonic waves are used, and the ultrasonic vibrations are transmitted into the part, pass through it, and are picked off its surface by a second crystal as a receiver.

Sokolov investigated the amount of couplant that was necessary and found that thin films were sufficient for very flat materials. However, where there was some irregularity of surface, he had more success with

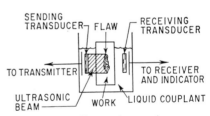

FIG. 8-3. Immersion testing.

mercury, which more nearly matched the impedance at the interface and therefore caused less reflection.

Sokolov[1] also had another arrangement in which the ultrasonic waves passed through a liquid, through the medium under test, and then through a liquid again. He claimed that with variations of this basic arrangement he could rapidly test large amounts of material.

He contributed the idea of a couplant that matches impedance and experimented with different indicators and frequencies. His work was of great importance in the pioneering of ultrasonic testing.

[1] S. J. Sokolov, Electro-Technical Institute, Leningrad, 1935.

Another of Sokolov's contributions to the art was a mechanism for getting an actual image of the flaw (Fig. 8-4).[1] This is described as operating on the following principle: The ultrasonic energy is transmitted through the part under test and received by a quartz crystal. However, this crystal does not integrate the electric charges produced, which remain isolated on its face. The face is then scanned either by a mechanical contactor or by electron beam.

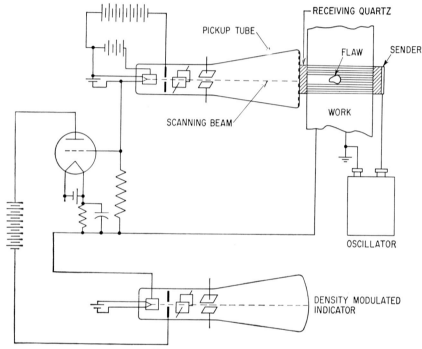

FIG. 8-4. Image system.

The operation of the scanning mechanism is synchronized with a suitable indicator such as a cathode-ray tube, which indicates on its face, by intensity modulation, a picture of the state of the sample. The picture on the tube face would therefore superficially resemble an X-ray film.

This patent is extremely important in that it is the first United States patent granted for this type of ultrasonic testing. Figure 8-5 shows Sokolov's method of scanning mechanically.

Various other systems have been suggested for obtaining an ultrasonic picture of an entire piece and are discussed elsewhere. The pictures obtained give ultrasonic testing a slight similarity to X ray, and transducers of this type could be of great value to the growth of ultrasonic applications.

[1] S. J. Sokolov, U.S. Patent 2,164,125 (1939).

Shraiber also contributed a great deal to the art of continuous-wave testing.[1] Among other things, he experimented with testing metals in oil, dust pictures of the ultrasonic beam, diffraction patterns, various types of transducers, a stepped sensitivity receiver, interruption of the beam by a nonconductor, etc. He built units that were used on airplane propeller blades and contained means for recording results on photosensitive papers by light.

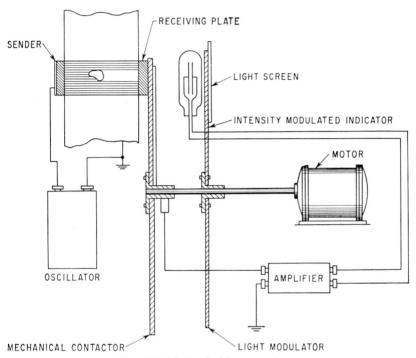

FIG. 8-5. Mechanical image system.

In one of these instruments, which is typical of the class, the oscillator and receiver were set up on rails over a long tank through which the propeller blades progressed. The transducers were mounted on long, waterproof cables and could be conveniently positioned by means of rails. Another tank was also provided with means for moving objects in the ultrasonic beam for test purposes and was used with samples other than the propellers.

Shraiber's driving oscillator operated from unrectified a-c voltages, and the signals were received and amplified by a superheterodyne type of receiver. This receiver was stepped in sensitivity so that it would indicate the energy only when it was greater than an arbitrary level. A neon bulb was used as an indicator. In order to investigate the possibility of

[1] D. S. Shraiber, All-Union Institute of Aviation Materials, *Z. Lab.*, **19** (1940) 1001.

electrical pickup between transmitter and receiver, Shraiber used a piece of nontransmitting material, which was interposed into the ultrasonic beam. This stopped the vibrational energy from passing; but if there was any electrical pickup, it still caused indications (see the section on wave interrupters in Chap. 3).

Shraiber[1] also mentioned the formation of resonance effects. Figure 8-6 is the schematic of his oscillator, and Fig. 8-7 of one of his receivers.

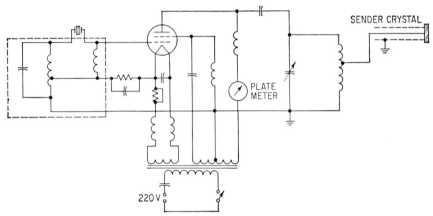

FIG. 8-6. Oscillator used by Shraiber.

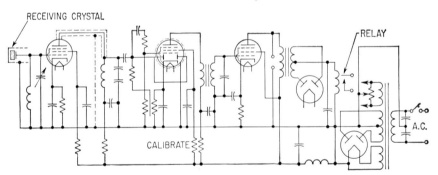

FIG. 8-7. Ultrasonic receiver.

It is interesting to note that the oscillator alone has all the necessary parts for resonance testing, using the plate meter as indicator.

Shraiber quotes the work done by Kruse,[2] who came to the conclusion, after some experiments with an ultrasonic generator operating between 30×10^3 and 10×10^6 cps, that it was impossible to test materials ultrasonically. The energy was sent through mercury, through the part under test, and finally picked up by a crystal transducer. A voltmeter was

[1] *Ibid.*

[2] F. Kruse, Doctorate Thesis, Hannover Technische Hochschule, 1938.

used as an indicator.   With this apparatus, the results were so erratic as
to be useless.   Shraiber analyzed Kruse's difficulty and hit upon the
greatest handicap to continuous-wave ultrasonic testing when he concluded that many other factors besides the mere defects in the material
influence the ultrasonic intensity of the test beam.   It was Shraiber's
idea that these difficulties in interpretation were caused by standing
waves, and he therefore suggested the use of stepped sensitivity to eliminate them.

Using stepped sensitivity, Shraiber successfully located drilled holes in
metal bars, as well as very small laminations in similar materials.   As
long as he confined his work to pieces whose sides were parallel, plane,
and not less than ½ in. thick, he was fairly successful.   With thinner
pieces he found himself unable to work consistently.

He therefore began to experiment with a "wobbulated" frequency in
order to avoid the standing waves.   He tried both continuous changing
of frequency and the simultaneous or alternate transmission of signals of
different frequencies.   He finally decided that
the use of two transducers and two oscillators at
different frequencies was most satisfactory.

Shraiber also experimented with lenses and
filters and with the use of spring-mounted transducers that followed the curvature of an irregular
part closely.

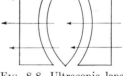

Fig. 8-8. Ultrasonic lens
system.

Figure 8-8 indicates a method of testing a
piece by means of metal lenses as suggested by
Shraiber.   The waves are affected by the lenses in the manner usual in
optics.   Ultrasonic lenses themselves are considered in Chap. 3.

He also attempted to find a couplant that would have the same velocity
for ultrasonic propagation as the common metals.   In this connection
experiments with oil and lead were carried out unsuccessfully.   An analysis of the common liquids indicates that such an ideal couplant does not
exist and strong reflections occur between most solids and liquids.

The work of these men laid the foundation for all continuous-wave
work.   However, although they pointed out certain basic difficulties in
ultrasonic testing, they did not entirely resolve them, and these difficulties
are still present in continuous-wave testing systems.   These difficulties
are:

1. The generation of standing waves from reflections
2. The lack of transparency of certain thicknesses of materials to
ultrasonics

The General Continuous-wave System.   From what has already been
said, it may be seen that all ultrasonic signaling systems which use con-

tinuous waves are made up of a driving oscillator operating at radio frequency, a receiving amplifier and indicator, and a sending and a receiving transducer.   Several of these elements may be combined in one unit, but all are always present.

The medium to be tested is almost always set between the two transducers, usually crystals.   A signal from the transmitting oscillator activates one crystal that vibrates and sends a steady stream of ultrasonic energy through a coupling material such as oil into the part under test. This energy is transmitted through that part, passes out of it into and through more coupling material, and activates another crystal transducer mechanically.   The receiving crystal transforms the mechanical energy into an electrical one, which is amplified by a vacuum-tube amplifier.   It is then impressed on an indicator, which interprets it in terms of whether or not the material is defective.

Almost all units of this nature use a tank of liquid in which to immerse the medium under test.   This liquid then acts as a continuous couplant, and the material can be freely moved between the transducers.   Most of these systems do not operate on the basis of fine quantitative measurement, but rather on a go or no-go basis.   The optimum condition is therefore one in which the flaw either interrupts 100 per cent of the ultrasonic beam or allows it all to pass.   This, of course, rarely happens, and variations in indicated signal level may then have to be interpreted.

A frequency range of 20 kc to 20 Mc may be used.   Since the crystal is immersed in a liquid in a holder, it is not subjected to hard wear as in the case of testing by direct contact.   It is therefore not critically fragile at higher frequencies.   However, most defects in metals may be found within the frequency range from 0.5 to 5 Mc.   For plastics, wood, glass, and similar materials, frequencies from 100,000 cps to 1 Mc are indicated.

Liquids suitable for application for immersing materials under test may be any of the same ones used as couplants.   Oil or water is most common. However, from the point of view of ultrasonic efficiency, almost any liquid can be used.   A wetting agent such as Aerosol should be mixed with the liquid; otherwise bubbles will form and deposit on the face of the crystal.   These bubbles can indicate in the same way as flaws.

The depth that ultrasonics can penetrate through solids in this type of test is essentially unlimited, and 25 to 30 ft is common in homogeneous media.   The energy should, however, be directed normal to any interfaces, since there will otherwise be great reflection and refraction from them.

The movement of the test piece should be regular and, if possible, should not have any component parallel to the ultrasonic beam, since such a motion will cause the system to act as a sort of ultrasonic interferometer and reflect more heavily at one position than another.   Since elimination of this motion is practically impossible unless the part is in direct contact with the transducer, spurious signals almost always result.

One limitation to the use of baths is the temperature which should be held within reasonable limits. Another is the fact that certain materials must not be wet because of their own characteristics. Currents in the test tank should be kept to a minimum, since they may affect the readings. This may be done by baffles mounted in the tank. In spite of these difficulties, immersion testing has become common in industry.

Even when transmitting into liquids and gases, coupling materials may sometimes be used and are described under crystal holders. In such cases they are almost always solids.

The Ultrasonic Oscillator. Almost any type of radio-frequency oscillator similar to those used in electronic work can be used to produce the power for vibrating the crystal transducer. Variable-frequency oscillators are most convenient except in those cases where frequency control

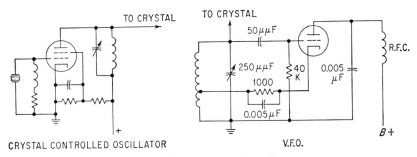

FIG. 8-9. Simple ultrasonic oscillator.

is necessary. Crystal-controlled oscillators may then be used. However, the crystal used for control purposes is normally a different one from that used for ultrasonic generation, since the latter is too heavily damped to be used as a control device, except in wave generation in gases and possibly in some liquids.

Although the frequency chosen will depend to some extent on the particular application, it should be continuously variable in the vicinity of the resonant crystal frequency so that it can be tuned to compensate for changes in the system, e.g., the cable lengths. In many cases the cable capacity is part of the tuned circuit. Oscillators for this purpose are shown in Fig. 8-9.

One-tube oscillators of this type will generate enough power for any ordinary testing use and also for short-range signaling purposes. A typical output would be less than 100 watts. The physical layout and construction of such an oscillator is extremely important, since any electrical coupling to the receiver, even if small, will be very troublesome. This type of difficulty can be visualized by considering the possibility of cross beats between the ultrasonically produced and electric signals. Moreover, the electric signals themselves may cause the indicators to give misleading readings.

The easiest way to isolate the oscillator is to keep it entirely separate in its own cabinet and with its own power supply. However, this may not be desirable from the point of view of economy, size, and portability. The oscillator can therefore be mounted on the same chassis as the receiver, enclosed in one or more concentric shields. The oscillator can also be constructed on a subchassis isolated from the receiver chassis but mounted physically on it and connected to it at carefully chosen ground points. The power supply, if it is a common one, is decoupled by suitable filters.

More complicated or higher power oscillators can be used for ultrasonic generation. Such oscillators may give an output from 10 watts up. For test purposes the additional power is not important, although it may be in signaling systems. Such units are made commercially for radio signaling.

Matching the transducer into the oscillator is very important. Any of the standard methods of matching can be used. When matching is accomplished, the crystal and cable capacity is no longer so troublesome, and increased output results. Matching technique is more fully considered on page 169.

The frequency at which the ultrasonic waves are produced is usually that of the crystal resonance, since at this point the signals are greatest. However, this is not always true, and a crystal may be driven at other frequencies. Theoretically, any frequency can be chosen, but they are usually ones below the crystal's resonance point.

Although a great part of the discussion refers to the transducer as a crystal, it should be understood that any type of piezoelectric, magnetostrictive (or other) unit may be used with minor changes in circuitry.

The Ultrasonic Receiver. Any ordinary radio receiver or amplifier that covers the required range, such as a standard communications type, can be used as an ultrasonic receiver. Vacuum-tube voltmeters fed by one or two stages of amplification can also be used. The output of the amplifier can be modified to operate suitable means of indication such as a cathode-ray tube, meter, light, or relay.

Since it is the amount of energy that is to be measured, the linearity of the receiver becomes of considerable importance, and steps should be taken to ensure it. Attenuators that allow the linear variation of sensitivity are very convenient.

Variations in signal level may occur very rapidly, i.e., as the material under test is passing through the transducers. The meter or indicator must be able to follow this variation. A quick-acting meter, such as a

decibel type, is most often satisfactory. A cathode-ray indicator is preferable from this point of view but not so satisfactory from the point of
economy and simplicity.

It is desirable to have the output of the receiver actuate a control
device such as a light or relay. This can then be used to control the
rejection of the faulty material. When only the signal level is of interest,
a circuit (Fig. 8-10) may be used on the output of an ordinary radio in
place of the audio system. This circuit is shown fed from the intermediate frequency of a superheterodyne receiver but could just as well be
inserted in any type of receiver. The detector output is impressed on a
gas trip tube such as a type 2050, in whose plate circuit there are a relay
coil and neon bulb. Whenever the 2050 fires, the neon bulb lights, and
the relay throws.

The gas tube must then recover quickly after breakdown in order to be
ready to fire again at the next indication. In order to accomplish this,

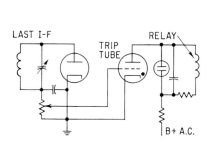

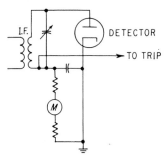

Fig. 8-10. Indicator circuit.   Fig. 8-11. Method of inserting meter.

alternating current may be used on the plate of the tube, or the d-c contact may be broken by the relay throw, since the tube will recover only
when plate voltage is removed.

In the most general case the polarity of indication may naturally be
adjusted to be in either direction, but it is more convenient to have the
light off and the relay open when the ultrasonic signal is being received.
The material is good at that time. When the material is faulty, the beam
is interrupted and the light flashes and/or the relay throws to "reject"
the flawed part.

If a meter is desired, it can be inserted in any convenient spot, e.g., as
in Fig. 8-11. This meter will then give a quantitative measure of the
actual amount of ultrasonic energy received. It may also be combined
with the circuit already described, and the trip tube set by a potentiom-
eter in its grid circuit to fire when convenient. In that case it is best to
have the meter inserted in such a manner that it will continue to read the
amplitude of the signal without reference to whether or not the trip tube
has been fired. This system has all the advantages of stepped reception

and at the same time gives the actual signal level. The step part of the indication is, of course, the trip tube. Figure 8-12 is a partial schematic of a superheterodyne receiver suitable for such work.

In short, any good radio receiver with a meter in its output can be used. The bandwidth need not be especially great, since very great resolution is not required.

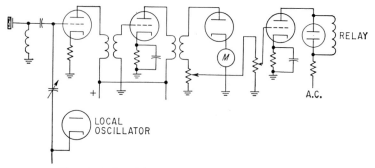

Fig. 8-12. Partial superheterodyne receiver circuit.

Radio-frequency amplifiers can also be used, and one such circuit is shown in Fig. 8-13. This has the same disadvantages of poor selectivity and low gain in this use as in ordinary radio work. However, radio-frequency or video amplifiers have been successfully used at times. The meter shown is a conventional audio-frequency output type.

Filters are sometimes used in such receivers to discriminate against signals of other than test frequencies. These are designed in the usual way, and their description can be found in radio texts. The presence of such filters is essentially to ensure that only the correct frequencies are feeding through to cause indication.

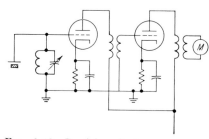

Fig. 8-13. Partial radio-frequency receiver circuit.

As mentioned, stepped sensitivity can also be used. In this method the receiver is arranged so that the indicator (relay or neon bulb) throws in at a predetermined point. The circuits already mentioned can be used for that purpose. This procedure is convenient for production methods, since it gives a very definite and strong indication.

When materials are being tested, the amplifier's sensitivity is set by experiment; i.e., a known sample is introduced into the beam, and the meter set at a standard indication for the flaw. When that is done, the receiver will act in order to reject flaws greater than the sample one.

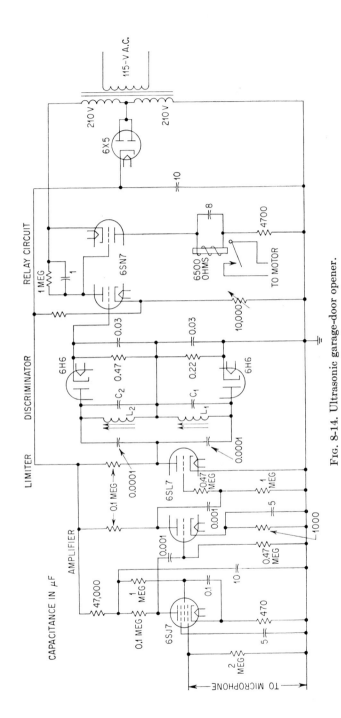

Fig. 8-14. Ultrasonic garage-door opener.

187

However, it is difficult to calibrate ultrasonic receivers exactly, since so many factors enter into the strength of the signal besides the flaw itself.

Another method of calibrating the receiver is by introducing a standard signal from a signal generator into the input of the receiver. The reading of the output meter or of a separate meter located across the output of the receiver will give the receiver's calibration.

This method gives a reading of the receiver's sensitivity, which can then be calibrated against the known flaws. It may be found that the different types of flaws give different indications, i.e., allow different amounts of energy to be indicated in the receiver output.

In ultrasonic signaling in air, the sensitivity of the receiver is not very important, since other factors cause greater changes in its response. These factors are discussed elsewhere. In test work the sensitivity of the receiver is almost always great enough, and a gain of 10,000 is about as much as can be used at present owing to various sources of noise. A receiver of such an order of gain is, however, very satisfactory. Receivers of a gain of a few hundred can sometimes be used in simple systems.

Besides being used for test purposes, ultrasonic amplifiers can obviously be used as control devices,[1] i.e., to operate a mechanism when an ultrasonic signal is either present or absent. Such devices as door openers, counters, etc., can be activated in this manner. In those cases the receiver causes a relay to throw at some specific signal level. Usually, the signal is amplified, limited, and then amplified again to introduce into the control circuit a signal that is always constant.

A circuit for this purpose is shown in Fig. 8-14. Any of the amplifiers already discussed can be used as a control device. Ultrasonic energy can be used in this manner much as light is used with the photoelectric cell. A whole field of control devices is therefore possible.

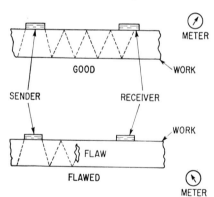

FIG. 8-15. Test method.

Transmission at an Angle. The continuous-wave method is sometimes used with the search units on the same side of a part. Such a method was disclosed by Muhlhauser and is illustrated in Fig. 8-15. The success of such a test depends on the spread of the beam of ultrasonic energy. Some of the energy travels at an angle that is determined by the beam spread and is reflected in a specular manner. It thus travels along in a direction essentially parallel to the front face of the transducer until it hits a flaw or reaches the receiver.

[1] B. A. Andrews, *Electronics*, **20** (1947) 116.

Bez-Bardili[1] experimented with solid plates at an angle to the ultrasonic beam in a liquid and from this found certain angles at which there was greater transmission than at others; i.e., he drew a relationship between angle of incidence and amount of transmission of the ultrasonics. An arrangement for introducing ultrasonics at an angle is shown in Fig. 8-16. Such angular introduction can obviously be used for test or other purposes.

This technique would be valuable for introducing ultrasonics into a curved surface or one on which it would be difficult to place the crystal. Angles may be chosen that will give optimum transmission, and such angles would be valuable for testing materials in a liquid bath. In addition, angles can be chosen to produce either shear or surface waves.

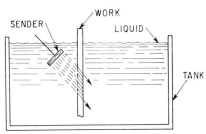

FIG. 8-16. Angular introduction of ultrasonics.

Wobbulated Systems. The effects of system resonances may be eliminated by varying the signal frequency, usually at a 60-cycle rate, and over a 2-to-1 frequency range—for example, 1.5 to 3 megohms. The 60 cycles are removed from the signal by a filter, leaving only test intelligence. The wobbled signal is applied to the sending crystal which produces a corresponding ultrasonic signal. This is sent through the test samples and couplants to a receiving crystal.

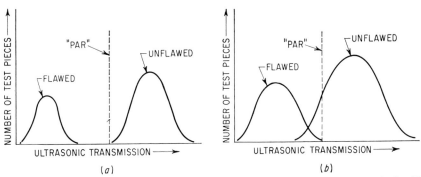

FIG. 8-17. Distribution curves. (*a*) Ideal one sets "par" at dashed line. This should reject all the flawed parts and pass all the good ones. (*b*) This curve rejects all flawed parts, but also rejects some good ones.

A standard reading is set by means of samples known to be good. This may have some tolerance but excludes definitely defective samples. Ideal and usual distribution curves are shown in Fig. 8-17.[2] Schematics of a typical unit are shown in Fig. 8-18.

[1] W. Bez-Bardili, *Z. Physik*, **96** (1935) 761.
[2] N. W. Schurberg, *Iron Age*, **176** (1955) 87.

Varying the Oscillator Frequency.   Any of the usual methods of varying oscillator frequency can be used.   However, the simplest method is to connect the rotor of the frequency-controlling capacitor to a motor that will rotate it and therefore periodically change the frequency.   Motors with ratings of $\frac{1}{75}$ hp are satisfactory.   In most cases the bearings of the capacitor must be changed for such service, and provision made for shock-mounting the tubes to prevent microphonics.   The condenser plates must also be dynamically balanced to obtain a smooth-running system.   For noise reasons, sleeve-bearing motors are preferable to ball-bearing

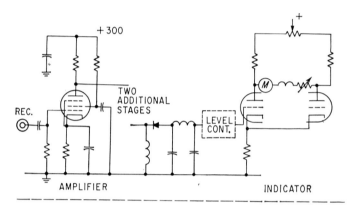

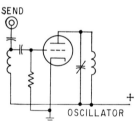

FIG. 8-18. Frequency-modulated tester.

types.   Frequency modulation by electronic means is also possible, and means for doing this will be found in the literature.

In the case of a rotating capacitor great difficulty is experienced in making satisfactory contact with the rotor and in eliminating hash caused by poor contacts.   When electronic modulation is used, care must be taken to prevent drift.   In order to avoid these difficulties the simultaneous transmission of several different frequencies may be resorted to.   In such a case several oscillators operating independently provide the frequency range necessary to avoid standing waves.   The same result can be accomplished by switching the different frequencies alternately rather than impressing them on the crystal simultaneously.

As indicated, filters[1] may be incorporated in the receiver or amplifier so that only the range of frequencies being used will be indicated. This is especially necessary where the range used is of the same frequency as extraneous sounds, i.e., in the audible range or near it.

Methods of Indication. As already discussed, the modulation of a light beam can be used to indicate the changes in the amount of ultrasonic energy transmitted in such a system. However, this method is so cumbersome that it is rarely used except in experimental work in a research laboratory.

The amount of agitation on the surface of a pool of liquid can also be used to indicate the emergence of ultrasonic energy. This, too, is a laboratory method.

In Germany several specialized methods were worked out during the Second World War for making the path of the ultrasonic waves visible after they emerged from the part under test. For example, the usual optical projection means were used together with small floating particles, which oriented themselves to provide a more visible signal.[2] Units of this type have also been built in this country.

Shielding. In continuous-wave ultrasonic systems, especially where the work is entirely immersed in a liquid, it is difficult to get satisfactory electrical isolation. The tank filled with liquid will pick up energy if it is placed near a source of such energy. Conductors, when they are placed in such a tank, will therefore pick up signals that will cause trouble.

Since the signal produced by the ultrasonic energy hitting the crystal will combine with the electrical pickup, extreme care must be taken to shield the apparatus and to ground all parts completely.

Sonic or Ultrasonic Signaling. Besides their use for testing purposes, ultrasonic waves can also be used for signaling and ranging. In many of these applications continuous waves are used.

Methods of ultrasonic communication and ranging are of particular concern in wartime, although not of great interest otherwise. The application usually takes two forms, i.e., the transmission of intelligence by modulated ultrasonic waves traveling either in the atmosphere or in the ocean and also the location of objects in the same media, without, however, transmitting intelligence.

Signaling by Ultrasonic Carriers. Ultrasonic signaling in the atmosphere is usually carried out at the very low ultrasonic frequencies, i.e., from about 20 to 30 kc. Such frequencies give wavelengths of approximately $\frac{1}{2}$ to 1 in.

Energy for such purposes may be produced by whistles, which can be driven either by the breath or by gas or air blasts. They can also be activated by vacuum.

---

[1] W. E. Morris, U.S. Patent 2,378,237 (1945).

[2] R. Pohlmann, *Physik Z.*, **113** (1939) 697.

Unfortunately, there is very great absorption in the atmosphere, as well as other factors that cause a loss in the ultrasonic signals. While all of these factors do influence the amount of transmission, it can be shown that no matter how much power is generated by the whistle, penetration in the atmosphere is limited to very little more than 1,000 ft even when parabolic reflectors are used to concentrate the energy.

Factors That Control Transmission. The transmission is influenced by many factors, chief among which are atmospheric conditions such as temperature, humidity, and wind.

As in other ultrasonic work, the frequency of signal also has great influence; and as the frequency becomes higher, the transmitted waves travel shorter distances. At about 20 kc, transmission with a given system might be about 200 ft; at 30 kc only about 100 ft would be penetrated. This indicates that the signal frequency should be as low as possible. This is always true where penetration is desired. At very high frequencies, of course, air is an excellent insulator to ultrasonic waves.

Another factor that affects the transmission is the height of the sending transducer above the ground, both because of the line-of-sight factor and also because of the influence of the ground on the ultrasonic waves that pass over it, especially when there is grass or shrubbery acting to interrupt the energy.

Many other specialized factors cause losses and therefore indirectly limit the transmission. Such factors are the spreading of the energy, molecular effects, shadows or reflections, conduction, damping or viscosity, etc. Most of these are natural limitations, which cannot be compensated for.

Ultrasonic signaling is also limited by noise naturally present in the atmosphere that is in the same general frequency range as the signal. This is, however, not so serious as the other factors.

It should be noted that although the transducer itself is not affected by air or water currents in the medium, the ultrasonic waves are affected, and greatly changed results may be observed when such currents are present.

For all these reasons it is unlikely that the transmission of ultrasonic energy traveling through the atmosphere will be widely used for signal purposes.

Methods of Use. The factors already mentioned naturally influence the ultrasonic signals no matter what applications are contemplated. The commonest use is in interrupted code transmission or in modulated systems. Listening systems are also used for location of objects, usually by triangulation, i.e., the use of several listening points with directional receivers, which give a bearing on the source of sounds.

Continuous-wave ultrasonic energy can also be used for object location by means of the Doppler effect. A moving object carrying an ultrasonic generator will produce marked Doppler effects when it approaches a reflecting surface, such as a wall. This type of device can therefore be used as a warning to indicate the proximity of a reflector. Units of this type utilizing ultrasonic signaling for burglar alarms, blind guidance, etc., are described in Chap. 11.

Signaling in the Ocean. Most subocean signaling is pulsed rather than continuous. However, continuous-wave listening is widely used in ocean warfare, and elaborate listening systems, consisting of banks of transducers of highly directional types, have accordingly been developed.

Telephoning on a subocean carrier, though possible, has never been widely used, although Langevin contemplated it as one of the major applications of ultrasonics. A tremendous amount of work has been done in sonar, which itself merits several books of consideration. However, a large proportion of this work has not been made public at present, and it cannot therefore be considered.

Tuning the Transducers. All continuous-wave signaling systems in common use are equipped with two crystals, one for sending and another for receiving. In such cases it is extremely important that the two crystals be tuned to exactly the same frequency, since the resonance curve of quartz is extremely sharp, i.e., a slight mistuning of one crystal will cause a sharp decrease in signal strength. It is very unlikely that two crystals of the same nominal frequency would be precisely the same, since there are usually differences in grinding or mounting, which may cause slight variations. Moreover, one or both crystals may be changed during the life of the instrument, and mismatch may occur in that way.

For these and other reasons both crystals are usually tuned in some way. This can be done in various manners, either by a condenser in series or parallel with the crystal or by movement of one of the crystal electrodes where that is possible. A series condenser is the simplest expedient for accomplishing the tuning.

Variation in the electrode distance is not ordinarily used (1) because it is critical and difficult to accomplish and requires a more complicated holder and (2) because crystals are usually plated by evaporation or deposit, thereby making the electrodes incapable of movement.

Resonance

The term *resonance* refers to a physical property possessed by a medium because of its dimensions. Such a characteristic may, for example, cause the body to begin to vibrate at a given natural frequency when it is brought into the neighborhood of another body that is already vibrating at that frequency. This action may be observed in a tuning fork or piano.

The induced vibration will continue, sometimes for considerable lengths of time, and will decay only when the natural friction of the medium causes it to do so. In some cases there may be several frequencies or modes in which such a body might vibrate, usually related to one another harmonically or in some other manner. Thus an article might, for example, oscillate at 60 cps and also at 120 cps, as well as at other frequencies.

Most bodies also exhibit another characteristic similar to the first. In this case the body will be forced to vibrate at a frequency determined by a neighboring vibrator. However, it is not a natural frequency due to its dimensions at which the body is oscillating. Therefore, when the medium that is inducing the vibration is removed, the driven unit will quickly stop its action. Moreover, the size of the oscillations will be considerably less than in the case of the natural ones. More driving power is therefore required. The operation is similar in theory to driving a crystal transducer at a frequency other than its resonant one.

Both these types of response are referred to as *forced responses*, since they are cases in which the vibrating body is actually driven. It may be shown, as indicated, that the first case, in which the driving frequency coincides with the natural one, is the one where a maximum motion or vibration occurs. Cases have been recorded in which such vibrations reached proportions where large structures were destroyed. It can therefore be seen that the force is a powerful one.

When resonance is referred to in ultrasonic systems, it is usually somewhat different from these cases, although the general nature is closely similar. The only response that is of much interest, because of the small amounts of power needed in most ultrasonic systems, is the type where the driving and driven resonances coincide. It has already been mentioned that in that case the motion is a maximum.

In most ultrasonic systems resonance occurs when the electrical frequency is varied until the ultrasonic wavelength is related to the distance traveled by an integer multiplier. In other words, there is a certain whole number of half wavelengths in an entire path of travel. In such a case the driving electrical oscillator will be called upon for a minimum amount of power output, and the greatest proportionate amount of ultrasonic energy will be produced in the material.

Testing Materials by Resonance. The principles of resonance have been successfully applied to the testing of materials, and several commercial instruments are now available.

Exciting Resonance. Almost any ultrasonic generator is capable of exciting resonance in thin sections. Radio-frequency oscillators of almost any sort are suitable for this method of operation. A generator that can be used for other methods of test will provide enough power for resonance methods.

Resonance Thickness Measurement. The relation between frequency and wavelength may be stated as follows, since ultrasonic waves travel at different velocities in different media. The formula is

$$\lambda = \frac{c}{f}$$

where λ = wavelength
c = velocity

or

$$f = \frac{ck}{2t}$$

where k = harmonic
t = plate thickness

All ultrasonic systems for measuring thickness by resonance are based on this relationship. The wavelength is varied until a point of maximum reflection is located. This is the resonant point. If the part under test is allowed to vibrate only in its fundamental mode, there will be only one such point.

In the case where the thickness of the medium is entirely unknown, the fundamental and a number of harmonics may all indicate. Under these circumstances two adjacent readings are taken. These will be $1/n$ and $1/(n - 1)$ of the total thickness t. By setting up two equations and solving them, a final equation for the thickness can be derived:

$$t = \frac{r_1 r_2}{r_1 - r_2}$$

Occasionally, when the resonance principle is applied to the testing of very thick sections, so many harmonics appear that it is difficult to interpret the pattern. In such situations every nth peak can be counted, and the results substituted in a revised form of the relation

$$t = \frac{N r_1 r_2}{r_1 - r_2}$$

The fact that only one pip occurs on a particular instrument obviously does not indicate per se a fundamental mode. The factor that determines the number appearing is, of course, the range of excitation and indication.

Therefore, when testing a material or reading its thickness by the resonance method, the most general information is not any one resonant point, but it is rather the distance in frequency between successive resonances. Pieces that are multiples of one another in their thickness dimension resonate at many of the same frequencies, but their total spectra will not be the same. Thus if a particular piece indicates resonance at 1, 2, 3 Mc, etc., it means that the actual fundamental frequency is the difference between two different frequencies at which higher modes of resonance occur. Thus, in this case the resonant frequency is 1 Mc. It may be seen from the above example that at least two harmonic resonant points are necessary in order to determine the fundamental resonance.

In a like manner any material—solid, liquid, or gas—can be investigated, and its thickness determined by getting two successive resonant points and subtracting them. It is always advisable to test the piece over as wide a range as possible, since the accuracy to which the readings can be made would be greater by testing over a range that makes small variations more readily noticeable. The wider the range the greater the number of harmonics that will indicate.

This does not mean that it is impossible to test in a fundamental mode, i.e., one where there is one nodal plane in the material. As a matter of fact, on a practical level it is possible to test on a fundamental up to about $\frac{1}{2}$ in. in steel under good working conditions. However, when parts are thicker than this, the fundamental mode is no longer used and harmonics must be used.

The accuracy of the resonance method of test is essentially limited only by the user's willingness or unwillingness to resort to very exact electrical and mechanical devices. For example, precise gear-driven knobs for controlling the frequency may be carefully calibrated and used with those types of screw drive common on interferometers. Moreover, the associated electrical circuits can be made tremendously selective, so that the resonant points are very narrow and frequency readings extremely exact.

Interferometers have been constructed with accuracies in the order of 0.2 per cent. However, the average ultrasonic resonance instrument for the testing of material probably approximates 2 per cent more closely.

This type of ultrasonic instrument has very wide applications in the measurement of the thickness of materials and in the testing of thin bonded articles such as silver-plated aeronautical bearings or bimetallic strip. It can also be used for measuring any thickness or for locating any flaw in a medium that is not more than about 4 in. thick. However, the instrument is most suitable when used on a large number of articles that are very similar to one another in thickness and in which small variations must be located. If the range of thicknesses that must be tested is very wide, separate ranges of test and separate crystals must be used. Generally speaking, the narrower the range over which a crystal is used and over which the oscillator operates, the sharper the resonant points will be. As the instrument is tuned away from crystal resonance, there will be a considerable loss in indication amplitude.

An instrument might therefore be reasonably set up to test from about 0.035 to about 0.075 in. in thickness. If it were also desirable to test an article 0.25 in. thick, a different range and a different crystal would have to be used. Generally a 1:2 thickness range is satisfactory in those instruments which have a swept frequency.

A number of studies have been made comparing theoretical calculated frequencies vs. thickness with measured ones, and some differences found.

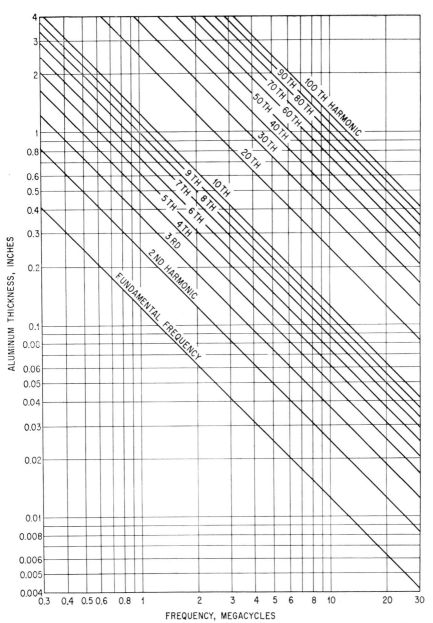

FIG. 8-19. Relation between aluminum thickness and resonant frequency. (*After Branson.*)

Of course the instrument calibration can be made to compensate for this difference.

Thus, certain valuable characteristics of resonance become immediately apparent. First, since ultrasonic resonance is defined as that condition (of dimensions) which requires a minimum of power to maintain, a part can continue to oscillate without requiring additional input power, except enough to overcome the material's internal damping. Therefore, in pulsed systems a sharp shock of excitation may be impressed on a material, and characteristics of that material deduced by the length of time that the system continues to ring. Again, a series of different frequencies may be applied to a medium, and its characteristics deduced by noting which frequencies require minimum driving power, i.e., resonate. Also since a part can be of such special dimensions that it will resonate at a particular frequency, it is obvious that the dimensions of a part can be deduced by noting which frequencies will resonate it. Resonance occurs only when reflected ultrasonic waves build up in the same phase with those transmitted. When this occurs, the thickness is an exact multiple of half wavelengths. It is therefore easy to make a table of material thickness vs. wavelength or frequency for any one material. Different tables are obviously required for different materials, since velocities differ in different media. Such a chart is shown in Fig. 8-19 for aluminum. By subtracting about 7 per cent from the thicknesses it may also be used for steel. If desired, a similar chart may be drawn up for steel, or a table, such as Table 8-1, may be used if it is more convenient. By the use of this information, the thickness of any medium that transmits ultrasonic waves can readily be determined.

To restate this in a slightly different way, the thickness of an article is inversely proportional to the frequency at which it will resonate and can be expressed for any material as

$$t = \frac{k}{f}$$

where f = frequency, kc

t = thickness, in. $\times 10^{-3}$

k = a constant, which for steel or aluminum is approximately 121,000

Constants for other materials can be calculated from

$$k = \frac{1}{2c}$$

where c is the ultrasonic velocity of the type of wave being used.

Any part that scatters the waves heavily, either by having a large number of inclusions or because of badly pitted or corroded surfaces, will not reflect enough energy for resonance use. Such media are very diffi-

TABLE 8-1. CONVERSION TABLES FOR STEEL*

($t = 0.116/f$; other frequencies by multiplying by factors of 10)

f	t	f	t	f	t	f	t	f	t	f	t
0.99	0.117	0.595	0.195	0.395	0.294	0.258	0.450	0.178	0.652	0.119	0.975
0.98	0.1185	0.590	0.1965	0.390	0.297	0.256	0.453	0.176	0.659	0.118	0.984
0.97	0.1195	0.585	0.1985	0.385	0.301	0.254	0.457	0.174	0.666	0.117	0.991
0.96	0.121	0.580	0.200	0.380	0.305	0.252	0.460	0.172	0.674	0.116	1.00
0.95	0.122	0.575	0.202	0.375	0.309	0.250	0.464	0.170	0.682	0.115	1.01
0.94	0.1235	0.570	0.204	0.370	0.314	0.248	0.468	0.168	0.690	0.114	1.02
0.93	0.125	0.565	0.205	0.365	0.318	0.246	0.472	0.166	0.698	0.113	1.03
0.92	0.126	0.560	0.207	0.360	0.322	0.244	0.476	0.164	0.707	0.112	1.035
0.91	0.1275	0.555	0.209	0.355	0.327	0.242	0.480	0.162	0.716	0.111	1.045
0.90	0.129	0.550	0.211	0.350	0.332	0.240	0.484	0.160	0.725	0.110	1.055
0.89	0.1305	0.545	0.213	0.345	0.336	0.238	0.488	0.158	0.734	0.109	1.065
0.88	0.132	0.540	0.215	0.340	0.341	0.236	0.492	0.156	0.744	0.108	1.075
0.87	0.1335	0.535	0.217	0.335	0.346	0.234	0.496	0.154	0.754	0.107	1.085
0.86	0.135	0.530	0.219	0.330	0.352	0.232	0.500	0.152	0.764	0.106	1.095
0.85	0.1365	0.525	0.221	0.325	0.357	0.230	0.505	0.150	0.774	0.105	1.105
0.84	0.138	0.520	0.223	0.320	0.362	0.228	0.509	0.148	0.784	0.104	1.115
0.83	0.140	0.515	0.225	0.315	0.368	0.226	0.513	0.146	0.795	0.103	1.125
0.82	0.1415	0.510	0.227	0.310	0.374	0.224	0.518	0.144	0.806	0.102	1.14
0.81	0.1435	0.505	0.230	0.305	0.380	0.222	0.523	0.142	0.817	0.101	1.15
0.80	0.145	0.500	0.232	0.300	0.386	0.220	0.528	0.140	0.829	0.100	1.16
0.79	0.147	0.495	0.234	0.298	0.389	0.218	0.532	0.139	0.835		
0.78	0.149	0.490	0.237	0.296	0.392	0.216	0.537	0.138	0.840		
0.77	0.151	0.485	0.239	0.294	0.395	0.214	0.542	0.137	0.846		
0.76	0.153	0.480	0.242	0.292	0.398	0.212	0.548	0.136	0.854		
0.75	0.155	0.475	0.244	0.290	0.400	0.210	0.553	0.135	0.860		
0.74	0.157	0.470	0.247	0.288	0.403	0.208	0.558	0.134	0.866		
0.73	0.159	0.465	0.250	0.286	0.405	0.206	0.563	0.133	0.873		
0.72	0.161	0.460	0.252	0.284	0.408	0.204	0.569	0.132	0.880		
0.71	0.1635	0.455	0.255	0.282	0.411	0.202	0.575	0.131	0.885		
0.70	0.166	0.450	0.258	0.280	0.414	0.200	0.580	0.130	0.892		
0.69	0.168	0.445	0.261	0.278	0.417	0.198	0.586	0.129	0.899		
0.68	0.1705	0.440	0.264	0.276	0.420	0.196	0.592	0.128	0.906		
0.67	0.173	0.435	0.267	0.274	0.424	0.194	0.598	0.127	0.914		
0.66	0.1755	0.430	0.270	0.272	0.427	0.192	0.604	0.126	0.920		
0.65	0.1785	0.425	0.273	0.270	0.430	0.190	0.610	0.125	0.929		
0.64	0.1815	0.420	0.276	0.268	0.434	0.188	0.617	0.124	0.933		
0.63	0.184	0.415	0.279	0.266	0.437	0.186	0.624	0.123	0.943		
0.62	0.187	0.410	0.283	0.264	0.440	0.184	0.630	0.122	0.951		
0.61	0.190	0.405	0.286	0.262	0.443	0.182	0.637	0.121	0.958		
0.60	0.1935	0.400	0.290	0.260	0.446	0.180	0.645	0.120	0.966		

* (After Branson)

cult to test.   Moreover, a material must not absorb energy strongly either within itself or at its boundaries or, generally, rest on absorbing surfaces. Under test conditions, for best results the part under examination is accordingly supported away from the table on which it rests.

In ultrasonic systems the transducers are sharply tuned, and the material itself often responds to frequency variations very sharply.   As damping is added to any part of the system, it tends to tune less sharply, i.e.,

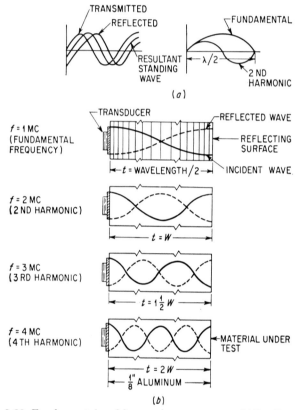

FIG. 8-20. Fundamental and harmonic resonances.   (*After Branson.*)

to become more broad band.   For resonance tests, it is naturally preferable that the tuning be as sharp as possible.   This sharpness is the usual rule, and as a result an ultrasonic system will vibrate at only one set of frequencies.

Although it is possible to get readings using shear waves, they are not as definite as using longitudinal ones, and together with the coupling difficulties, this has made the use of shear waves undesirable.

Standing Waves.   If a wave is sent out into any type of finite system, sooner or later it will reach the end of the medium in which it travels, be reflected, and return toward its source. However, during the time of travel other waves have been continually sent out, and each, in turn, is reflected. After a given time the whole system may reach a state of equilibrium, in which all the waves, both transmitted and reflected, are summed up (Fig. 8-21). However, this summation will not necessarily be uniform over the entire transmission distance. For example, considering only two waves, if the time of travel is correctly chosen, they may be found to be 180 deg out of phase at certain points, entirely in phase at other points, and at varying phases at still other points. If the resultant disturbance is then measured over the entire path, that disturbance may vary in amplitude at different points because of addition and cancellation effects. These variations may and usually do become fairly regular over the transmission path; and since they do not seem to vary with time once the system reaches its equilibrium, they are referred to as *standing waves*.

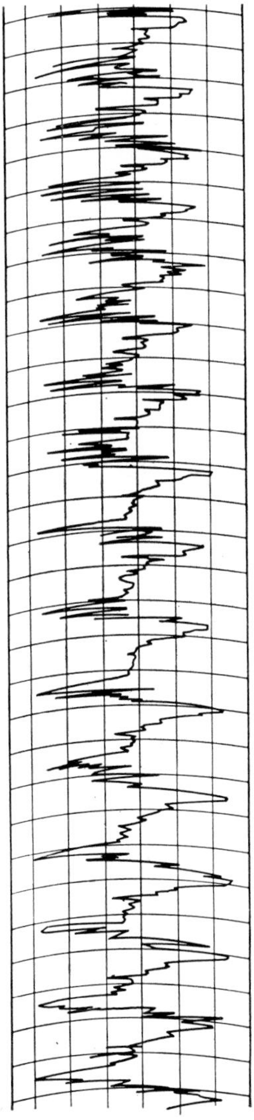

The relation between resonance and standing waves is readily apparent. Actually the formation of standing waves may be considered as a sort of resonance. Figure 8-20 shows how resonances are set up in a part at the fundamental and various harmonics.

The case above can be applied to ultrasonic waves. When an ultrasonic wave is transmitted into a medium and the path it travels is greater than a half wavelength (which it practically always is), the wave will be reflected from an interface or from any change in elasticity or density. This reflected wave will combine with the transmitted one, and a set of standing waves will result.

The first mention of standing waves in continuous-wave systems occurred in Shraiber.[1] He pointed out the possibility of interference between those ultrasonic waves reflected by a part and those being transmitted toward it. The particular case of interest to him was that in which nodes formed on the surfaces of the media where the waves were being reflected. Since he was trying to transmit ultrasonic energy through these mate-

Fig. 8-21. Standing waves in liquid bath.

[1] D. S. Schraiber, Testing of Metals by the Use of Ultrasonics, *Z. Lab.*, **9** (1940) 1001

rials, this was particularly troublesome.   If the piece had a varying thickness, no energy seemed to be transmitted through it (at those thicknesses where standing waves formed), and the receiver acted as though the energy were interrupted by a discontinuity in the material.   The person operating the instrument in such a case could not interpret his results. Such conditions were considered theoretically in Chap. 1.

It is, however, more common for the standing waves to indicate as differences of energy level as the part is moved between two transducers. This occurs because of minute differences in distance among various parts of the system, which are nonetheless appreciable fractions of ultrasonic waves.   The entire standing-wave pattern may thus continuously shift as a test is carried out, and all sorts of extraneous responses occur.

One of the main problems in the use of continuous ultrasonic waves lies therefore in the fact that these resonances or standing waves may occur in the medium itself, in the coupling medium, in a submerged part, or in any part of the entire ultrasonic signaling system where there is a reflection from a change in the acoustic impedance.   The indicator may then be influenced more by the difference caused by the standing waves than by the ultrasonic signal itself, and the system becomes useless, since it is impossible to interpret the results.

Figure 8-21 is an oscillogram of an actual ultrasonic test in a liquid bath.   The variations are caused by standing waves and not by flaws in the material.   These standing waves shift with movement of the piece under test.

The presence of standing waves or reflections in a medium that attenuates the ultrasonic signal causes additional losses of energy.   Ultrasonic waves will be attenuated by any medium that has viscosity.   This, of course, is a characteristic of all materials to some degree.   Since the amount of ultrasonic attenuation is a function of the size of the signal and since the reflections of energy cause a rise in the internal signal intensity, it may be qualitatively stated that the greater the amount of reflection in a part, the greater will be the attenuation of energy within it. Thus, for a fixed amount of incident ultrasonic power, if the reflections become larger, the losses also become greater.

Since any sharp difference in acoustic impedance will cause a reflection, and since any boundary between materials or within a material constitutes such a difference, there will always be reflections at boundaries. This reflected energy will combine to form standing waves.

In order to do away with standing waves, reflections must also be eliminated.   To accomplish this, it is essential that the media in the path of the ultrasonic beam be matched acoustically.   In other words, the transducer must be matched to the media, the media to the receiver, etc.

However, matching two media ultrasonically poses certain problems.

For example, resonances may be avoided at a certain set frequency; but when the frequency is varied, the same result will no longer be accomplished.

The greater the amount of reflection in a body, the more it will discriminate with respect to frequency (the more sharply tuned it is). A piece in which an ultrasonic standing wave exists acts something like a resonant electrical circuit. It will pass only a small range of frequencies. In other words, the more gradual the change in acoustic impedance is between parts of an ultrasonic system the less selective to frequency those parts are, and the fewer reflections there are.

Another approach to the problem is commonly used in ultrasonic light cells, where the ultrasonic energy is to be continuously modulated. In such cases, an absorbing material is so placed that it absorbs the ultrasonic energy after the modulation effect has taken place. There is no reflection and accordingly no buildup of energy and no resonance or standing waves.

This effect may be observed in testing materials for thickness by resonance, where placing a finger or other absorbing medium on the back of the part causes all the resonance peaks to disappear because of the loss of reflection.

The phenomenon has been applied in tanks, etc., to kill reflection. Various absorbing media such as animal wool, gelatin, and similar substances have been used. Scattering media may also be applied in this manner. In that case the wave is broken up into many small parts and therefore cannot reinforce itself. A material with many small irregular protrusions will accomplish this.

Acoustic Impedance. The acoustic impedance represents a characteristic of the medium that is closely akin to electrical impedance. It is determined by all the elastic properties of the material. Such an impedance may be thought of as "characteristic" in a technical sense when it is the impedance that would be offered by an infinite extent of the media, i.e., when there are no variations in that impedance within the material (and therefore no reflections). In a like manner the electrical analogy may be carried further, and it may be considered that when a piece of any given impedance is matched into another medium of the same impedance, or when a medium is terminated in its own characteristic impedance, then the combination will act like a single part of identical material, and there will be no reflections at the interface. Such a condition is difficult to attain in ultrasonics.

Matching Impedances. Impedances can be matched by keeping them alike; however, it is obvious that situations often occur in ultrasonics where energy must be transmitted from one medium into another of vastly different impedance. When that occurs, some method of matching impedance becomes necessary.

One possible suggestion is the addition between the two media of another part that has an impedance of approximately the geometric mean of the other two impedances.   Even better results may be accomplished by interposing a number of such parts, each having an impedance that is the mean of that of its two neighbors (see Fig. 8-22).

Such a combination acts as a sort of impedance transformer.   Naturally, the greater the number of sections the less the reflection at any one interface and the more efficient the matching.

Moreover, if the intermediate material is of the proper wavelength dimensions, reflections from the two sides will have a tendency to cancel out.   This may be approximated with sections of a quarter wavelength.

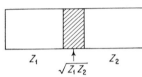

FIG. 8-22. Matching impedances.

Very few net reflections will result in such a system.

When a crystal is used, one material to be matched is quartz, and the matching media can be fastened directly to the crystal face if desired.   It will then also act as a protecting faceplate (see Fig. 3-15).

Standing-wave Ratio.   As already indicated, whenever an ultrasonic wave travels in a material with boundaries and the part is more than a half wavelength in length, some standing waves will result.   Since this condition always occurs, it is convenient to have a method of indicating it.   However, a similar situation occurs in electrical systems, and the analogy is obvious.   The same nomenclature will therefore be used here.

The standing-wave ratio in ultrasonics will therefore be defined as the relation between the energy of the ultrasonic wave at its loop and that at its node.   This in turn depends on the relation between terminating and characteristic impedance.   The ratio is defined by the formula

$$\text{SWR} = \frac{Z_t}{Z_0}$$

where SWR = standing-wave ratio

Z_t = terminating impedance

Z_0 = characteristic impedance

A medium that is terminated by an ultrasonic impedance equal to its characteristic impedance acts exactly like a single part of homogeneous material.   There are therefore no standing waves; both impedances are equal, and the standing-wave ratio is 1.

History—Submarine Apparatus.   German interest in submarine warfare led to what may have been the first practical application of resonance to the measurement of thickness, although in this case the thickness was the depth of water in which a submarine or ship was traveling.   A patent was issued for this purpose in 1921 and is illustrated in Fig. 8-23.[1]

[1] A. Behun, German Patent 464,516 (1921).

The operation of this apparatus is of interest, since it represents the action of all systems of this class and depends upon the fact that a signal of the greatest intensity will be indicated by an instrument when the standing-wave system is so set up that the wavelength is a specific submultiple of the thickness of the material. The submarine apparatus consists of an oscillator that transmits ultrasonic vibrations and of a receiver with indicating meter. The transducers are crystal plates.

The frequency of the transmitting oscillator is varied over a range that includes in it those frequencies necessary for measuring the average depth of the water. This range covers a frequency that is specifically resonant at the depth under test. At the same time that the transmitter is swept,

the receiver frequency is also tuned in a like manner over the same frequency range. In this particular piece of apparatus both oscillator and receiver are controlled by capacitors that are rotated on the same shaft. If at any point the transmitter is sending out some one frequency, the receiver is therefore also tuned to that same frequency. The receiver will indicate a maximum voltage at the point where the depth of the water is resonant to a frequency being transmitted by the oscillator. The indicator is a neon bulb, which is in the output

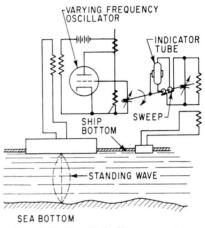

Fig. 8-23. Depth-finding apparatus.

of a receiving amplifier and which glows with a varying degree of brightness as the received voltage changes. This is somewhat difficult for the operator to interpret. Therefore, in this particular patent the light also rotates on the capacitor shaft behind a calibrated dial. When the bulb flashes, the calibrated dial can be directly read in frequency, wavelength, or depth of water. Obviously any other form of indicating system may be used.

The disclosure also indicates that a second crystal for reception can be placed either directly next to the sender or anywhere else in relation to the transmitting crystal.

Interferometry. The interferometer is an instrument for exactly measuring the wavelength of any wave motion. These instruments are made for ultrasonic use and operate on the same principle as those made for use with other kinds of radiation. Generally speaking, an interferometer can be used only in liquids or gases, since it works on the principle of movement within the media. The instruments measure the distance between successive nodes. The measurement is accomplished by very exact calibration of the movement of a mechanical part of the system. The principle of the interferometer in ultrasonics was first stated by Pierce in 1925.[1] The general operation is as follows:

A crystal source transmits ultrasonic waves into the medium; they impinge upon a parallel reflector and are reflected back to the source. This parallel reflector is ordinarily mounted on a very fine screw, which can move the reflector small fractions of a centimeter at a time. As the reflector is moved through a given distance, the plate current of the oscillator that provides the driving force for the sending crystal is observed and points during which the current is a minimum are noted. Naturally, the principle can be applied to instruments that are built in various forms, and there has been considerable literature on interferometry. A more refined instrument, for example, was designed by Hubbard and Loomis.[2]

However, all these instruments are essentially of the same class and are capable of very fine adjustment and measurement. For example, instruments can be made that will give an accuracy of approximately 1 part in 2,500 when used for wavelength measurement. Because of the relation between wavelength and frequency, this same instrument can be used for the measurement of velocities in liquids or gases, and a good many velocity measurements have been made in all types of liquids using it.

As already indicated, there has been considerable experimentation in the field, most of which is not of any great interest to anybody except the specialist in interferometry. However, a few of the more significant experiments may be mentioned. Klein and Hershberger[3] built a modification of the instrument, which uses Rochelle salt as the driving element, and also tried magnetostrictive materials for transducers. They also worked out methods for measuring the characteristics of minute quantities of liquids. Various other experimenters have measured reactions under special conditions such as low temperature, etc. Values obtained by the interferometer are usually more accurate than those required for practical work.

Another method of interest in measuring wavelength was suggested by Brillouin. His system is based upon the fact that when the standing waves are set up ultrasonically in a translucent material, the pattern formed in the material by successive rarefactions and condensations affect the light, and the resultant pattern can be investigated by optical diffraction methods. Such methods are described at greater length elsewhere.

The interferometer depends for its accuracy upon the care with which it is mechanically designed and constructed. Figure 8-24 shows a pic-

[1] G. W. Pierce, *Proc. Am. Acad. Arts Sci.*, **60** (1925) 271.

[2] J. C. Hubbard and A. L. Loomis, *Phil. Mag.*, **5** (1928) 1177.

[3] E. Klein and W. D. Hershberger, *Phys. Rev.*, **37** (1931) 760.

torial diagram of a simple interferometry system. More complete units are shown in Fig. 8-24.

Indicating Resonance. Resonance may be indicated by two basic methods, i.e., by either the effect upon the ultrasonic signal or that upon the electrical system which generates it. Thus in the former case the transmitted ultrasonic wave may be received after reflection, indicated on a cathode-ray tube, and viewed. The maximum amplitude of signal will indicate a resonant condition.

In the second type of instrument the fact that the ultrasonic system is resonant causes it to draw less power from the plate circuit of the driving oscillator. A plate current meter will therefore show a drop when resonance occurs. Other conventional methods of indicating the change in plate dissipation are also satisfactory.

Complete Resonance System. Resonance systems are of two types because of the phenomena described

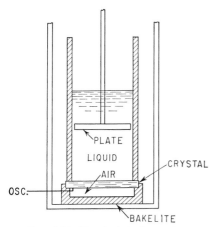

FIG. 8-24. Simple interferometer.

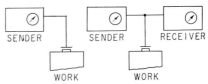

FIG. 8-25. Types of resonance instruments.

above. These two systems are indicated in Fig. 8-25. The first system is simpler but sometimes not so convenient. In it the effect of resonance upon a transmitting system is used to indicate results. This effect may be indicated directly or amplified. The sender is swept over the entire frequency range necessary for the test, and resonances indicated. It is then necessary to take several different resonances and calculate the fundamental. This is ordinarily done by having a chart calibrated against thickness or by having some kind of automatic device for indicating the thickness directly.

The system may also consist of separate senders and receivers, using either one or two transducers. In that case the amplifier must be capable of receiving the transmitted signal, either by being tuned to it or by being of sufficiently broad band to pick up the entire spectrum of the oscillator. The oscillator is swept over a frequency range in the usual manner. The output of the receiver is indicated in some fashion and calibrated in the same manner as the first type of unit.

The above principles apply equally well to continuously oscillating or pulsed systems. The most successful method of avoiding standing-wave problems in test systems that do not operate by resonance consists in pulsing the ultrasonic energy. When this is done, the ultrasonic vibrations will decay between successive pulses and standing waves cannot build up to the same degree as in continuous systems.

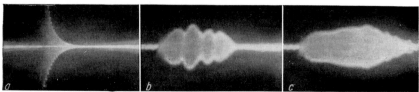

FIG. 8-26. Resonant indications on a pulsed instrument: (*a*) pulse alone; (*b*) nonresonant; (*c*) resonant.

Nevertheless, pulsed ultrasonic systems may be successfully used for resonance work.[1] Almost all these systems use separate oscillators and receivers, since the change in output at resonance is so minute that it is difficult to measure. When a pulsed system is used for resonance, that condition indicates as a swelling out of the pulse; Fig. 8-26*b* shows a nonresonant condition and Fig. 8-26*c* illustrates a resonant one.

Resonant test equipment may use either crystals or magnetostriction devices, but crystal use is far more common. The entire discussion is applicable to either type of transducer.

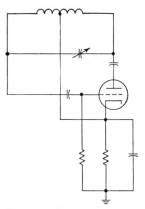

FIG. 8-27. Simple oscillator.

The Oscillator. Any of the common types of oscillators, such as that indicated in Fig. 8-27, may be used. For wobbulated systems, a mechanically tuned condenser may be used.

The oscillator should be designed to give as constant an amplitude of output as possible. If the amplitude of the radio frequency produced is not constant, the trace of an oscillographic indicator will be displaced and the pips appear on the displaced sweep. An oscilloscope is probably the most satisfactory indicator, although a plate-current meter is occasionally used. However, the output of the oscillator must be amplified before it is fed into the plates. A typical system is shown in Fig. 8-28. Filters are sometimes included to eliminate the radio frequency, but the ordinary amplifier will do this in any case. The gain needed is not great and is usually between twenty and several hundred. No compensation of any type is required for frequency.

Each coil used in the oscillator should cover one testing range. These

[1] J. B. Butler and J. B. Vernon, *JASA*, **18** (1946) 212.

ranges are usually about a 1:2 ratio, i.e., from 0.010 to 0.020 in. thickness in steel, 0.020 to 0.040 in., etc. Since most thickness testing is carried out on parts whose dimensions are at least approximately known, each range should have the dimensions most commonly measured in its center

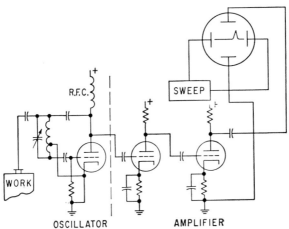

FIG. 8-28. Typical indicator system.

so that it is easier to read and also so that harmonics do not appear. When harmonic indications do appear, they must be distinguished from the primary indication by their height. If this is not possible, a number of readings are taken, and the thickness found by substitution into the harmonic formula. If the range is just under a 2:1 ratio, no harmonics of measurements within that range can appear.

The sweep should be as linear as possible; otherwise the calibration marks will be irregularly spaced. In any case the sweep would normally be calibrated against standard samples, i.e., pieces whose thickness was known. Separate calibration marks must be provided for different metals whenever the velocity of ultrasonic propagation

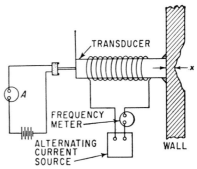

FIG. 8-29. Magnetostrictive resonance system.

is different. Calibration can also be carried out electronically, by feeding a signal of proper frequency into the unit and noting where the beat falls.

Magnetostrictive Resonance System. A resonance measuring system that illustrates many of the characteristics of all similar systems is shown in Fig. 8-29.[1] This happens to be a magnetostrictive instrument, but there is no real difference between it and crystal ones, except in detail.

[1] H. C. Hayes, U.S. Patent 2,105,479 (1938).

The operation of the unit is as follows: A rod or bar of suitable magnetostrictive material is either placed against or permanently fastened to a medium whose thickness is to be measured. Separate readings are naturally taken at those different sections where the thickness variation may be of interest. A coil is set around the bar in the usual manner; and when this coil is magnetized by passing a current through it, the rod is affected according to the magnetostriction effect. It will therefore oscillate at the exciting frequency and will transmit the vibrations into the medium under test.

The frequency of oscillation may then be varied over a range until a resonant condition results. In the figure a special indicator is used. This is a microphone which is mounted on the magnetostriction rod and connected across a metering circuit. The current flow through the microphone will then change at resonance, and the thickness of the wall can be calculated from the frequency indicated.

The velocity of ultrasonics in the medium must be known in advance in order to determine the wavelength. The formula for thickness then is (according to the inventor)

$$t = \frac{c}{2f - L}$$

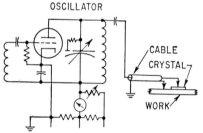

OSCILLATOR

FIG. 8-30. Basic Sonigage. (*General Motors.*)

where c = velocity
f = frequency
L = rod length

Any convenient system of units may be used. Only the general principle is indicated here. However, there is no reason except the intrinsic limitations of magnetostriction why that phenomenon should not be applied to resonance.

The Reflectogage. A more recent instrument for measuring thickness ultrasonically when only one surface is available is the Sperry Reflectogage, which is illustrative of a class of instruments now appearing commercially. The work is set into resonant vibration, and the frequency at which this occurs is automatically indicated. Since this resonant frequency, as already indicated, will be directly related to thickness, the instrument may be and is directly calibrated.

The Reflectogage is based on the General Motors Sonigage[1] (Fig. 8-30),[2] which originally consisted of a variable-frequency oscillator and a

[1] W. S. Erwin and G. M. Rassweiler, The Automatic Sonigage, *Iron Age*, **160** (July 24, 1947) 48.

[2] W. S. Erwin, Supersonic Measurement of Metal Thickness, *S.A.E. Journal*, **53** (March, 1945) 25.

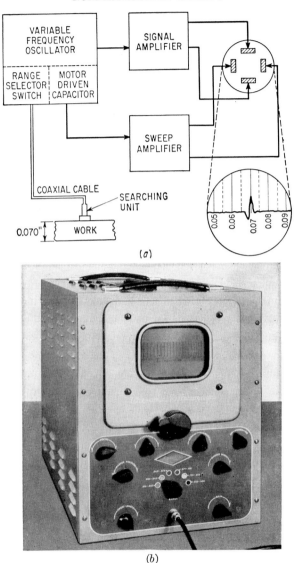

FIG. 8-31. Resonance instrument: (*a*) block diagram; (*b*) photograph. (*Sperry.*)

transducer. The crystal was pressed on the material, and the oscillator turned until a resonant point was reached. Owing to the losses in the system, power was necessary to maintain the vibrations and was drawn from the oscillator. An output meter was used to indicate the frequency at which minimum power was drawn from the oscillator. Specifically, the oscillator was a one-tube variable-frequency affair, with a d-c milliammeter in its plate circuit. A sharp change in the current indicated resonance.

Inasmuch as crystals are resonant at their own natural frequencies, the transducers are always chosen with a resonant frequency higher than any likely to be met in the particular range of measurement, so that the oscillator must force them to vibrate at its own frequency rather than the natural one of quartz. In this case the crystal resonance will have little effect. Resonances in the crystal will otherwise indicate in the same way that thicknesses do.

The dial of the instrument was then calibrated to read thickness rather than frequency. The inventor claimed that he could rapidly read the thickness of sections in the range from 0.020 to 0.400 in. with an error of less than 2 per cent.

An instrument of this class will indicate not only the primary resonances but also the harmonics. However, the amplitudes of the successive harmonics are less than that of the fundamental, and they can be recognized by this means. Also, the approximate thickness of the part under measurement is often known, so there is no question of which indication is correct.

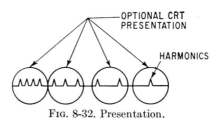

FIG. 8-32. Presentation.

The Reflectogage differs from this original prototype, since it is automatic in operation, i.e., the frequency is automatically varied over a given range by a motor-driven rotating condenser and resonances indicated on an oscilloscope (Fig. 8-31). Ranges are so chosen that the thickness of test falls in the center of a range. In this manner only one resonance pip will appear at a time and can be read directly from a calibrated mask. The complete range of harmonics possible is indicated in Fig. 8-32, as well as the manner of choosing a part of it for presentation.

Very thick parts can be tested by resonant methods by noting the appearance of the pattern and seeing if there is any gross change as a part is tested. Generally a multiplicity of pips appear on a sweep when this method is used, and the number and spacing of those pips change as the character of the work varies. Other forms of resonance instruments are considered in Chap. 11.

Drop Tests. Other types of resonant tests that are closely related to those already mentioned are the hammer and drop tests, which have been tried more or less successfully for several years. Primarily, the procedure for the hammer test was as follows: A mechanic with keen ears tapped the surface of a steel sheet with a hammer and listened for the false note, which indicated to him the presence of a flaw.   Unfortunately, such tests were not always successful; but with the advent of sonic and ultrasonic methods, electronic analysis has been applied to them.   The system suffers from the obvious defect that the flaw may be a very small portion of the entire tested area and it is therefore difficult to determine when the article is bad and when good.   However, although the test has been mainly unsuccessful in use on large parts, it has found a variety of applications in devices designed to test small articles, which can be rung either by dropping them on an anvil or by other means.   In most cases the sound is picked up by a microphone or other transducer and analyzed in one way or another.

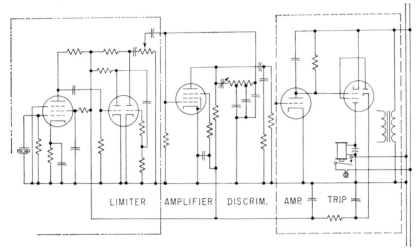

FIG. 8-33. Drop tester.

The basic operation of a drop tester can be analyzed as follows: The article under inspection, which is usually metallic, is dropped on an anvil or struck in such a position that free vibration is possible.   Vibrations are set up at a frequency that is generally determined by the structure and dimensions of the material.

In this simplest form the total sound is received on an amplifier whose frequency response can be adjusted so that other sounds than the free vibration of an unflawed piece can pass through it and actuate an indicator.   In the more elaborate types complicated frequency-analyzing circuits may be included (Fig. 8-33).[1]

It is sometimes desirable to ensure that the sounds, even if of different frequency, are of the same amplitude so that spurious results are not obtained.   Electronic limiters for such purposes are well known in the

[1] B. A. Andalikiewicz et al., U.S. Patent 2,352,880 (1944).

art. Another means of accomplishing the same object is to ensure uniform drop of the article as far as height and force are concerned. Waves produced in such tests may be either sonic or ultrasonic.

Ultrasonic waves have also been produced for other purposes in England by dropping a pellet or hammer on an article in which the waves are to occur.

Pulsed Resonance Systems. Pulsed systems may also be used to excite and measure resonance. A typical pulsed system,[1] is shown in Fig. 8-34. In this case the initial oscillogram is an exponential pulse viewed directly, the second one shows a nonresonant condition which takes the form of a series of reflections falling closely after each other so that they partially run together, and the last one a resonance condition where the signal bellies out smoothly Pulsed resonant systems follow all the general laws of resonance.

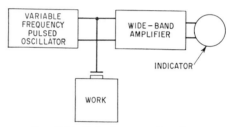

FIG. 8-34. Pulsed resonant system.

Limitations of Resonance. Resonance systems work poorly on highly corroded or absorbing surfaces. A very smooth surface without paint or scale is usually required, without excursions of more than a fraction of a thousandth of an inch. For curved surfaces, curved crystals must be used. Resonance crystals for this purpose are much harder to manufacture than for testing or other purposes. Certain types of bonds cannot be tested ultrasonically, since there is always some adhesion, although the bond itself may be either good or bad.

Testing Bond. Another instrument very similar in its approach is one referred to as the *Stub-meter*, which tests material for its mechanical impedance.[2] Basically, the instrument is very similar to a resonance indicator and consists of an oscillator which is varied or swept and an indicator. The range of frequency through which it is swept, however, is much less than is common in resonance testing, and the shape of the resonance curve itself is used as an indication of the condition of the material. The crystal is operated below its own resonance, so that it does not affect the shape of the curve, and the only thing which remains is the

[1] F. A. Firestone, U.S. Patent 2,439,131 (1948).

[2] J. S. Arnold, *WADC Tech. Rept.* 54-231 (1955).

character of the material. This reacts on the transmitter in such a way as to affect its indication. Figure 8-35 shows a block diagram of such a unit and typical indications. Unfortunately, the type of indication is complex and requires skill to interpret.

Ultrasonic Liquid-level Sensors. Liquid-level systems using ultrasonic probes have also been used. These systems consist of a transducer, an

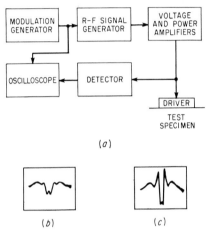

(*a*)

(*b*) (*c*)

FIG. 8-35. The Stub-meter and typical indications: (*a*) block diagram; (*b*) normal material; (*c*) poor bond.

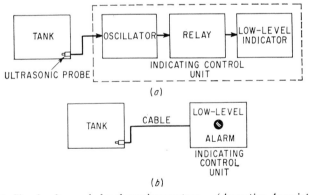

(*a*)

(*b*)

FIG. 8-36. Simple ultrasonic level-sensing system. (*Acoustica Associates, Inc.*)

oscillator, and a relay or other indicator. The oscillator and probe are designed so that the loading of the liquid on the transducer causes the oscillator to stall and stop oscillating. As soon as the liquid is removed, oscillations start again. This in turn causes changes in plate current which are used to activate some sort of indicator such as a relay.

CHAPTER 9

NONDESTRUCTIVE TESTING OF MATERIALS: PULSED

Testing Materials with Pulsed Ultrasonics.   Work in the use of pulsed ultrasonic energy for the testing of materials was disclosed in U.S. Patent 2,280,226, issued in April, 1942, to F. A. Firestone.   This invention solved many of the problems that had been plaguing users of ultrasonics and gave great impetus to ultrasonic research, leading to many later inventions and refinements.   The method is simple, quick, and positive and has essentially eliminated most of the difficulties inherent in all systems developed prior to that time.   It has suggested the use of such techniques in all sorts of test applications, as well as in theoretical investigations.

Dr. Firestone calls his instrument the *Reflectoscope*.   It locates defects by means of the echo principle, which had been extensively used in both sonar and radar, to which ultrasonic testing by the pulse method bears striking and basic similarities.

As in these other fields, the basic principle of operation consists of the transmission of a pulse of vibration into the part or medium to be inspected and the measurement of the time intervals between the initial pulse and the arrival of the reflections from internal defects and from the opposite side.

When the medium is metal and a few inches thick, the reflections return a few microseconds after the pulse is emitted, and the Reflectoscope accordingly provides a method of measuring these small time intervals.

Such a method offers great possibilities in testing objects where only one face is available or which are many feet long, where the defects lie totally within the part and may not be found by any other means.   Moreover, the method is totally nondestructive and can also be used to determine physical properties of the material, such as the amount of absorption or velocity of ultrasonics.

In most cases 30 ft of material can be easily penetrated and therefore tested with one application of the testing transducer.

A major advantage of ultrasonic testing is that the thickness of the medium does not dictate the size of the flaw that can be located (it does, for example, in X rays), and a very small defect is practically as easily found in a part 6 ft thick as in one 6 in. thick.

The exact operation of the Reflectoscope and of other devices of the same type is disclosed in the patent (Fig. 9-1b),[1] which includes the elements of the operation, as well as the waveshapes associated with each.

The pulse generator produces a radio-frequency pulse a few microseconds in duration and between a few hundred and several thousand volts in amplitude. Raising the voltage does not necessarily raise the sensitivity proportionately, and 500 volts will work very well. This oscillation is then impressed on a crystal, which is placed up against the article under test, with the usual thin film of couplant between.

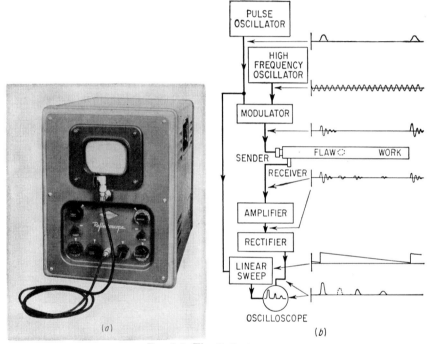

FIG. 9-1. The Reflectoscope.

The receiving crystal may be the same one that sends out the energy, i.e., the one used during the time it is quiescent, or it may be a separate crystal placed anywhere on the work. The time elapsed between the pulse and reflection is indicated on the cathode-ray tube. When the crystal is off the work, only the initial pulse shows, giving a starting indication from which the time is to be measured. After contact is made with the work, subsequent reflections are received by the amplifier, and each reflection is indicated at a particular time after the initial pulse, which represents the distance that some part of the energy has traveled.

[1] F. A. Firestone, U.S. Patent 2,280,226 (1942).

Thus, if an oscilloscope (which is the most convenient method to date) is used for the indicator, the initial pulse would occur to the left of the line, and the echoes spaced after it to its right.

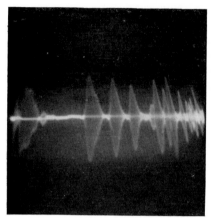

Fig. 9-2. Typical signal.

The reflected energy will bounce back and forth in the medium, indicating over and over again until it is damped or attenuated by the physical properties of the medium and also by losses in other parts of the system. The instrument should be so designed that the reflections from one pulse entirely die out before the next one is sent out; otherwise reflections from the successive pulses will overlap each other, and it will be impossible to tell which is which. The time between pulses is accordingly made long enough so that this does not occur. A 60-cycle repetition rate has proved satisfactory, although other rates up to 1,000 cps have been used.

A typical picture of a pulse and its successive reflections is shown in Fig. 9-2. It will be noted that the energy is reflected within the material many times.

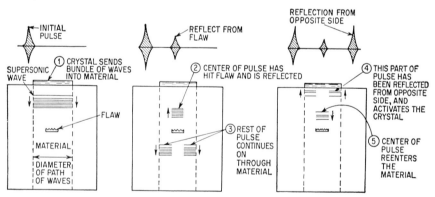

Fig. 9-3. Action of the ultrasonic pulse.

The action of the ultrasonic energy can be visualized from Fig. 9-3.[1] The pulse is impressed on a block of material and also appears on a sweep at the same time. It then begins to travel through the material until it hits a discontinuity, where part of the energy is reflected and the remainder continues to travel through the article under test. The reflection is

[1] B. Carlin, *Product Eng.*, **18** (1947) 113.

thus picked up by the crystal, which now acts as a receiver, and is impressed on the sweep as a pip.   Then, after a further interval of time, the reflection from the back face returns and indicates on the screen. The whole process repeats over and over, providing a stationary pattern that can be easily read by the operator.

A number of manufacturers have produced essentially the same instrument here and abroad.

Hughes Ultrasonic Instrument.   Henry Hughes and Sons, in England, has produced an instrument[1] operating on the reflection principle but differing considerably from the Firestone one in certain respects.   Figure 9-4 shows the operation of the instrument.   Certain basic similarities

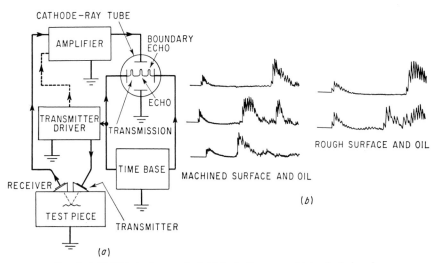

FIG. 9-4. British instrument: (*a*) block diagram; (*b*) typical signals.

may be noted.   In the unit a triggering circuit supplies firing signals to the sweep and after a short delay to the pulse generator.   The pulse generator is a gas tube, the British equivalent of the 884.   A pulse of energy, i.e., of logarithmically damped ultrasonic waves, is then sent out by the transmitting crystal, shown mounted on a wedge.

This wedge directs the beam of ultrasonic energy into the part under test, and the receiving crystal is also tilted so that it is sensitive only to the energy from the particular region under test.   There should be no refraction due to the wedge, which is of the same material as the medium. This wedge method of test suffers from certain basic difficulties of application.   It is hard to handle, and the wedges must be continually readjusted if an area is to be tested.   However, flat crystals can also be used,

[1] C. H. Desch et al., *J. Am. Welding Soc., Suppl.* (January, 1947).

but the instrument can operate to date only with two separate crystals, which makes it cumbersome. The received signal is amplified and appears as a vertical detected pip on the screen of a cathode-ray tube.

The crystals used are about 0.75 in. in diameter and operate at a resonant frequency of $2\frac{1}{2}$ Mc. They are therefore about 0.1 cm thick. The transmitter pulse generator generates a pulse of approximately 300 volts amplitude on the sending crystal. This pulse is produced, as indicated, by discharging a condenser through a thyratron.

The amplifier is a video type, inductance-compensated, with a response flat up to $2\frac{1}{2}$ Mc and then gradually falling off up to 5 Mc. The triggering circuit is a generator of square waves, which is followed by means of differentiating them to produce the short sharp pip used in the triggering action.

There are no markers, except a rulerlike etching on a screen placed over the tube. The sweep must therefore be linear and is produced by a thyratron being fired in the usual manner through a pentode, which gives greater linearity. Blanking voltage is applied to the cathode-ray tube to obliterate the return trace.

The Hughes company claims to be able to find flaws between $\frac{1}{2}$ in. and 12 ft from the testing surface in steel.

Figure 9-4b shows a typical indication on a Hughes-type instrument. One interesting feature of this instrument is the fact that only one crystal is used for all frequencies. The instrument operates at $\frac{5}{8}$ Mc, $1\frac{1}{4}$ Mc, $2\frac{1}{4}$ Mc, and $2\frac{1}{2}$ Mc to date; but a $2\frac{1}{2}$-Mc crystal is used throughout and is driven at the other frequencies. This makes the handling of crystals and cables simpler and easier.

In addition to their use in testing materials, the pulsed tester has been used for medical diagnosis and in measurement and other fields. However, the principle of operation and the circuitry remain the same or very similar. Similar apparatus has been produced in many other countries and under various company names, but they are all similar in principle to those described. The major modifications have been in methods of indication.

Pulsed Systems—Electronic Considerations. The late war contributed greatly to the development of electronic measurement techniques and particularly to those which were related to pulse production and measurement. Such developments have had wide influence on all forms of equipment; and since ultrasonics has come to depend almost exclusively on electronic equipment for the production of energy and for its measurement, it also has felt the results of this work.

Although, strictly speaking, the electronic considerations are not a part of ultrasonic knowledge, the fields are now so connected that no treatment of ultrasonics is complete without consideration of the associated devices. Therefore, a brief discursive description of the typical circuits used in pulsed ultrasonic equipment may be of considerable value in defining some critical aspects of the problem. More complete discussions may be found in many books and articles in the technical press and are too extensive to quote here.

This treatment will indicate the types of circuits used. Block diagrams will be used whenever possible, since once the type of circuit is known, design considerations can be found in any engineering text. However, those electronic problems which are characteristic of ultrasonics will be considered in greater detail. Naturally engineering texts can be consulted for circuitry detail.

The Pulsed Ultrasonic Unit. The type of systems and circuits discussed hereafter is particularly adapted to test and signaling purposes. However, by minor changes in circuit constants, the apparatus can be adapted to other types of ultrasonic application. The principles apply equally well to all phases of the work.

The fundamentals of the pulsed ultrasonic system may be seen in Fig. 9-1. In its most general form, the system is similar to a pulsed radar unit, and such devices can sometimes be adapted for ultrasonic work. However, ultrasonic apparatus is of lower frequency and power.

The ultrasonic system usually produces a pulse ranging in length from 1 to 10 μsec. This length may be adjustable. It may operate over a frequency range of 100,000 cycles to about 30 Mc and have a peak-to-peak pulse voltage of 300 to 1,500 volts. The amplifier may be either tuned or untuned, with a gain of about 10,000 or greater.

The system consists of a pulse generator, which produces the pulses mentioned and impresses them on the crystal. This initial pulse provides the starting point from which all time is measured; and in those cases where two crystals are used and the coupling between transmitter and receiver is insufficient for this indication to be picked up and appear on the screen, part of the signal may be taken and used for this purpose.

The pulse is synchronized to the sweep generator in those cases where a cathode-ray tube is used as indicator. In the discussion here, that method of indication is considered exclusively, since it is at present the simplest and most economical. However, there is no electrical or ultrasonic reason why other types of indication should not be used. The pulse and sweep must be synchronized so that there will be no mutual jitter between them, which makes the signals fuzzy and hard to read.

The synchronization, or sync, signal is usually taken from the sweep circuit. If it is desirable to delay the pulse after the start of the sweep, the signal from the sweep can be used to actuate a suitable delay circuit, which may be fixed or variable, and the delay circuit will produce another signal, after a suitable time delay, which performs the function of triggering the pulse. In some cases, both sweep and pulse may be synched from a separate source.

The transducer is coupled into both the transmitter and receiver. Either two separate transducers or a single one may be used. The amplifier acts upon the received signal, which is then impressed on the indicator and appears as a series of pulses or pips after the initial pulse. The bandwidth of the amplifier must be sufficiently great to produce separation of the signals without great loss of gain.

The time is then read between the initial and reflected signals. To do this, either a calibrated linear sweep must be used or suitable marks for timing purposes impressed on the sweep.

Sweep. Any of the ordinary circuits used for generating a sweep can be used on the cathode-ray tube. The duration of the sweep should be so chosen that it is sufficient for the longest possible range which would result from sending the ultrasonic energy through a very large mass of material. At the same time it must be sufficiently fast so that variations occurring close to the initial pulse can be observed. For this reason, sweep circuits used in ultrasonics are usually variable by either switched or continuous means.

A sweep allowing enough time for about 30 ft of steel or aluminum would be very difficult to use in a few inches of the same material or in other materials except those where the speed of transmission is much slower, as it is in plastics and some liquids. Since ultrasonic waves travel about 1 ft every 100 μsec, a 30-ft sweep would be one of about 3,000 μsec. The shortest range for ordinary work is usually about 2 in., which corresponds to about 16 μsec in aluminum. Thus a sweep to be completely satisfactory should be variable over a range from 16 to 3,000 μsec for testing materials.

Sweeps for other purposes can be computed in the same manner after the minimum and maximum range has been determined from velocities of travel in the medium in question.

Circuits may be of either the hard or gas-tube type and of any of the conventional kinds. The start of the sweep would normally be on the charge side; otherwise the action will commence with a flyback, and a corresponding delay must be introduced to get the pulse to occur on the usable sweep. The sweep need not be particularly linear, since in most cases where exact distances are to be measured, marker circuits will be included. These markers may be either fixed or movable.

Sweep Operation. The simple sweep circuit (Fig. 9-5) illustrates the operation of all gas-tube sweeps. The condenser and resistor values determine the time of the sweep, which can then be varied by switching the condenser or resistor when a gross change in frequency is desired or by varying the resistor when a vernier on the large changes is more desirable.   The condenser will periodically charge up in the usual exponential manner while the tube is not conducting until it reaches a point at which the voltage on it causes the tube to fire.   The voltage will then discharge rapidly through it.   If it is desired to have the tube fire before the voltage reaches the breakdown point, a synchronizing signal may be introduced on the grid.   The point at which the tube fires is then determined by the grid voltage.

When the voltage on the tube drops to a point so low that plate current cannot be maintained, the tube will recover and the condenser again charge.

The flyback time is the time required for the discharge through the tube, and the sweep time is the time that the condenser takes to charge. Flyback time should naturally be kept as low as possible in order to keep the flyback trace from being too bright and interfering with the actual

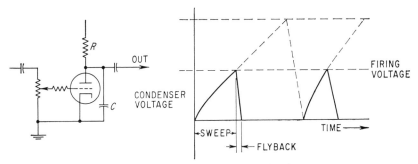

FIG. 9-5. Elementary sweep circuit.

working sweep.   In certain cases it is necessary to bias out the flyback voltages by means of a blanking signal on the cathode-ray-tube grid or cathode.   This is sometimes known as a *flaw gate*.

A sweep can be constructed so that the flyback occurs before or after the working sweep; i.e., the tube may be normally conducting or noncon- ducting and thrown into the opposite condition to produce the sweep.

Either a portion of the saw-tooth produced or the whole signal can be used on the cathode-ray tube depending on the linearity desired and the length of sweep desired.

As already indicated, if the trigger for the pulse is taken from the sweep, the sweep should start with the charge of the condenser; otherwise the additional delay interposed by the flyback time will cause the pulse to appear on the back trace unless it is suitably delayed.

Such a sweep may be satisfactorily used to give time axes of the order necessary.   If desired, the circuit can be adjusted by one or two potenti- ometers to the full extremes of the times necessary without the necessity of additional switching.

Delay Circuits. The term *delay circuit* may be taken to refer to any circuit that can be activated by a suitable signal and that some time later delivers another signal which can be used to control some process. The order of delay usable in ultrasonic work may vary between zero and a few hundred microseconds and usually, though not necessarily, represents the time delay between the start of the sweep and the firing of the pulse (or vice versa in the case of long water delays due to tank coupling). If this delay is variable, it will allow the movement of the pulse together with all succeeding reflections relative to the sweep, so that they can be placed on whatever portion it is most convenient to work with. Delay circuits may be of various types. They are generally used to compensate for long coupling paths (water) between crystal and work, or to allow expansion of various parts of the returned signal; i.e., in testing a long part it may be desirable to look only at its far end. Terms such as *water gate*, etc., are sometimes used to refer to delays.

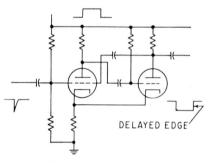

FIG. 9-6. Delay circuit.

A simple variable type of delay is shown in Fig. 9-6. The operation of this type of circuit may be visualized in the following manner. The circuit is essentially a single-shot multivibrator. In other words, it has a two-stage resistance-coupled amplifier, in which one of the tubes is cut off while the other is conducting. When a certain point is reached, the tube that has been shut off starts to conduct, and the other tube cuts off. The circuit continuously fluctuates back and forth in this manner with the time of conduction determined by the circuit constants. Since the oscillation is extremely sharp, square pulses are produced. Since this tube is biased to be a single-shot type, it will produce one square pulse and then turn itself off.

The time that the tube remains in its unstable condition is determined by the time constant of the circuit elements. Therefore, the length of the output pulse, which is a function of oscillation frequency, is also determined by these circuit constants. It can therefore be varied by altering either a capacitor or resistor. If the square-wave output is now differentiated, the signal that results will be made up of a sharp pip in one direction, either negative or positive, followed after an interval by a sharp pip in the other direction. If the circuit elements are variable, this second pip may be moved with respect to the first one, thus giving a delay between them. If a positive pip is used to fire the delay system and a positive pip derived from it, there is a delay between the start of the sweep, which coincides with the firing signal, and the positive pip, which is produced by the multivibrator. The time delay will be equal to the time duration of the square wave that the multivibrator puts out. Many other systems of time delay have been used, but this one is particularly easy to set up, economical, and foolproof. This type of circuit may also be used to provide a movable marker for measuring time.

Differentiation. In order to produce short sharp marks such as pips from a square wave, a circuit referred to as a *differentiator* is usually used. This type of circuit produces a voltage whose amplitude is approximately proportional to the input voltage's rate of change. The circuit consists of a capacitor and resistor as shown in Fig. 9-7.

The time constant of the combination is extremely short, much shorter than the length of the input signal. The capacitor therefore charges in a small part of this length; and that part of the signal which does not

contribute to the capacitor charge appears at the output as the differentiated signal. Figure 9-7 also shows the voltage waveshape on the output.

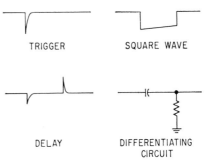

FIG. 9-7. Waveshapes from delay circuit.

Marker Circuits. The marker circuit is included to provide timing marks, which are impressed on the cathode-ray-tube sweep. These marks are usually introduced on the lower plate, while the signal is impressed on the upper one. However, either plate can be used for either function. The signal and the marks should not both be introduced on the same electrode, since considerable loss in signal strength may ensue owing to the resulting interaction.

Any of a number of well-known marker circuits can be used, and marks may be either of the deflection or intensity type. The first appear as pips; the second show as bright or dark spots. When intensity marks are used, the signal is introduced on the cathode or grid of the cathode-ray tube rather than on its plates.

The marks must be synchronized with the sweep. This is usually accomplished by gating them, i.e., turning them on only for the sweep duration. This may be done by a square pulse, starting with the sweep and lasting as long as the sweep. The two signals are locked together and cannot jitter.

The time of travel in steel is about 8 μsec/in. If time marks are desired, they may be arranged to occur once every 8 μsec/in. of travel or at suitable intervals for feet or other distances. They may be fixed or

variable.   One wave every 8 μsec will be provided by 125,000 cps of oscillation, and that frequency can therefore be used if inch marks are desired.

The simplest type of marker is the sine wave, which can be provided
from an oscillator.   Of course, these marks are not very sharp.   Square
waves or pips are therefore preferred.   Pips may all be of the same height
or include periodically spaced marks higher than the others to facilitate
reading.   In some cases, very accu-
rate marks, such as those produced
by a phantastron, may be used.

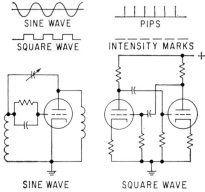

FIG. 9-8. Marker circuits.

The production of square waves
by means of a multivibrator or other
form of relaxation oscillator is well
known.   Circuits for this purpose
are shown in Fig. 9-8.   The waves
are usually most nearly square on
the tube cathodes.   However, they
may also be coupled from the
plates, and this is sometimes desirable, since the gating signal may
appear across the cathode.

These markers can be applied directly to the sweep or shaped into
sharper pips by means of a differentiator or other circuit.   When the output is too low for direct connection, amplification by one or more stages
may be applied.   If the marker squareness is not satisfactory, they may
be clipped or shaped by auxiliary circuits.   In any case, the oscillator is
usually biased off and gated on as described.

The Cathode-ray Tube.   Power circuits for actuating cathode-ray tubes
are well known in the art or can be obtained by request from any manufacturer of tubes.   The voltages provide the necessary electron beam,
and the deflections are provided by the amplifier and sweep circuits.
Sweep signals are ordinarily impressed on the horizontal plates, and signals on the vertical ones.   Short-intensity phosphors are commonly used
for A scans (P1), and long-intensity for cross-section views (or other picture scans) (P7 or P27).

Pulse Forming.   The signal derived from the delay must, in turn, be
used to fire or trigger some kind of circuit that will produce a square or
nearly square wave of suitable polarity, duration, and magnitude to control the action of the pulse generator.

If there is no delay, this signal is still necessary, but it is supplied
directly from the sweep.   It takes the form of a semisquare wave of the
order of a few hundred volts in amplitude and of a width of 1 to 10 μsec.
The control signal must not be of a greater length than the radio-frequency pulse itself, since its trailing edge will cause spurious signals that

appear as pips following the actual pulse.   In those cases where the radio frequency itself is varied in duration, the triggering pulse must be extremely short, in fact shorter than the shortest pulse used.   Where the duration of the pulse is varied by the trigger pulse itself, the trigger is always of the same length as the final pulse.

These pulses are usually positive, and one of the simplest methods of producing them is by using a circuit such as Fig. 9-9.   In this case a tube is operated with very high plate current normally flowing.   When a positive signal hits the grid, it therefore has very little effect.   However, when a negative one is used, the tube is momentarily cut off, plate current stops, and the voltage at the plate rises, producing the desired square waves.

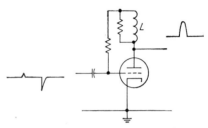

Shock-excited oscillators or blocking oscillators with resonant circuits of low frequency can also be used to produce the pulses when actuated by a suitable triggering signal.

FIG. 9-9. Pulse-forming circuit.

In the case of a shock-excited circuit, the operation is the same as for the overdriven oscillator except that upon being cut off, the resonant coil momentarily rings at its own natural frequency.   If this frequency is chosen correctly, it will produce pulses of any specific length.   That is, each such pulse is $\frac{1}{2}$ cps of oscillation, so a $\frac{1}{2}$-Mc oscillator would produce a pulse 1 μsec in length, etc.

Critical damping must be provided by a resistor across the ringing circuit, so that the ringing voltage is damped in only $\frac{1}{2}$ cps; otherwise the circuit will produce an oscillatory pulse.

In the overdriven amplifier the length of the pulse is a function of the amplifier; in the shock-excited one it may be independent.

There are many more complicated systems, but either of the above is satisfactory.   Whatever the type of pulse-forming circuit, extreme care should be taken to have only one trigger pulse.   Any extra or extraneous signals may have the effect of firing the radio-frequency pulse extra times or producing extra oscillations, which appear on the trace and obscure the actual signal.

Pulse Generator.   Ultrasonic pulse generators are similar to those used in other forms of radiation.   A complete circuit, as shown in Fig. 9-10, may consist of a delay, differentiator, amplifier, and pulse generator.   It may also consist of a simple pulse generator without delay.   In fact, there may not necessarily be synchronization.

Naturally, many circuits are capable of producing pulses.   Those mentioned are illustrative only and in all cases the simplest possible ones.

Pulse generators may be of any kind and are usually classified as either hard or gas-tube types. Each has its own intrinsic advantages, largely determined by the particular application for which it is used. Since, in general, the high-vacuum tube may be either pulsed or continuously running while gas tubes can be only pulsed, and since there are a very large number of receiving and transmitting tubes that make excellent pulse generators, the hard type is slightly preferable, especially since it is not so erratic in action as the gas one and usually requires much less service. However, circuitry for gas types is somewhat simpler.

Moreover, in certain cases the recovery time of the tube may affect the recovery of the sensitivity of the receiver, particularly immediately after the pulse. All other things being equal, the high-vacuum tube is superior in this respect. Pulses may be step or square waves, or trains of r-f waves. Both have been used successfully.

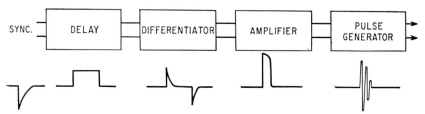

Fig. 9-10. Complete pulse generator.

GAS TUBES. Any gas tube such as the 884, 2050, 3C22, etc., can be used to provide pulsed oscillations. Also a number of thyratrons have been developed for radar work that can be used. Most of these latter types are of greater power-handling capabilities than needed in test work but may be useful in some signaling applications.

In all gas tubes the general operation is to maintain the grid negative and then trigger it with a positive pip. The tube will fire, as, for example, when used as a relaxation oscillator. If its plate current flows through a tuned circuit, this circuit will ring at a frequency determined by its own characteristics and for a period determined by its damping.

If necessary, artificial damping in the form of additional resistance can be introduced either in series or in parallel so that the damping can be varied, together with the pulse length (and unfortunately the amplitude also). The resulting pulse will be exponential, since each successive sine wave will be smaller in amplitude than its immediate predecessor, because of the losses already mentioned. An illustrative system is shown in Fig. 9-11.[1] The output pulses produced by this oscillator are represented in Fig. 9-12.

An additional capacitor may be connected into the plate circuit of the

[1] F. A. Firestone, U.S. Patent 2,398,701 (1946).

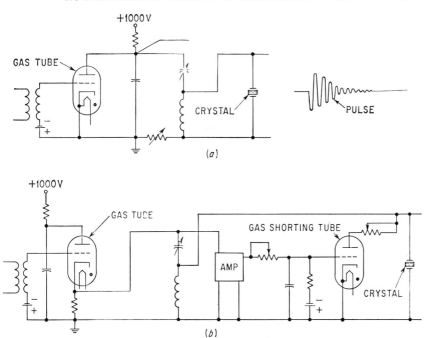

+1000V

GAS TUBE

CRYSTAL

PULSE

(a)

+1000V

GAS TUBE

GAS SHORTING TUBE

AMP

CRYSTAL

(b)

Fig. 9-11. Gas-tube pulse system: (a) without shorting tube; (b) with shorting tube.

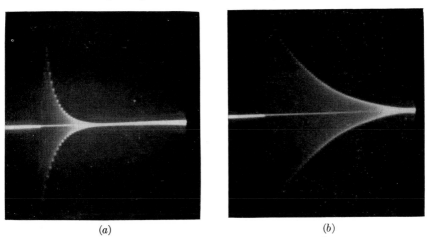

(a)   (b)

Fig. 9-12. Pulses: (a) damped; (b) undamped.

tube, where it will charge up and then discharge through the tube, further exciting the ringing circuit.

The Firestone patent discloses an additional variation. A complete train of damped waves is often undesirable. It may, for example, be better to have several large waves followed by essentially no oscillation.

The small waves at the end of an exponential pulse contribute little to the pulse power in any case and interfere with the received signals.

In order to cut off these small waves, a cutoff tube can be used and may be another gas tube, such as a second 884. This tube can be connected across the tuned circuit (Fig. 9-11). At a predetermined time after the pulse is fired, the tube is tripped and shorts out the tuned circuit, thus stopping the oscillations suddenly. Again, in this case, the recovery time of the tube is of great importance, since the resonant circuit in a pulsed reflection system is connected directly across the input receiver unless special circuits are used. If the cutoff tube has a long recovery time, the receiver will be unable to receive signals close to the pulse. Gas tubes can also be used to trigger hard ones. This method was fairly common in radar systems.

Gas pulse oscillators have been widely and successfully used. They are simple and economical but erratic in action. The tube itself often produces extraneous signals, and each tube may act differently even in a group bought at the same time from the same manufacturer.

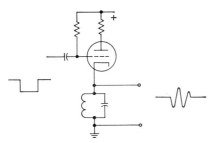

FIG. 9-13. Ringing oscillator.

As already indicated, the duration of the pulse in a gas-type pulse generator is essentially independent of the synchronizing signal and is controlled only by the decay time of the tuned resonant circuit. Variable resistors added to this circuit will make the duration adjustable. About 0 to 500 ohms is satisfactory when the resistor is in series with the coil and about 0 to 25,000 ohms when in parallel.

THE HIGH-VACUUM PULSE. High-vacuum tubes can also be used to produce pulses in any one of a number of ways. For example, they can be used to shock-excite a resonant circuit in the same manner as the gas tube just described. In such a case they may either start or interrupt a high current flowing through that circuit. The latter is the more common arrangement. Figure 9-13 is a typical hard-tube shock-excited oscillator.

The tube that acts as the switch may have the tuned circuit anywhere in the path of its plate current. If the grid is held positive by returning it to a suitable voltage, the tube will conduct very heavily, and the resulting current will flow through the tank inductance. A large negative pulse is then applied to the tube grid, cutting off the current and shocking the resonant circuit into oscillation. This operation has already been described in the section on pulse forming.

The number of cycles of oscillation will depend on the length of the triggering signal and on the damping in the circuit.   Since the tube acts as a switch, it does not influence the frequency of oscillation.

When the trigger ends, however, the tube rapidly returns to the state where it is conducting heavily and the oscillations abruptly stop, owing to the shunting effect of the tube.

Other types of circuits are also possible.   Possibly the simplest method is to have an oscillator of any of the familiar kinds, e.g., Hartley, with a high negative grid bias to keep it from oscillating.   The trigger pulse is then used to remove this bias and allow the tube to oscillate.   The triggering pulse may, of course, be either delayed or not, in the usual manner.

The oscillator should be so designed that it is self-starting, and oscillations should build up quickly.   Normally, the first half cycle is extremely large owing to transient effects, so the rapidity of starting is not a difficult problem.

When the trigger is removed, the pulse should cut off immediately. This does not always happen, and the oscillator may continue to ring for a few cycles.   This is not of any consequence, since damping may be introduced to stop it quickly. The oscillator usually builds up in about $\frac{1}{2}$ cps and stops entirely in $1\frac{1}{2}$ cps.

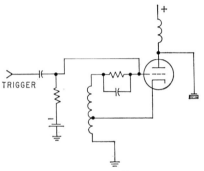

FIG. 9-14. Oscillator.

It is more troublesome when the oscillator stops before the end of the trigger signal, since the end of the gate itself may produce spurious signals on the indicator.

The schematic of a conventional Hartley-type oscillator is shown in Fig. 9-14.   If the cable to the crystal is directly across the tank circuit, without special coupling means, it must introduce very little capacitance into the circuit.   The tank should also be designed to resonate with the tuning capacitor as close to all the way out as possible; i.e., the coil and its distributed capacity should resonate at a frequency very close to that desired.   The minimum capacity controls the range over which it is possible to tune the circuit.

As far as sensitivity is concerned, connecting the cable directly across the resonant circuit is satisfactory.   If any direct voltage is present, it must be blocked out by a suitable capacitor.   Adjustment of either the grid leak or bias voltage will prevent any tendency the circuit has to multiple-fire.

The oscillator can be modulated on any electrode.   However, for one-tube systems, the results are satisfactory when the control grid is used, and the amount of power required to pulse the oscillator is usually less than with other methods. Moreover, it is easier to keep the impedance of the circuit into which the triggering pulse is fed high enough to prevent deformation of the control voltage.

Low-level oscillators can be easily pulsed and then followed by several stages of radio-frequency amplification. Such systems have the advantage of greater stability and more output but require more space and parts than the one-tube variety.

A Hartley oscillator, such as the one described, can be made self-pulsing by a change in its components. This is explained in the following manner: If the grid leak and capacitor have a sufficiently long time constant, the capacitor charges up on each cycle, but this charge cannot escape entirely between cycles. Finally the charge on this capacitor becomes so large that oscillations stop entirely. The oscillator then quits until enough charge drains off so that it can again operate. Thus, pulses of oscillation interposed with longer periods of no oscillation result.

The period of oscillation is the time during which the capacitor is charging and is therefore determined by capacitor size. When the capacity is small, the pulse is accordingly short, and vice versa.

The time between pulses is determined by the total time constant of the resistor and capacitor. When this is large, the time between pulses is also large, since the charge takes a long time to leak off.

Self-pulsing oscillators are somewhat more difficult to synchronize than other types. However, they can be synchronized, or the sweep can be synchronized from them. The self-blocking characteristic can also be used in conjunction with other types of operation to get sharper cutoff.

One of the chief advantages of a hard-tube generator is the fact that the successive waves are all of about the same height; i.e., they are not exponentially damped.

Ultrasonic Receivers for Pulsed Energy. Amplification of pulse-type high-frequency signals requires an amplifier of considerable bandwidth in order to have satisfactory resolution. The term *resolution* refers to the ability of a system to distinguish among signals following very closely upon one another. This property of an amplifier is directly dependent upon its bandwidth.

In other words, the more closely together the signals fall in time, the greater will be the bandwidth required to distinguish them. If they are, for example, 1 μsec apart, a bandwidth of 1 Mc is required; if they are $\frac{1}{4}$ μsec apart, a bandwidth of 4 μsec is necessary. This relation is therefore a fundamental one; i.e., the resolution is the reciprocal of the bandwidth.

Generally, a bandwidth of 1 Mc is sufficient for most ultrasonic testing systems, although for greater resolution, ones of as great as 4 Mc may be used.   However, it is not usually necessary to distinguish the cycles of high frequency in a signal.   All that is required is the resolution of the envelope, and signals closer together than 1 μsec are rare.

The amplifier may be of two basic kinds, i.e., superheterodyne or video. These two systems are indicated by the block diagram (Fig. 9-15).   The main difference is that in the superheterodyne receiver, the signal is changed to an intermediate frequency by mixing with a local oscillator voltage while in the video it is directly amplified at the frequency of ultrasonic test.

Both systems are satisfactory and have worked excellently in practice. Whatever slight advantage there may be is probably in favor of the superheterodyne type.   For one thing, as the frequency of operation becomes

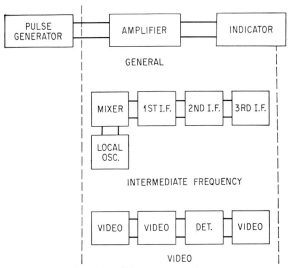

Fig. 9-15. Ultrasonic receivers.

greater than about 5 Mc, most video systems lose gain; and for another, it is difficult to keep video systems from oscillating.

The intermediate-frequency amplifier is well known in television work, where very similar requirements must be met.   An amplifier with a bandwidth of 2 Mc or more, center frequency of about 10 Mc, and gain of 10,000 is satisfactory.   Three or four intermediate stages will provide this.

Where the local oscillator must run very close to the frequency of the amplifier bandpass, such as in the case where the testing frequency is very low, a reject circuit must be provided to sharpen one side of the pass characteristic and make it fall off more quickly than it would otherwise. Rejects are also well known in television, where they are used to keep the audio signals out of the picture.   They may take the form of series traps, resonant circuits in the cathodes of the tubes, etc.   Balanced mixers are sometimes used to suppress the oscillator frequency.

The local oscillator is of the conventional type.   It is generally advisable to use a separate mixer and oscillator rather than a single tube.   The oscillator may operate either above or below the intermediate frequency.   Operating at the lower frequency has some advantages in gain.

One of the greatest difficulties in pulse transmission and reception is the effect the pulses have upon the input of the receiver when they are impressed directly across it.   However, if only one crystal is to be used, there is no other simple way of connecting the circuit.   These effects are likely either to block the amplifier totally for a time that is appreciable in comparison with the time of transmission and reflection or to produce extraneous signals, such as long tails on the pulse, which have the effect of blotting out the received signals.   Because of this blocking, it is very difficult to receive signals close to the surface from which the pulse is being transmitted.   As the distance between transmitter and reflector gets shorter and shorter, the problem becomes more and more difficult.   The most obvious expedient is to place a very low time constant in the input stages so that signals will not block them for any appreciable time.   Keeping all capacitors and resistors as small as possible will accomplish this.   Unfortunately, it also has the effect of sharply lowering the gain.

Keeping the voltage supply to the tubes regulated will also facilitate recovery.   Moreover, certain specialized procedures and circuits may be resorted to in order to stop the blocking of the amplifier.

Possibly the simplest method of avoiding the problem is the use of separate transducers for sending and receiving.   This will provide a great deal of improvement, since only stray electrical coupling will remain to bring the initial pulse into the receiver.   However, it makes necessary the use of separate cables and crystals.   The desire to avoid this complication has resulted in the use of concentric or side-by-side crystals, which can be set in a single mount and connected by two separate cables to the receiver.   However, the capacity between such cables may lead to additional undesirable coupling.   The much greater simplicity, economy, and ease of single-crystal work has led to its widespread adoption and the minimizing of blocking by various types of special circuits.

Methods of Gating the Receiver.   Gating refers to turning a system on or off according to an arbitrary signal.   Signals may be used to render an amplifier insensitive, so that troublesome indications will not pass.   This system has certain drawbacks; i.e., the gating signal must be of the same size as the signal it is to stop, and it may therefore cause transient effects of its own.   Its duration must be closely controlled, since it will otherwise block out signals that are wanted.   Any method for producing these gates can be used, and they may be of either polarity.

For purposes of illustration, some connections for gating procedures are briefly illustrated (Fig. 9-16). In the first instance a tube is inserted between the pulse generator and receiver, and its impedance varied so that it is very high during the transmission of the pulse and very low at all other times. This has the desired effect of discriminating against the pulse and in favor of the reflections.

In the second case the tube acts as a grid resistor, which can be varied to place various amounts of negative bias on the amplifier tube and thus cause it to allow signals to pass or not.

A number of gas-tube applications have been suggested. Inasmuch as the same problem is intrinsic to radar, the TR and anti-TR boxes were developed for the same purpose. In those cases, cavities filled with gas were used. The gas broke down during pulse transmission (because of the high associated radio-frequency voltages) and short-circuited the receiver input. The radio-frequency pulses associated with ultrasonic transmission are not sufficiently great and of high enough frequency for

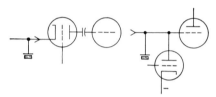

Fig. 9-16. Gating circuits.

use with those TR devices which are available. Use of conventional gas tubes such as the 884 has been suggested, but the time of ionization and deionization is always high, and hash is introduced by erratic behavior of the gas.

The gating signal must usually be higher than the radio-frequency pulse itself, and this is difficult where about 1,000-volt, 1- or 2-μsec pulses are used. For this and other reasons, gates with simple ultrasonic signals have not been very successful to date.

Other Means of Presentation. As indicated, the first ultrasonic pulse systems used the A scan as the indicator. A typical scan was shown in Fig. 9-1. It is obvious that the operator had to learn to interpret the condition of the material in terms of a series of pulses. While, in general, this is a practical thing to do, other presentations have also been studied.[1]

It has been felt that the amount of information present in the ultrasonic signal is not completely used by means of the A scan and that it would be possible to more completely evaluate the condition of the material if other types of scans were used, in particular, that the B scan and C scan be

[1] R. W. Buchanan and C. H. Hastings, "Ultrasonic Flaw Plotting Equipment," Watertown Arsenal.

used. The C scan refers to a view looking directly into the material similar to that given when an X ray is taken of a part. The B scan is a cross section of the same part, that is, a view which would be obtained by looking down into the material at right angles into the C scan. It is understood that the B scan gives the view at any one cross section as though the material had been cut and the operator were looking down from

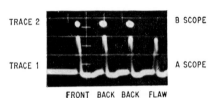

FRONT BACK BACK FLAW

FIG. 9-17. Comparison of A- and B-scope presentation of data from a single search position.

above. Figure 9-17 shows the comparison between a B scan and A scan. The A scan merely indicates the location of some sort of flaw. In most cases, it is also necessary to remove multiple reflections by some sort of gating system to get a B scan which looks like a picture of the material. Figure 9-18a shows a complete B-scan picture.

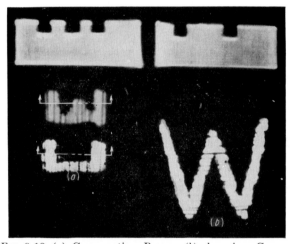

FIG. 9-18. (a) Cross section, B scan; (b) plan view, C scan.

The C scan is a picture of the flaw itself; both the front and back indications are removed. When enough points on the flaw are picked up, a picture of the total flaw can be seen. A typical C scan is shown in Fig. 9-18b.

These scans are most satisfactory when used with a water coupling and a scanning head which may be moved back and forth. When used in that manner a picture appears which is usable.

Other presentations may be derived from the same information.   In medical work, for example, other angles of view may be preferable,[1] although the C scan has been successfully used to show tumors, etc.

Pulse-technique Applications.   In addition to material testing, the pulse technique has been applied to a number of fields.

Attenuation Measurements.   It has been obvious from the first experiments with pulsed ultrasound that the amount of attenuation is a function of the internal characteristics of the material in which the waves are traveling.   It is likely that some change in velocity may also be a function of the same sort of thing or of the attenuation itself.   Attempts were made to correlate this information, but it was found that it was much

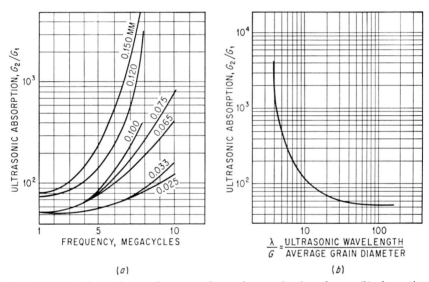

FIG. 9-19. (*a*) Absorption vs. frequency for various grain sizes, brass; (*b*) absorption for brass.

more difficult to test materials using attenuation as the factor involved than to test them using the time of travel of pulses, and the method has therefore been a secondary one up to the present time.   However, recently, a number of studies have been made to get more information on attenuation as correlated to the characteristics of materials.[2]

The losses seem to be a function both of scattering and of absorption and are measured by allowing the pulse to travel back and forth between

[1] D. H. Howry et al., Use of Ultrasonic Pulse Echo Techniques for the Visualization of Soft Tissue Structures and Disease Processes, *Sci. Proc. 3d Ann. Conf. Ultrasonic Therapy* (1954).

[2] R. Truell, Ultrasonic Attenuation Measurements, *ASME paper* 55-2-17 (1955).
    A. Hikata, R. Truell, A. Granato, B. Chick, and K. Lucke, *J. Appl. Phys.*, **27** (1956) 3967.

two parallel faces of a sample.   The decay of the pulse is measured as a function of the number of reflections.   The pulse has completely died out before another pulse is introduced, repeating over and over the same test.   The crystal may be either in direct contact with the specimen or coupled through liquid in the usual manner used in ultrasonic material testing.

Even in equipment which is very carefully designed, however, it is difficult to circumvent the problems which were originally apparent with ordinary pulse equipment.   These problems include conversion of wave types, lack of parallelism, use of waves which are not plane, losses caused by coupling or pressure, etc.   An interesting analysis of the various types of ultrasonic energy losses in solids is shown in Fig. 9-19.   On the purely electronic side is the difficulty of measuring the attenuation per pulse accurately and correlating this information with the internal characteristics of the material.

Equipment has been constructed to measure grain size by pulse attenuation.[1]   The part is immersed in a water bath, and a pulse sent through it.   Curves relating absorption to frequency were worked out (Fig. 9-19) and from this a formula for grain size:

$$g = \frac{4.2}{fN} \quad \text{mm}$$

where g = grain size, mm (for $1\frac{1}{2}$-in. brass cylinder)
$\quad f$ = frequency, Mc
$\quad N$ = $\lambda : g$ ratio
Figure 9-19b shows a single curve derived from Fig. 9-19a.

[1] D. L. Worlton, *J. Soc. Non-Destructive Testing*, **11** (1955) 24.

CHAPTER 10

EFFECTS

General. The study of ultrasonics may be broadly separated into two phases:

1. The study of the equipment for generation, reception, measurement, etc.

2. The study of the physical, chemical, biological, etc., effects of ultrasound.

While the primary approach here is to the first aspect of the science, some consideration will also be given to the second one.

The results of investigations into the effects of ultrasonics will be given briefly together with the apparatus suggested for undertaking such investigations, wherever available. Among the effects to be discussed are the physical, biological, chemical, medical, metallurgical, gaseous, and photographic. Wherever possible, references to review articles are included.

This section may be read in conjunction with Chap. 11, to which it is related. However, if an attempt were made to even partially cover all the investigations, a good-sized library would result. It has therefore been the function of this discussion to briefly indicate major reports, in such a way that reference to them would give additional bibliography. Whenever possible, emphasis has been on effects which may have practical or commercial use.

Physical Effects. Some physical effects have been briefly mentioned. Among the most outstanding are (1) cavitation, (2) local heating, (3) local pressure, (4) quartz wind, and (5) production of fog.

Cavitation. Cavitation has already been discussed in Chap. 1 but merits further attention. At present, *cavitation* is a generic term applied to a number of ultrasonic effects characterized by the formation and collapse of bubbles in a liquid. These bubbles may be empty or filled with gas or vapor. These cavities are not necessarily only produced by ultrasonic waves, but may accompany high-intensity ultrasonic effects. The results of cavitation can be spectacular, and many ultrasonic effects are ascribed to the accompanying cavitation. Such effects are the erosion of propellers, cleaning of metal parts, chemical effects, etc.

Cavitation seems to be basically of two types, bubbles filled with the gas which was in the liquid, and (much smaller) bubbles filled with liquid vapor.   The former appear at lower power levels and do not have the effects which the latter do.   These bubbles are accompanied by a hissing sound.

Most investigators attribute many of the effects of ultrasonics to cavitation, i.e. the mixture of immiscible liquids, depolymerization, the destruction of bacteria, etc.

Among the factors which govern the onset of cavitation are the presence of dust particles, small gas bubbles,[1] the gas content,[2] the intermolecular bond,[3] dissolved air, frequency, system pressure, etc.

Cavitation may be formed by ultrasonic or other methods, and results in the formation of gas-filled, vapor-filled, or empty bubbles or cavities. Experimentally it usually forms at the point of greatest intensity, i.e., on the transducer face for a plane transducer, or at the focus for a focusing unit.   In standing-wave systems the bubbles are trapped in the nodes.

Cavitation is formed by a more or less regular process.   The mechanism appears to be as follows:[4]

1. Nucleii must be present.

2. Bubbles start and gradually become larger (initiation).

3. Bubbles become resonant and radiate shock waves and produce microcavities (catastrophic phase).

4. Noncollapsing gas bubbles are produced (bubble phase).

The number of articles on cavitation and the opinions offered are numerous.   Table 10-1[5] shows a list of various experimenters in the field and the frequencies at which reactions occurred.

Thermal.   Experiments carried out in various materials at 4 Mc indicate that sound energy transforms into heat with a definite ratio (Joule's equivalent).[6]

Many early experimenters noticed the thermal effects in test tubes filled with water, stirring rods held in an ultrasonic field, etc.[7]   Particularly strong effects are noted at interfaces, either of solids within a bath or of bubbles.   Heating becomes greater with increase of frequency (above about 300 kc) because of increased absorption.   The thermal effects may be the cause of results listed under other headings, i.e., medical, chemical, etc.

Fog Production.   When intense waves hit an interface between a liquid and air, a jet of liquid is thrown up, and a fine mist or fog is produced. The intensity of the fog is a function of the surface tension and the power,

---

[1] H. B. Briggs, J. B. Johnson, and W. P. Mason, *JASA*, **19** (1947) 664.

[2] A. Weissler, *J. Appl. Phys.*, **21** (1950) 171.

[3] J. P. Horton, *JASA*, **25** (1953) 480.

[4] G. W. Willard, *JASA*, **28** (1953) 670.

[5] W. Gaertner, *JASA*, **26** (1954) 977.

[6] S. Parthasarathy, S. S. Chari, and D. Srenwasan, *JASA*, **25** (1953) 335.

[7] R. W. Wood and A. L. Loomis, *Phil. Mag.*, **4** (1927) 417.

TABLE 10-1. REPORTS ON CAVITATION WITH REFERENCE TO
FREQUENCY DEPENDENCE*

Frequency of sound field, kc	Phenomenon	Reference
0.4	Weak degassing and emulsification	H. Freundlich: *Trans. Faraday Soc.*, **35** (1939) 319.
\-100	Dispersion of metals, after Claus	B. Claus: German Patent 663,927 (1934).
2, 7	Effects in colloid chemistry	H. A. Wannow: *Kolloid Z.*, **81** (1937) 105.
3	Cavitation	R. Esche: *Akust. Beih.*, **2** (1952) 208.
4, 8	Depolymerization	G. Schmid: *Physik. Z.*, **41** (1940) 326.
7, 5	Weak effect on virus	G. A. Kausche: *Naturwiss.*, **29** (1941) 573.
8	Dispersion	L. Chambers: U.S. Patent 1,992,938 (1935). W. H. Ashton: British Patent 433,583 (1934).
8, 9	Luminescence of cavitating liquids	L. Chambers: *J. Chem. Phys.*, **5** (1937) 290.
9	Depolymerization	G. Schmid: *Physik*, **2**, no. 41 (1940) 326.
9	Cavitation	H. G. Moeller and A. Schoch: *Akust. Beih.*, **2**, no. 6 (1941) 165.
9	Effect on molten metals	G. Schmid: *Z. Elektrochem.*, **43** (1937) 869.
15	Cavitation	R. Esche: *Akust. Beih.*, **2** (1952) 208.
20–100	Depolymerization	H. Mark: *J. Acoust. Soc. Am.*, **16** (1945) 183.
25	Cavitation	Briggs, Johnson, and Mason: *J. Acoust. Soc. Am.*, **19** (1947) 644.
100	Peptization	H. W. Dangers: *Z. Physik*, **97** (1935) 34.
100–500	Chemical effects	W. T. Richards and A. L. Loomis: *J. Acoust. Soc. Am.*, **49** (1927) 3086.
100–500	Photoemulsions	B. Claus: *Z. tech. Physik*, **15** (1934) 74.
160–250	Dispersion of graphite, steatite, and sulfur	S. S. Tumanski: *Colloid J. (USSR)*, **5** (1939) 517.
150	Very good emulsion of petroleum and water	S. S. Daniewski: *Acta. Phys. Polon.*, **2** (1933) 45.
175	Cavitation	R. Esche: *Akust. Beih.*, **2** (1952) 208.
194	Degassing	C. Sorensen: *Ann. Phys.*, **26** (1936) 121.
200–500	Emulsion	P. Freeman: British Patent 332,533 (1929).

TABLE 10-1. REPORTS ON CAVITATION WITH REFERENCE TO
FREQUENCY DEPENDENCE* (*Continued*)

Frequency of sound field, kc	Phenomenon	Reference
200–840	Mixture of liquids	O. E. Whiteley: U.S. Patent 2,407,462 (1946).
200–2,000	Halogen-silver-gelatin emulsions	B. Claus: Z. tech. Physik, **16** (1935) 109.
214	Good degassing, cavitation, and emulsion	H. Freundlich, Trans. Faraday Soc., **34** (1938) 649.
250	Liquification of thixotropic systems	Freundlich, Rogowski, and Sollner: Kolloid-Beih., **37** (1933) 223.
284	Depolymerization	G. Schmid: Physik. Z., **41** (1940) 326. G. Schmid: Z. physik. Chem., **A186** (1940) 113.
289	Chemical effects	W. T. Richards and A. L. Loomis: J. Acoust. Soc. Am., **49** (1927) 3086.
300	Cavitation	T. Lange: Akust. Beih., **2** (1952) 74.
300	Depolymerization	H. Mark: J. Acoust. Soc. Am., **16** (1945) 183.
300	Physical and biological effects	A. Wood and L. Loomis: Phil. Mag. **4**, no. 17 (1927) 417.
300	Depolymerization	E. Thieme: Physik. Z., **39** (1938) 384.
300–600	Dispersion of metals, after Claus	B. Claus and E. Schmidt: Kolloid-Beih., **45** (1937) 41.
330	Strong effect on virus	G. A. Kausche: Naturwiss., **29** (1941) 573.
350	Depolymerization	A. G. Krupp: British Patent 502,891 (1936).
350	Destruction of fibrils	R. Pohlmann and C. Wolpers: Kolloid-Z., **109** (1944) 106.
365	Cavitation	R. Esche: Akust. Beih., **2** (1952) 208.
380	Strong precipitation of hardening agents	H. Beuthe: Z. Akust., **4** (1939) 209.
380	Strong degassing	C. Sorensen: Ann. Phys., **26** (1936) 121.
380	Chemical effects	H. Beuthe: Z. physik. Chem., **A163** (1933) 161.
395	Emulsion	S. S. Daniewski: Acta. Phys. Polon., **2**, 45 (1933).
400	Depolymerization	A. Weissler: J. Appl. Phys., **21** (1950) 171.
450	Dispersion of mercury	N. Sata: Kolloid-Z., **71** (1937) 48.
450–600	Effect on solidifying Zn	F. Seidl: Osterr. Chem. Z., **45**, 103 (1942)
500	Luminescence through cavitation	H. Frenel and H. Schultes: Z. physik. Chem., **B27,** 421.

TABLE 10-1. REPORTS ON CAVITATION WITH REFERENCE TO
FREQUENCY DEPENDENCE* (Continued)

Frequency of sound field, kc	Phenomenon	Reference
500	Cavitation	R. Esche: Akust. Beih., 2 (1952) 208.
530	Strong degassing	C. Sorensen: Ann. Phys., 26 (1936) 121.
575	Cavitation	Ibid.
600	Dispersion	A. Mathieu-Sicaus and G. Levavasseur: Compt. rend., 227 (1948) 196.
600–700	Emulsion, dispersion	C. E. Weaver: U.S. Patent 2,163,649 (1935).
722	Depolymerization	A. Szalay: Physik. Z., 35 (1934) 293.
723	Depolymerization	A. Szent-Gyorgyi: Nature, 131 (1933) 278.
800	Cavitation	T. Lange: Akust. Beih., 2 (1952) 74.
940	Dispersion	A. Mathieu-Sicaud and G. Levavasseur: Compt. rend., 227 (1948) 196.
950	Degassing of water only	C. Sorensen, Ann. Phys., 26 (1936) 121.
970	Preparation by ultrasonics	G. Millot and G. Noisetts: Compt. rend., 227 (1948) 974.
1,160	Weak emulsion of petroleum and water	S. S. Daniewski: Acta. Phys. Polon., 2 (1933) 45.
2,500	1.8 kw/cm², cavitation	B. Claus: German Patent 663,927 (1934).
3,000	No emulsion of petroleum and water	S. S. Daniewski: Acta. Phys. Polon., 2 (1933) 45.
4,250	575 watts/cm², no cavitation	F. E. Fox: J. Acoust. Soc. Am., 21 (1949) 352.
5,000	No cavitation in spite of great intensity	J. F. Muller and G. W. Willard: J. Acoust. Soc. Am., 20 (1948) 589.
9,000	No emulsion of petroleum and water	S. S. Daniewski: Acta. Phys. Polon., 2 (1933) 45.
15,000	No cavitation in spite of great intensity	J. F. Muller and G. W. Willard: J. Acoust. Soc. Am., 20 (1948) 589.

* From Gaertner.

focusing, etc. Mists have been produced with water (at about 3 watts/cm²), with molten metals, and with other liquids. The size of the particles seems to be a function of frequency. Distribution of size at given frequencies has been measured,[1] using a microscope and camera. The formation of fog has been shown to be unrelated to thermal effects; instead it seems to be a function of cavitation.[2] Thus, a degassed liquid

[1] T. K. McCubbin, Jr., JASA, 25 (1953) 1013.
[2] K. Sollner, Trans. Faraday Soc., 32 (1936) 532.

sealed in a test tube does not produce fog. The fogs produced are in general very unstable.

Volatile liquids produce fogs more easily than others and are merely placed in an ultrasonic field. Oils, however, must be placed in a special container, which is in the form of a test tube with its walls drawn together in the center (Fig. 10-1). This thin section vibrates very vigorously and produces a fog from the oil wiped on its surface. The remainder on the tube forms into spots from which the mist comes.

Degassing. The term *degassing* is applied to the expulsion of gases from a liquid or solid. This action is particularly valuable in metals, where inclusions of gas can cause imperfections. Ultrasonic waves can bring about a degassing action.[1] However, the application is influenced by frequency and operates better at lower frequencies (about 200 kc).

The degassing appears to be caused by the collection of the gas at the nodes of the waves and by cavitation. The effect has been applied on a laboratory scale to degassing molten metal (aluminum) and glass.

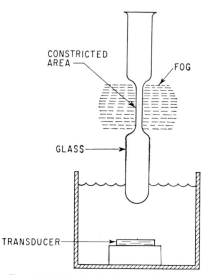

FIG. 10-1. Device for fog production.

Biological Effects. One of the original phenomena noted by Langevin during his experiments was the lethal results that ultrasonic waves had on small marine life that wandered into the path of his submarine beam. These fish were rapidly killed by the energy, and this action has suggested the use of ultrasonics for so-called "death rays" although these applications have never actually been extensively explored.

The biological effects of ultrasound, as discussed here, are separated from medical ones. Experiments carried out so far have used widely differing apparatus and have been qualitative in nature. However, it appears likely that the results are due to one or all of the following characteristics of ultrasound:

1. High pressures and accelerations which cause motions within cells
2. Locally generated heat
3. Cavitation

[1] R. W. Boyle and G. B. Taylor, *Trans. Roy. Soc. Can.*, **20** (1926) 245.

Experimentation has been mainly carried out in test tubes (in vitro). However some live experimentation has also been done. The effects of ultrasound in air on humans have been observed but not widely experimented with. In an intense field fatigue, nausea, dizziness, and local heating may occur.

Nevertheless, there has been much experiment on the biological effects of ultrasonics, particularly on the effects produced by very strong ultrasonic fields on small life, such as various frogs, animals, and fish (see Table 10-2). Certain of these small animals may be either killed or

TABLE 10-2. GENERAL ARTICLES ON BIOLOGICAL EFFECTS

Subject	Reference
Cell changes	F. O. Schmitt and B. Uhlmeyer: *Proc. Soc. Exptl. Biol. Med.*, **27** (1930) 626.
Carcinoma cells	C. Dittmar: *Strahlentherapie*, **78** (1948) 217.
Yeast cells disintegration	D. Hamre: *J. Bacteriol.*, **57** (1949) 39.
Killing bacteria	M. Ronyer and P. Grabar: *Am. Inst. Pasteur*, **71** (1945) 378.
Genetic changes	R. H. Wallace: *Am. J. Botany*, **36** (1949) 230.
Tuberculosis	G. Veltman and K. H. Woeber: *Proc. Erlangen Congr.*, **15** (1949) 230.
Blood PH	K. Stuhlfauth: *Proc. Erlangen Congr.*, **15** (1949) 189.
Nerve effects	P. D. Wall, P. Tucker, F. Fry, and W. H. Mosberg: *JASA*, **25** (1953) 281. W. J. Fry: *JASA*, **25** (1953) 1.
Heart effects	W. D. Keidel: *Arch. ges. Physiol. Pflüger's*, **252** (1950) 381.
Germs	F. Kress: *Proc. Erlangen Congr.*, **15** (1949) 225.
Abnormal embryonic development	G. G. Selman and S. J. Counce: *Nature*, **172** (1953) 503.
Destruction of enzymes	L. A. Chambers: *J. Biol. Chem.*, **117** (1937) 639.
Tissue	W. J. Fry and R. B. Fry: *JASA*, **25** (1953) 1.

damaged by the rays, and similar effects occur when experimenting with different types of nerve cells, protozoa, and blood corpuscles. The particles of matter are actually torn to pieces. Rapid and radical changes in body or skin temperatures are also produced. These effects seem to be caused by the formation of bubbles of gas within the body and by cavitation.

The heart action of animals may be changed by ultrasonics.[1] Artificial

[1] F. Forster and A. Holste, *Naturwiss.*, **25** (1937) 11.

fever may be produced by the waves, and they have also been suggested for diathermy and knifeless surgery.

A list of other common biological phenomena follows: changes in seed-germination time, destruction of reproductive ability of cells, disintegration of bacteria to release enzymes, etc., separation of antibodies, changes made in the character of milk, changes in albumin, etc.

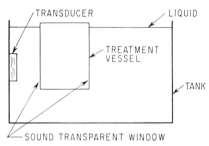

FIG. 10-2. Typical biological apparatus.

Figure 10-2 shows a typical biological apparatus as recommended for such experiments. The material to be irradiated is in a cylindrical container larger than the beam diameter and closed at both ends by ultrasonically transparent diaphragms. Temperature and gas content must be carefully controlled.

Chemical Effects. It is well known that ultrasonics effect chemical changes which cannot be accomplished in any other manner. These

TABLE 10-3. ARTICLES ON CHEMICAL EFFECTS

Effects	Experimenters
Review	A. Weissler: *JASA*, **25** (1953) 651.
Review (bibliography)	D. Thompson: *Virginia Polytech. Inst. Eng. Exp.*, no. 75.
Iodine reaction speeded	R. W. Wood and A. L. Loomis: *Phil. Mag.*, **4** (1927) 417.
Heterogeneous reactions	N. Moriguchi: *Intern. Congr. Acoustics Unesco*, **28** (1934) 398.
Oxidation (many experimenters)	J. Leiseleur: *Compt. rend.*, **218** (1944) 878.
Luminescence	S. E. Bresler: *Acta Physicochim. URSS*, **12** (1940) 323.
Decomposition	L. Lliboutry: *J. Chem. Phys.*, **41** (1944) 183.
Inversion	S. Sokolov: *Tech. Phys. U.S.S.R.*, **3** (1936) 176.
Crystallization	R. Berlaga: *J. Exptl. Theoret. Phys. U.S.S.R.*, **16** (1946) 647.
Molecular properties	A. Weissler: *J. Chem. Educ.*, **25** (1948) 28.

changes are generally attributed to cavitation, although exactly which aspect of cavitation is not agreed upon. Among the opinions advanced are (1) temperature rise,[1] (2) pressure change,[2] (3) electrical phenomena,[3]

[1] V. Griffing, *J. Chem. Phys.*, **18** (1950) 997; A. Weissler, *J. Chem. Phys.*, **18** (1950) 1513.

[2] M. Kornfeld and L. Sumov, *J. Appl. Phys.*, **15** (1944) 495.

[3] R. Kling, *Rev. sci.*, **85** (1947) 364.

(4) separation of water into ions, and (5) internal resonances, etc. In addition, a number of experimental conditions may be varied and will affect the results. Among these are frequency, intensity, time duration, temperature, pressure, etc. Each of these has been investigated at some length (see Table 10-3).

Frequency. Most experimenters agree that frequency has no appreciable effect on chemical effects, except possibly in so far as cavitation is one of its functions.

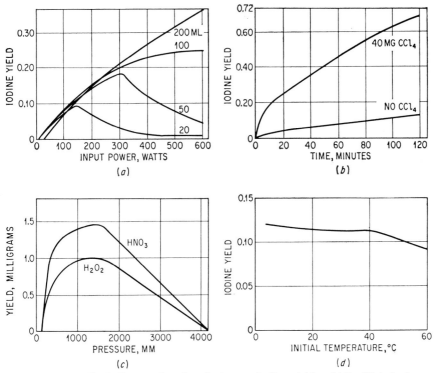

FIG. 10-3. The influence of various factors on iodine yield. (*After Weissler.*)

Intensity. Chemical effects do not occur at very low intensities. As the intensity is raised the chemical effects appear at the threshold of cavitation and increase approximately linearly with increase in intensity. Some experimenters mention an optimum intensity above which the effects decrease. This may be due to a buildup of cavitation bubbles or the removal of air. An example of this phenomenon is shown in Fig. 10-3a, which indicates the point of ideal intensity for a number of different volumes for iodine yield. Iodine yield from KI solution is used as an example of ultrasonic effects. The reference[1] is recommended as a general survey article.

[1] A. Weissler, *JASA*, **25** (1953) 651.

Duration of Time. Yield appears to increase with duration of exposure, although there is still some question if a late drop takes place. Figure 10-3b shows the yield of iodine as a function of time.

Pressure. Since cavitation is a function of pressure, it would be expected to have a great effect on chemical effects and does. Some pressure may aid the effects, but above about 1,500 mm the pressure is too great to allow bubble formation (see Fig. 10-3c).

Temperature. The effect of temperature on iodine yield is shown in Fig. 10-3d. It is difficult to control temperature during ultrasonic irradiation and the results are still undecided.

Specific reactions will not be discussed at length here. The investigator is referred to the literature for that. However, a brief mention of some of the applications may be apropos.

Increases in quickness of reaction, separation of certain chemicals, oxidation, decomposition, crystallization, changes in boiling points, etc., are some of the common effects. Oxidation effects take place more quickly when treated ultrasonically. Especially affected are chemical bonds,[1] such as colloidal systems, and intermolecular bonds, such as the van der Waals type. High polymers can be broken up by ultrasonics, starch can be changed, etc. Molecule chains may be disintegrated. As already indicated small particles will gather together in groups when so treated.

Photographic emulsions rise in sensitivity and resolution when exposed ultrasonically. Color sensitivity becomes greater, and grain size smaller.

Other experimentation[2] showed that ultrasonics will vaporize certain volatile liquids and melt wax.

Electrochemical Effects. Ultrasonic applications to electrochemical effects may be divided into:[3]

1. Effects on electrode processes
2. Electrokinetic phenomena
3. Studying electrolytic solutions

If an electrode is irradiated ultrasonically while liberating gas by electrolysis, an alternating potential is produced on it. Moreover, the potential at which metals are deposited is changed, and the structure of the deposited metal modified. Many studies have been made and will be found in the literature. Corrosion is also affected.

At the boundary between a solid and electrolytic solution, a thin layer of ions appears and, when this is disturbed, certain phenomena appear, referred to as electrokinetic phenomena. This phenomenon has been used as the basis for transducers in which a wire covered with a porous material

[1] H. Mark, *JASA*, **16** (1945) 183.
[2] R. W. Boyle et al., *Trans. Roy. Soc. Can.*, **111** (1929) 187.
[3] E. Yeager and F. Hovorka, *JASA*, **25** (1953) 443.

is exposed to ultrasonics in a dilute electrolytic solution.[1] One such unit is shown in Chap. 6. The amount of electricity produced is a function of the power in the ultrasonic field.

Electrolytic effects have been studied by studying electrical conductivity, velocity, absorption, and other phenomena. Because of these effects it would be supposed that ultrasonics would change the efficiency of deposition, grain of the depositing metal, composition, etc., in plating.[2] This has turned out to be the case. Among metals which have been treated successfully are nickel, chromium, copper, silver, and zinc. Work has been done at both high and low current densities. The arrangement for electrolyte dispersion (after Claus) is shown in Fig. 10-4.

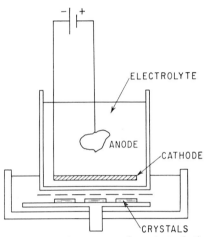

FIG. 10-4. Apparatus for electrolytic dispersion.

Emulsion and Dispersion. Dispersion and coagulation are effects in liquids closely related to chemical effects. Both dispersive and coagulative effects occur under ultrasonic irradiation, and oscillations of frequencies between 20,000 and 100,000 cps have been used, with oscillators that could produce from 10 to 20 watts/cm² of ultrasonic energy (maximum).

One of the more common effects is emulsification, i.e., the mixing of several ordinarily immiscible liquids such as water and benzoil. Several experimenters have investigated such action, and it has been shown[3] that the mixing is strongest at the boundaries of the system. i.e., between the liquid and the walls of the container and also between the liquid and the vibrating system. The greatest effect seems to be due to small particles of one liquid such as water being forcibly propelled into a second one by the vibration. It appears likely that the presence of gases, pressure, etc., also influences the action.

Strangely enough, although strong dispersive actions seem to occur as above, equally strong coagulative effects come about under some conditions. This type of action is more noticeable in the case of aerosols, i.e., systems consisting of small particles of some foreign substance dispersed in a gas. The commonest form taken by such a medium is a smoke or mist. The attractive action depends on various details of the system such as

[1] H. Dietrick, E. Yeager, J. Bugosh, and F. Hovorka, *JASA*, **25** (1953) 461.

[2] E. Kelsen, Austrian Patent 121,986 (1931).

[3] W. T. Richards, *J. Am. Chem. Soc.* **51** (1929) 1724.

frequency.[1] In other words, there are always optimum frequency conditions for each size of particle in a certain suspension.

The formation of emulsions has been described in the following manner.[2] The amount of pressure must be correct, as the action does not occur when it is either too great or too little. When the ultrasonic wave travels through liquids, it forms compressions and rarefactions that actually disrupt the media. Incidentally, when a liquid is undergoing ultrasonic irradiation, a strong hissing noise should be heard. Many small bubbles are being produced within the liquid and collapsing, producing tremendous pressures. This action was originally pointed out by Lord

TABLE 10-4. ARTICLES ON EMULSIFICATION AND DISPERSION

Material	Reference
Mercury-water	W. T. Richards: *J. Am. Chem. Soc.*, **51** (1929) 1724.
Mercury-water	K. Sollner and C. Bondy: *Trans. Faraday Soc.*, **31** (1935) 843.
Oil-water	K. Sollner: *Colloid Chem.*, **5** (1944) 337.
Solid in liquid	B. Claus: *Z. tech. Physik.*, **16** (1935) 80.
Milk	L. A. Chambers: *J. Dairy Sci.*, **19** (1926) 29.
Gels	H. Freundlich, F. Rogowski, and K. Sollner: *Kolloid-Beih.*, **37** (1933) 223.
Gelatin and starch	A. Syalay: *Physik. Z.*, **35** (1934) 293.
Gums	H. Freundlich and D. W. Gillays: *Trans. Faraday Soc.*, **34** (1938) 649.
Fogs	S. S. Urasowski and J. G. Polotzki: *Colloid J. USSR*, **6** (1940) 779.
Colloids	K. Sollner: *Trans. Faraday Soc.*, **34** (1938) 1170.
Photographic emulsions	B. Claus: *Z. tech. Physik*, **15** (1934) 74.

Rayleigh. It is this production and collapse (cavitation) which causes the emulsification (with the possible exception of metal-liquid mixtures).

Any strong ultrasonic action is accompanied by stirring of the entire material, due to irregularities in the way the material is being agitated.

The presence or absence of gases seems to have a strong influence on what happens. When gas is entirely absent, many actions do not occur, whatever changes appear are unstable, and the chemicals shortly revert to their original state.

Commercial application of this type of operation has to date been slight although it appears promising for the future. One of the main things delaying application has been the design of suitable transducers, since the ones used to date are low in power output and cannot be used for processing large volumes, although reports have been appearing to the

[1] O. Brandt, H. Freud, and E. Hiedemann, *Kolloid Z.*, **77** (1936) 103.
[2] E. N. Harvey, *Biol. Bull.*, **59** (1930) 306.

effect that such use has been growing and experimental transducers of novel design are being built.   Table 10-4 shows some of the applications which have been carried out in this field.

Medical Effects.[1]   As indicated elsewhere, medial effects (see Table 10-5) may be divided into therapy and diagnosis.   Biologic effects are considered separately.   The first effect noticed was heating.   Since most

TABLE 10-5. ARTICLES ON MEDICAL EFFECTS

Effect	Reference
Heating	H. Freundlich, K. Sollner, and F. Rogowski: *Klin. Wochschr.*, **11** (1932) 1512.
Cancer	J. D. Schroder, J. F. Herrick, and A. G. Karlson, *Arch. Phys. Med.*, **33** (1952) 660.
Bone effects	P. A. Nelson, J. F. Herrick, and F. H. Krusen: *Arch. Phys. Med.*, **31** (1950) 6.
Nerve effects	H. Rosenberger: *Chirurg*, **21** (1950) 404.
Brain diagnosis	T. F. Hueter and R. H. Bolt: *JASA*, **23** (1951) 160.
Cancer location	J. J. Wild and J. M. Reid, *JASA*, **25** (1953) 270.
Gallstones	G. D. Ludwig and F. W. Struthers: *Naval Med. Research Inst. Rept.* 4 (1949) NM004001.

early measurements were qualitative, there have been periods of enthusiasm and discouragement about ultrasonic use.   At present the following opinions appear most general:

Therapy

1. Ultrasound does not selectively destroy malignant tissue.
2. Heating in bone is more rapid than by any other means.
3. Heating in nerves is done selectively.

Diagnosis

1. It appears possible to locate changes in tissue, in the brain, in cancer tissue, etc.
2. Gallstones can be located.
3. Blood flow may be measured.

Surgery

1. It is possible to selectively destroy certain tissue.

Therapy.   The use of ultrasonic therapy has resulted in the common use of instruments such as those described on page 275 for the treatment of arthritis and similar diseases.   These are in everyday use in thousands of physicians' offices.

Diagnosis.   For diagnosis, the use of the pulse-reflection method is rapidly being perfected.   This is practically the identical apparatus to the equipment used for material testing.   Fifteen megacycles has been used as a satisfactory frequency for tissue definition.

[1] J. F. Herrick, *JASA*, **26** (1954) 236.

Indication may be in any one of a number of types of display.   Figure 10-5 shows the relationship between the A scan and breast-cancer location.   Figure 10-6 is the transducer.   Figure 10-7 shows a picture-type scan employed in locating bowel lesions.   Similar apparatus has been

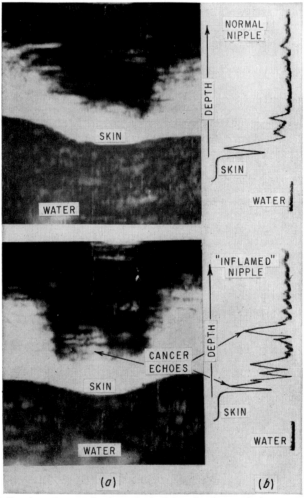

FIG. 10-5. Indications from pulsed method of locating breast lesions: (a) B scan; (b) A scan.   [J. J. Wild and J. M. Reid, Am. Inst. Ultrasonics Med., **4** (1955) 59.]

built by a number of investigators.   It is obvious that the apparatus techniques are very similar to those described at length in Chap. 9.

The location of gallstones is based on a different principle, i.e., ringing of the transducer in contact with a hard substance.[1]

[1] H. P. Kalmus, Natl. Bur. Standards Tech. News Bull., **37** (1953) 30.

The use of ultrasonic techniques for measuring the flow of blood has also been suggested. This has been accomplished only on models to date (see Flowmeter, p. 296).

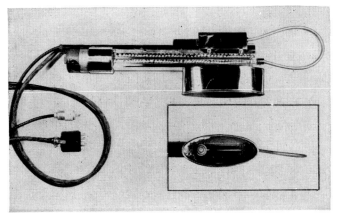

FIG. 10-6. Transducer for B-scan medical use. [(*J. J. Wild and J. M. Reid, Am. Inst. Ultrasonics Med.*, **4** (1955) 59.]

Neurosonic Surgery. Work has been done recently on the use of ultrasonics to produce lesions in various parts of the brain.[1] Extensive experiments have been carried out on cats and monkeys. The transducer used (Fig. 10-8) is a four-beam focusing unit producing great concentrations

TABLE 10-6. METALLURGICAL EFFECTS

Effect	Means	Frequency, kc	Reported by
Reduction in grain (finer needles tin-zinc)	Mechanical	10	Muhlhauser
Solidification of tin, zinc, and aluminum—produce dendritic structure	Crystal	600	S. Y. Sokolov
Solution of iron in zinc—rate increase	....	9	G. Schmid and A. Roll
Zinc grain size reduced	....	10	G. Schmid and L. Ehret
Antimony brittleness decreased	....	...	G. Schmid and L. Ehret

of energy in a relatively small space. Precision apparatus for positioning the subject's head is obviously necessary. A frequency of about 1 Mc was used. Dosages of the order of 300 to 1,200 watts/cm² were used to produce lesions, at about 980 kc.

[1] W. J. Fry, *Am. Inst. Ultrasonics Med., 4th Ann. Conf.* (1955) 41.

Lenses have also been used to focus the ultrasound producing a beam of about 1.5 mm in diameter.   Coupling is by means of sterile physiological saline.   This liquid is first degassed to prevent bubble scattering of the energy.

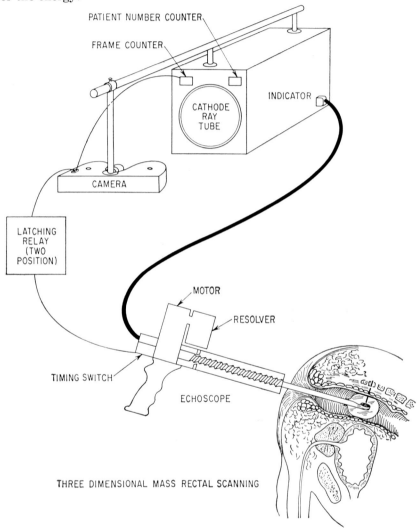

PATIENT NUMBER COUNTER

FRAME COUNTER

INDICATOR

CATHODE RAY TUBE

CAMERA

LATCHING RELAY (TWO POSITION)

MOTOR

RESOLVER

TIMING SWITCH

ECHOSCOPE

THREE DIMENSIONAL MASS RECTAL SCANNING

Fig. 10-7. Rotating transducer for tumor location.   [*J. J. Wild and J. M. Reid, Am. Inst. Ultrasonics Med.*, **4** (1955) 59.]

Metallurgical Effects.   The metallurgical effects of ultrasound have been often mentioned in the literature (see Table 10-6).   Among the more prominent effects are reduction in grain size, degassing of melts, dispersion of various foreign materials into melts, acceleration of rate processes, etc.

One thing of particular interest in metal treatment is the induction of ultrasound directly into the molten metal. The force between the induced electric currents in the melt and the current in the heating coil will cause motion directly in the melt.[1] Additional force may be obtained by adding a static magnetic field to the alternating field produced by the heater. Conventional methods may also be used to produce the ultrasound in the melt.

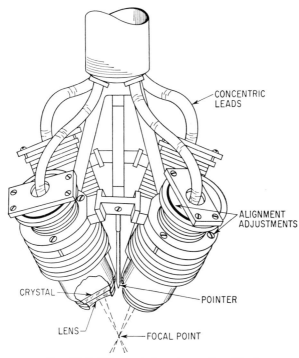

FIG. 10-8. Ultrasonic focusing unit. (*Fry.*)

Metallurgical applications may be classified as (1) grain refinement and (2) dispersion.

Grain Refinement. Sokolov mentions that melted metals when ultrasonically treated solidified more quickly and were of finer grain. This has been shown in the case of aluminum and magnesium.

Dispersion. One of the chief metallurgical applications is that of dispersion, i.e., mixing small particles of metal throughout some sort of solution, e.g., copper and water. This has been successfully done with many common metals. Very fine particles with a diameter of a few microcentimeters may sometimes be obtained. Frequencies of about 400 kc were used.

[1] W. Esmarch, T. Rummel, and K. Beuther, *Wiss. Veröffentl.* (1940) **78.**

As already mentioned, the passage of ultrasonics through a liquid may be indicated by means of small particles that orient themselves in the beam. In a like manner, any suspended particles will orient themselves, particularly if they are of rodlike or similar shape.[1]

These experiments were carried out with metals merely placed in a solution. Further work[2] was done while depositing metals electrolytically, and much finer and more highly dispersed deposits of metal were accomplished. Work was also done by Claus on photographic plates, and he claimed superior resolution, etc.

Other work was as follows: Metals that would usually not mix can be kept mixed by ultrasonics while solidifying. The magnetic properties of nickel are changed (using a frequency of about 20 kc).[3] Alloys and metals in which nitriding takes place have their structure improved and the process speeded up.[4]

The metallic action was described by Richards[5] in the following manner (applied to metals in a liquid state): The walls of the container have strong S waves set up in them; these waves fling drops of water into the metal. These drops each become covered with a thin film of metal, which breaks and throws minute particles of metal into the water.

Most solid bodies such as metals, which exhibit considerable adhesion between the parts, are not easily broken down by ultrasonic action. Some slight breakdown may be sometimes noticed in those solids which have poor cohesion, but generally this phenomenon is not efficient enough to be useful. The possible extension of the field of ultrasonics in this direction must await the design of generators of much greater power capabilities.

A transducer setup suitable for experimental use with small amounts of molten metal is shown in Fig. 10-9.

Welding. As with most aspects of ultrasonics, there is a considerable history of suggested application to spot welding. Behr,[6] Alexander,[7] Willrich,[8] and others describe experiments or suggestions for this use. The objectives are improvements in shear strength, grain refinement, elimination of cracks, etc.

Equipment operating at about 2 kw at 15 kc has been used in recent experiments.[9] The generator used was of a conventional type. High

[1] N. Marinesco, *Compt. rend.*, **196** (1933) 346.
[2] B. Claus, *Z. tech. Physik*, **15** (1934) 74.
[3] G. Schmid and U. Jetter, *Z. Electrochem.*, **47** (1940) 155.
[4] G. Mahoux, *Compt. rend.*, **191** (1930) 1328.
[5] W. T. Richards, *J. Am. Chem. Soc.*, **51** (1929) 1724.
[6] A. Behr, *Metal Ind.*, **63** (1943) 422.
[7] P. Alexander, *Bios* 1504.
[8] H. O. Willrich, *Welding*, **18** (1950) 61.
[9] Aeroprojects, *Natl. Bur. Standards Research Rept.* 50-5.

frequencies were also tried without success. The transducers for the
15-kc unit were magnetostrictive and of two designs: the first was integral
with the upper electrode, and the
second with the lower.

Use of the ultrasonics seems
to reduce cracking, improve shear
strength, reduce variation, etc.

Precipitation. Among the earliest effects noticed in applying ultrasonic waves were precipitation
and agglomeration of particles (see
Table 10-7). This indicates the
possibility of an application using
ultrasonics for the removal of particles from gases in order to clean
the atmosphere or recover materials. For example, it has been suggested many times in the past that
ultrasonic waves could be used for
removing fog from airplane run-
ways or smoke particles from industrial chimneys. Several attempts
have been made to do this, but so
far as is known at this moment

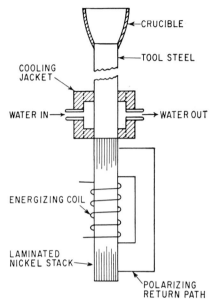

FIG. 10-9. Transducer for treating liquid
metals. (*J. B. Jones and J. G. Thomas,
ADC Tech. Rept.* 53-527.)

there is no generally accepted large-scale industrial use. Among the
materials which have been worked with have been carbon black, sulfur,

TABLE 10-7. PRECIPITATION AND AGGLOMERATION

Subject or material	*Reference*
Gas:	
Aerosol collections	E. P. Newmann and J. L. Norton: *Chem. Eng. Progr. Symposium Ser.*, **47** (1951) 4.
Quartz	K. Sollner and C. Bondy: *Trans. Faraday Soc.*, **32** (1936) 616.
Gas bubbles	*Ibid.*
Mercury	*Ibid.*
Oil	*Ibid.*
Colloids	*Ibid.*
Silver iodides	J. J. Hernais: *Rec. trav. chim.*, **58** (1939) 139.
Liquid:	
Milk treatment	L. A. Chambers: *J. Dairy Sci.*, **19** (1936) 29.
Wood pulp	A. Frey-Wyssling and K. Muhlethaler: *Textile Research J.*, **17** (1947) 32.
Survey	C. A. Stokes and J. E. Vivian: *Chem. Eng. Progr. Symposium Ser.*, **47** (1951) 11.

and ash.   In addition, it has been suggested that solids could be precipitated from liquid materials in place of gravity separation.

One of the earliest means of measurement was discussed by Kundt, who suggested the use of lycopodium powder to indicate the nodule processes of ultrasonic waves.   The particles (which are very fine) arrange themselves at the nodes.   A number of studies have been made attempting to relate the amplitude of vibration particle size and frequency.   It can be said in general that the rapidity of action is a function of the energy. About 2 watts/cm^2 is required to bring about any real agglomeration.

In Gas.   An aerosol is a mixture of solid or liquid particles in a gas (as in a dust, mist, smoke, etc.).   The advantage of collecting these particles is obvious, and ultrasonic methods have been applied to this problem. The important sonic conditions are frequency, intensity, exposure time, particle size, and density, etc.

The best and commonest example is the well-known Kundt dust figures, which represent a coagulating effect of ultrasonics in a gas.

The reason for this action seems to be that the particles do not travel the same paths because of their different sizes and because of characteristics of the system (such as frequency).   Electromagnetic whistle or siren generators are commonly preferred in gas work, and frequencies of 15,000 to 30,000 cps are common.

In Liquid.   Results similar to the agglomeration of particles in the gas may be obtained in liquids.   It is interesting to note that both agglomeration and separation may be brought about by ultrasonic waves.   In general, the concentration in mixing two liquids reaches a limiting value which may be lower than that obtained by other means.   Although agglomeration may occur below cavitation ranges, it requires cavitation to bring about any appreciable mixing.   The widespread use of ultrasonic waves for precipitation and agglomeration will probably wait upon an economical means of producing these waves in considerable powers.   The effect seems to be due to (1) collision of particles and (2) adherence.   The adherence may be due to electric charges, or removal of surface films, etc.

Photographic Effect.[1]   It has been known for some time that ultrasonic waves will produce a latent image on a photographic plate[2] as a result of mechanical action.   The action is present on wet plates but not on dry ones.   However, some investigators[3] feel that this is a secondary effect, caused not by the ultrasonics itself, but by the associated luminescence. Recent experiments[1] again indicate both types of effects, i.e., direct and secondary.   These experiments used a barium titanate transducer at 2,390 kc.

[1] G. S. Bennett, *JASA*, **25** (1953) 1149.
[2] N. Marinesco, *Compt. rend.*, **202** (1936) 757.
[3] R. Pinoir and J. Ponradier, *J. Chem. Phys.*, **44** (1947) 261.

CHAPTER 11

APPLICATIONS

One of the major problems in the proper use of ultrasound is the practical solution of application problems. As a matter of fact, this may very often be the major engineering difficulty encountered. It is therefore important to show how certain specific problems were approached and solved and what the general characteristics of the resulting equipment were. At the present time, equipment has been designed and used in the following fields (among others). In general, equipment shown may be applied to allied uses.

1. Nondestructive testing of materials
   a. Pulse technique
   b. Resonance technique
   c. Through technique
   d. Testing characteristics of materials
2. Medical applications
   a. Diagnostic applications
   b. Therapy equipment
   c. Biologic instrumentation
3. Cleaning, both high and low frequency
4. Soldering of materials without fluxes
5. Drilling, both industrial and dental
6. Ultrasonic alarm systems
7. Miscellaneous applications such as flow meters, viscosity meters, television, etc.

Pulse Technique. The most practical means of testing ultrasonic material is the echo method,[1] wherein a pulse of ultrasonic energy is sent out and the time between this transmission and the reception of an echo is measured. Such a system labors under the disadvantage that the apparatus is comparatively complex and expensive. Block diagrams and descriptions of such apparatus have already been given in Chap. 9.

In setting up the pulse system, the length of the pulse should be adjusted according to the minimum distance of transmission. For exam-

[1] B. Carlin, "Location of Internal Defects of Plant Equipment," American Gas Association, June, 1947.

ple, if an operator were testing a part that was 1 in. thick, he would want the pulse to be a very small fraction of an inch. The time it takes for ultrasonic waves to travel 1 in. in steel or aluminum is about 8 μsec; so a good length for the pulse would be 2 μsec. If he were testing a part that was 20 ft long, the operator could have a pulse length of 5 to 10 μsec. This longer pulse enables him to get somewhat more power into the medium and therefore greater penetration. Above a certain amount, usually about 10 μsec, additional length does not seem to help the penetration, and the only effect is to make the reflected signal appear broader.

For convenience, the indicating sweep may be designed so that any portion of it can be placed upon the screen and expanded to take up the entire visible space. This enables the operator to examine one particular part of the entire pattern. If the part being tested is 4 in. long, 4 in. of the sweep can be placed upon the screen and expanded. If only 1 in. is being tested, that length can be examined as a complete sweep. If a part in the center of a 30-in. block or even a 20-ft block shows some indication of a defect, the operator should be able to position the significant section of the sweep at the center of the screen and expand it so that it covers the complete area. In cases where very thin bonded films are to be tested, the difference in time between the reflection of a flaw and the reflection of the opposite side may be too slight to be noticed; in such cases, through pulsed transmission can be used. However, the through method of testing is generally used with continuous waves, since the systems are cheaper and simpler.

The amount of transmission is also of value in testing whether or not a given part will absorb large amounts of ultrasonic energy. If it is discovered that the amount of absorption is within certain limits for a standard part, defective material can often be differentiated from good material because of the fact that it will absorb more energy.

It has been noted that the amount of reflected energy depends upon the relation between the size of the reflecting surface and the wavelength at the particular frequency being used. This information gives a measure of the frequency which can be used in testing materials. Of course, it may not be necessary to detect flaws of the order of size of the wavelength. Lower frequencies can therefore be used as long as the flaws being detected are not too much smaller than the wavelength at the frequency of test.

For example, if the part is a very fine homogeneous structure such as steel or aluminum, it would be advisable to use a 5-Mc frequency, which will find very fine flaws and will not be affected by the grain boundaries of the material. On the other hand, if the material is of somewhat coarser consistency and it is desirable not to have any interference from the structure, a 2½-Mc frequency will be used. If the material is of very coarse structure such as brass or bronze, the higher frequencies will be reflected and scattered at the grain interfaces and will not penetrate the material, so it would be advisable to use a frequency of 1 or $\frac{1}{2}$ Mc, which will pass these boundaries.

It is possible to get a measure of the grain size of a particular material by noting the amount of ultrasonic attenuation. However, the most important fact to remember is that as the interferences within the material become of the order of length of the wavelength at a particular test frequency, it gradually becomes impossible to penetrate the material at that frequency, and it is then necessary to go to a lower frequency, which would have a correspondingly longer wavelength and which is no longer interfered with. The best frequency from the point of view of general use is one of about $2\frac{1}{2}$ Mc.

Distance Tested. The pulsed ultrasonic tester can satisfactorily test for flaws lying between $\frac{1}{4}$ in. and 30 ft from the face of the transducer. It is possible to find discontinuities closer to the surface than this, but more skill is required in interpreting the oscillograms. Greater distances can also be penetrated by raising the power output. The size of the flaw that is found does not appear to be a function of its distance from the testing probe. In other words, the pulsed tester will find a No. 60 hole $\frac{1}{8}$ in. in length at 1 or 2 in. from the testing unit and will find it practically as well at any distance between its testing limits. The amount of penetration does not depend upon the frequency of testing except in those cases where the ultrasonic waves are scattered by discontinuities in the material that are of the order of magnitude of the wavelength at which the testing is taking place. In other words, a particular billet may not transmit 5-Mc ultrasonic vibrations because of inclusions or grain-size characteristics, which possibly would interfere completely with the transmission of the 5-Mc beam. Thus, one of the experimental uses of the ultrasonic test method might be in a metallurgical laboratory, where exact measurements of grain-size characteristics or plastic properties of particular metals or alloys are of interest. However, in routine testing, a crude indication of the character of the material being tested can be easily determined by trying various frequencies. The instrument must be carefully calibrated for the purpose. Unless very exact measurements are made, this method cannot be used for routine tests of materials. Table 11-1 shows a chart of the distance in common materials that a low-power (1,000 volts peak to peak, 2-μsec pulse) ultrasonic tester will penetrate.[1]

Testing Materials. Ultrasonic methods are applicable to the testing of most metals and are particularly successful for metals that are reasonably homogeneous and close grained (see Table 11-1). These methods can also be applied to many of the denser plastics and glasses, and to other materials of lower density by using special frequencies. Tool steel is one

[1] B. Carlin, *Product Eng.*, **18** (1947) 113.

TABLE 11-1. ULTRASONIC PENETRATION INTO MATERIALS*

Type material	Testing frequency, Mc				Remarks
	0.5	1	2.25	5	
	Range, in feet unless otherwise marked				
Steel:					Generally, depth of penetration into steel depends on the amount of working and processing of the material. Finer grain structure usually permits greater penetration
Ingots	4–6	2–4	1–2	1	
Billets, blooms	5–12	6–8	3–4	1–2	
Rolled	22–25	22–25	10–25	5–8	
Cold drawn	22–25	22–25	16–20	7–10	
Forged	22–25	22–25	22–25	22–25	
Tool steels	22–25	22–25	22–25	22–25	
Spring steels	22–25	22–25	22–25	22–25	
Stainless steels	....	....	....	....	
Steel castings:					Cast steels in the lower carbon range permit greater supersonic penetration
Carbon cast steels:					
Low carbon	15–20	15–20	10–15	7–10	
Medium carbon	14–18	14–18	8–12	5–8	
High carbon	13–16	13–16	7–10	4–6	
Low-alloy castings	17–20	17–20	12–15	7–10	
High-alloy castings	17–20	17–20	12–15	7–10	
Cast iron:					"Scattering" of supersonic vibrations results where excessive porosity exists
Gray iron	1–2	6–12 in.	2–4 in.	....	
Malleable	7–10	7–10	3–5	6–12 in.	
Wrought iron	7–10	7–10	3–5	6–12 in.	
Aluminum:					Coarse structure or porosity will interfere with penetration. Finer grain structure permits greater penetration
Cast	12–15	12–15	8–10	8–10	
Extruded	22–25	22–25	22–25	22–25	
Worked	22–25	22–25	22–25	22–25	
Magnesium:					Physical properties similar to those of aluminum
Cast	12–15	12–15	8–10	8–10	
Extruded	22–25	22–25	22–25	22–25	
Worked	22–25	22–25	22–25	22–25	
Copper:					Coarse grain structure disperses vibrations
Cast	....	....	....	....	
Worked	0–6 in.	0–12 in.	....	....	
Brass and bronze:					Heat treatment will substantially extend limits of penetration
Cast, fine grain	0–1½	0–1½	....	....	
Cast, coarse grain	....	....	....	....	
Worked	1–5	1–3	....	....	
Lead	....	....	....	....	Physical properties absorb vibration

TABLE 11-1. ULTRASONIC PENETRATION INTO MATERIALS (*Continued*)

Type material	Testing frequency, Mc				Remarks
	0.5	1	2.25	5	
	Range, in feet unless otherwise marked				
Nickel:					Greater porosity is
Cast	1–3	1–3	1–2	6–12 in.	usually present in
Worked	1–15	8–10	5–8	3–5	cast materials
Monel—worked	10–15	8–10	5–8	3–5	
Gold—worked	0–1	0–1	. . . .	. . . .	Testing experience very limited
Silver—worked	5–10	2–5	1–2	0–1	Application usually confined to small pieces
Platinum	7–10	7–10	3–5	3–5	Figures are relative
Tungsten	7–10	7–10	3–5	3–5	penetration. Sizes tested were not in this range
Sintered carbides	0–12 in.	0–6 in.	0–3 in.	0–3 in.	Most of testing done at high frequencies because of nature of flaws to be found
Molybdenum:					
Sintered	5–10	5–10	1–5	0–2	
Worked	21–25	21–25	21–25	15–18	
Wood:					Direction of grain
Hard	0–8 in.	0–4 in.	. . . .	. . . .	and amount of mois-
Soft	. . . .	. . . .	. . . .	. . . .	ture in the wood
Masonite	0–8 in.	0–4 in.	. . . .	. . . .	affect transmission into medium
Plastics:					Depends on amount
Vinylite	6–12 in.	6–12 in.	6 in.–6 ft	6 in.–6 ft	of filler in material
Catalin	6–12 in.	6–12 in.	6 in.–6 ft	6 in.–6 ft	
Bakelite	6–12 in.	6–12 in.	6 in.–6 ft	6 in.–6 ft	
Lucite or Plexiglas	6–12 in.	6–12 in.	6 in.–6 ft	6 in.–6 ft	
Oil	24–25	24–25	24–25	24–25	Indication of penetration limited only by capabilities of instrument
Water	24–25	24–25	24–25	24–25	

* Experimental values of approximate maximum depth of penetration, in specific samples; not computed values or absolute indication of penetration in any single material.

example of a material that can be easily tested for flaws by ultrasonic methods. These steels can be used for cutting, shearing, or forming tools. The types of flaw ordinarily encountered are blowholes, bursts, flakes, inclusions, seams, segregations, and laps. All these are easily detected and located.

Forgings are also well adapted to ultrasonic testing. Common examples of forgings are bearings, axles, shafts, turbine blanks, hammers, rotors, rolls, die blocks, billets, bars, piston rods, studs, pressure vessels, guns, etc. In every one of these cases the article can be quickly and easily tested.

Many ferrous castings can be tested. Steel castings take the form of cylinders, gears, wheels, rolls, etc., while iron castings are used on boat frames, gears, crankshafts, rolls, etc. Many castings can be satisfactorily tested, although as the grain sizes increase, it becomes more difficult to do a satisfactory job.

Type and Size of Flaw. An ultrasonic tester will find any appreciable discontinuity or inhomogeneity of elasticity or density in the material; thus it can find any holes or cracks within a solid mass of material and locate them exactly. It makes little difference exactly what causes the variation; i.e., a drilled hole and a blowhole indicate in the same manner. It should be realized that the flaws which the operator wishes to find must be larger than natural discontinuities or changes in grain size within the material. Within certain limits the ultrasonic unit is able to distinguish between reflections from small and large flaws by variations in frequency or by differences in the amplitude of the reflected signals, but it should be obvious that if the material is naturally full of porosities of $\frac{1}{8}$ in. diameter, it will be difficult or impossible to find a $\frac{1}{16}$ in. flaw. Moreover, even if the material is full of $\frac{1}{16}$-in. inclusions, it may be impossible to distinguish $\frac{1}{8}$ in. flaws. Ultrasonic waves will be affected by all of these without regard to the difference in size. However, if the material is uniformly homogeneous except for the flaws, or if the flaws are larger than any natural discontinuity within the material, an ultrasonic instrument can usually locate them easily.

SIZE. The actual size of a flaw that can be found is rather difficult to state, but practical experimentation seems to indicate that the situation is as follows:

When the flaw is below a certain size, approximately the size of a No. 60 drill (0.04 in. in diameter) and about $\frac{1}{8}$ in. long, the ability of an instrument to find it varies somewhat with distance; thus it is usually easier to find a flaw of this size 6 in. away than 6 ft away. As long as the dimension is smaller than that stated, it may roughly be stated that the ultrasonic unit will find a flaw of a size approximately 0.1 per cent of the thickness of the part. Whenever the flaw becomes larger than one of those dimensions, the relation no longer holds and the instrument seems to work on a more or less absolute basis. Thus it will find a ⅛-in. hole 1 ft away or 10 ft away in steel or aluminum with not too much difference in sensitivity.

In other words, if the discontinuity is greater than the diameter of a No. 60 drill, then the thickness of the part can be disregarded and the flaw will be located in almost any case.

ORIENTATION. The orientation of a flaw can be very important if it is a very fine hairline crack of no appreciable thickness. If the crack is normal to the face of the transducer, it will not offer so much surface for reflection as otherwise. The section of a flaw in a plane parallel to the face of the crystal offers reflection. However, in a practical sense, this has never been a disadvantage, since there is almost always some component of the flaw in the proper direction to reflect energy to the transducer. Figure 11-1 indicates the action of a flaw lying at an angle to the crystal face upon the ultrasonic energy.

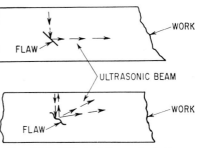

FIG. 11-1. Effect of flaw orientation.

Wall Thickness. Ultrasonic testers can be used to measure wall thickness from one side by the reflection method in exactly the same manner as that used to find flaws. If the wall, however, is less than ½ in. in thickness, the number of reflections per section of trace must be counted, and the thickness computed by division into the total number of indications. For this reason it is difficult to measure walls less than ½ in. thick. In testing walls on tanks where the surface is very badly pitted or corroded on either side, the ultrasonic waves may be scattered, and it will be difficult to get definite indication. Generally speaking, each new application must be tried before it can be definitely stated whether or not the instrument will operate satisfactorily.

One of the major problems in ultrasonics today is the successful application of the method to badly corroded or rusted parts. Smooth walls of more than ½ in. in thickness can be satisfactorily measured by pulsed instruments.

Shape. The chief disadvantage in ultrasonic testing is difficulty in testing small articles of involved shapes and sizes. Ultrasonic instruments can test a part wherever the surface on which the crystal is to be placed is at least ¼ in. wide; but if the part is very small and has a large number of offsets and holes in it, it is practically impossible to interpret the results.

Ultrasonic testing in general therefore shows its greatest value in the examination of parts of large size such as huge steel ingots where it is possible to shoot through 30 ft of steel and find a small flaw. Any part that is regular in shape and has a thickness in excess of 1 in. can easily be tested if the material permits ultrasonic transmission. On the other hand, a part under 1 in. thick can very often be tested as long as its shape is not too involved.

Curvature of the material, such as that in a pipe, is not a disadvantage, since either curved crystals or special methods of using flat crystals have been successfully used. If the diameter is large, flat crystals can be used

TABLE 11-2. SURFACE FINISH

General Electric			Surf Check and others	Acceptance for ultrasonics
Symbol	Roughness, μin.		Roughness, μin.	
	Average	Average peak to valley		
F4	63	220	60–80	Preferred finish for detecting defects as small as 0.005 in.
F5	125	455	100–150	Satisfactory for average testing for defects
F6	250	875	250 and up	Can be tolerated but not entirely satisfactory, as this finish may reduce sensitivity owing to poor surface contact

without any special couplant.   If the diameter is small, it is usually easy to fit a curved crystal to it.

The use of immersion techniques has made possible many applications where shapes were too complex to use direct contact.

Surface.   The surface of the material under test should be as smooth as possible.   Where the material is very irregular, the irregularities have the effect of supporting the crystal away from the work so that it is not in intimate contact, and therefore the amount of energy transmitted into it is too slight for satisfactory testing.   This may take place where the surface is badly pitted, rusted, or covered with heavy coatings of paint; and although general rules for ultrasonic testing can be set up, it is usually advisable to try the instrument on any particular surface in order to determine whether or not great enough penetration will take place. Where the surface is irregular and the transducer cannot get into contact, a suitable surface can be provided by smoothing with a hand grinder. This must be done on most sand-cast surfaces. Machined surfaces are satisfactory within the limits of roughness given in Table 11-2.[1] Rolled or forged surfaces do not require extensive grinding but should be cleaned and scale may be left on the material as long as it is securely attached. As a matter of fact, it is not advisable to remove tightly adhering scale from steel surface, since the surface below a layer of scale may be wavy. The most desirable surface for routine tests is a ground surface with a tight scale adhering to it.

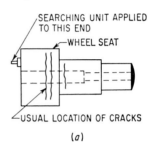

(a)

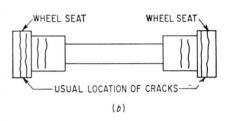

(b)

In most cases where the surface is concave, curved crystals must be used and flat ones are not applicable. Generally speaking, a special crystal or coupling device can be used with any surface of regular curvature. Where the curvature is very irregular, the surface must be smoothed off so that the crystal can fit against it.

The standard reference is from the General Electric Roughness Standards and from the Surf Check Roughness Standards. These refer to machined surfaces and are self-explanatory (see Table 11-2).

Fatigue Testing. Ultrasonic methods are of particular value when used for locating fatigue failures. Testing can be carried out immediately after an article is assembled in order to see whether or not the assembly or machining process has contributed to the production of fatigue cracks within it.

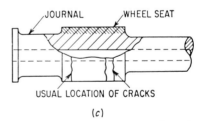

(c)

Fig. 11-2. The testing of axles and crankpins.

However, the commonest use is for periodic checks of materials that are under strain due to the way in which they are being used to determine whether or not flaws have developed. One example is the testing of locomotive axles and crankpins while they are in use on the locomotive. The same items can also be tested after the wheels are pressed off during a routine overhaul. In a like manner, ultrasonic testing has been used to test fatigue of steel plates used on the hulls of large ships, of

[1] B. Carlin, *Prod. Eng.*, **18** (1947) 113.

backup rolls in use in steel mills, of shafts in large machines such as generators, and in many similar applications. The testing of crankpins and axles is done from the ends (Fig. 11-2). Typical locations of flaws are also shown in the figure.

Absorption Testing. The ultrasonic tester has been successfully used in the testing of materials by noting the absorption pattern. A typical pattern is indicated in Fig. 11-3. These results can be correlated to differences in grain structure or the internal condition of the material. One successful application has been the testing of materials in plates where the thickness of the plate was too small to permit ordinary reflective thickness measurements. On a plate that is sound, a series of reflections of considerable height and spaced the proper distance will be clearly noted. When the plate is laminated, the reflections entirely disappear, thus giving a very strong and sharp indication of the defects. The laminated

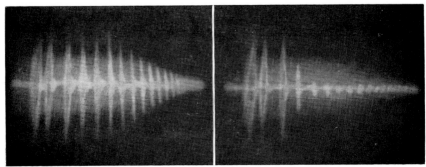

Fig. 11-3. Typical absorption pattern.

parts can be located exactly because of the directional characteristics of ultrasonics.

Technique for Close Testing. When using pulsed ultrasonic testing, it is difficult to test within less than $\frac{1}{2}$ in., because of the very short times involved. Certain techniques may, however, be worked out to circumvent this. One method is the use of total patterns to indicate differences in material characteristics. Another is the use of wedge methods. Still others include the use of delays, spacers, etc. However, in spite of all these systems it is difficult to test closer than $\frac{1}{4}$ in. from the surface in aluminum.

Setting Standards for Ultrasonic Testing. Many older methods of test have the advantage that standards for testing materials are already set. This is not as yet completely true for ultrasonics. However, it is possible to set them. One procedure is more or less as follows: First, the size and frequency of crystal is chosen, e.g., 1-in. square crystal at $2\frac{1}{2}$ or 5 Mc. The sensitivity is also chosen by locating certain standard holes in a standard metal block. The surface is standardized, and the test specified as satisfactory on certain distances of penetration.   Parts within those limitations are then checked and passed or rejected by comparison with the standard.

Sets of standard test blocks are now available in which standard holes are drilled and which may be used to calibrate ultrasonic pulse testers.

These blocks must be chosen with careful attention to material, size of block, direction, number and spacing of holes, frequency and size of crystals, size of holes, etc.   They are used to obtain measurements of performance of instruments and search units, so that consistent results may be obtained, and so that results can be expressed on a common basis.

Resonance Technique.   The resonance method can satisfactorily test the thickness of parts between about 0.005 and 0.5 in.   Besides measuring the thickness it can find flaws as well.   However, its use as a flaw-finding mechanism is questionable, except in comparatively thin stock.

The resonance method can be used on any material that transmits ultrasonics satisfactorily.   As with pulsed methods, Table 11-1 can be used to indicate which those materials are.   Inside or outside surfaces can be used as the test surface. Resonance instruments must be separately calibrated for every material.   Besides metals, some glasses, plastics, and rubbers can be examined.   As usual, when the

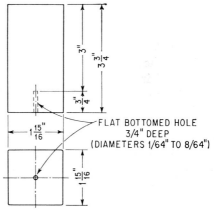

FIG. 11-4. Ultrasonic standard reference block.   (*Alcoa.*)

material is nonconducting, the face of the transducer must be returned to ground by a foil facing, although some results can be obtained without that expedient.

The use of the fundamental for resonance indications is not completely satisfactory, as it limits the thickest part easily tested to about $\frac{1}{4}$ in. By using harmonics, 4 in. can be tested.

Resonance testers can most easily be used as flaw detectors by using them as simple comparators; i.e., the transducer is placed on what is known to be a good part and then tried on a large succession of parts. The tested items are considered good if the pattern is identical.   Resonance (as other ultrasonic means) will respond to extremely thin separations.

The indications will often completely disappear.   This merely means that the energy is being diverted, as by an angular opposite face; absorbed, as by very viscous material; or scattered, by small inclusions.   This action may be taken as cause for rejection, but the actual reason for the phenomenon may be unknown, and the method is therefore not to be recommended. Indications will usually be obtained in using resonance methods under conditions similar to those on which other ultrasonic methods are successful.

Resonance testing is particularly valuable in the inspection of bond, such as the silver bond on aeronautical bearings. The tester is set at the thickness of the entire part and indicates resonance; when the indication disappears, it shows that the part is defective.

Another method is to adjust the resonance instrument to the thickness of the bond only. In that case it will indicate only when the bond is separated from the main body of metal and show a defect then.

A number of resonance instruments have appeared, and in general two approaches have been made commercially. One is the use of an oscilloscope type which is arranged to produce a single marker and generally to operate at the fundamental frequency. A second method which is theoretically the same uses some other form of indication (such as an audible note) and is generally much simpler from an electronic point of view. This type of instrument satisfactorily operates on a harmonic, and the indicator is a dial which can be varied at a wide frequency range. The point at which indications are obtained are noted, and the thicknesses are computed or read from a chart or graph according to the distance between successive indications. The schematic diagram for such a unit is shown in Fig. 11-5, and an instrument of this type is also shown in the photo. The transducers are the same.

Bond Testing. Bond between metal and other materials can be shown. However, when those materials are highly damping ones such as rubber or wood, the test must always be made from the metal side. The material fastened to the back of the metal will then always dampen out reflections except when the bond is defective. This method can also be used with any other kind of ultrasonic testing depending for its action on reflected energy.

Transmission of Continuous Ultrasonics. Systems that use continuous waves for flaw testing are rarely used because of the troublesome reflections existing within the system, which make it nearly impossible to interpret results. However, modifications of the systems have been used when the flaws to be located were large enough to interrupt substantially the entire testing beam. These are discussed at length in Chap. 7.

Swept-frequency methods are used for such instruments, an example of which is shown in Fig. 8-18.

Medical Equipment. The application of ultrasonics to medicine is probably in its infancy. Basically, ultrasound lends itself to several different types of applications: (1) diagnostic and (2) therapeutic.

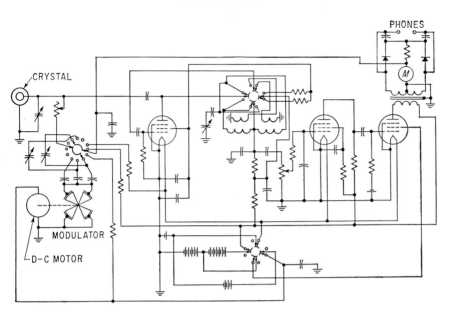

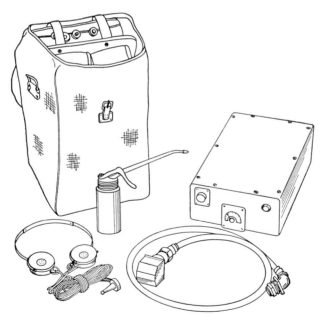

FIG. 11-5. Audigage.   (*After Branson.*)

Diagnostic. One of the earliest diagnostic devices was the stethoscope, which is basically acoustic, but the same principle may be applied in the ultrasonic region. For example, a recent device has been used for locating gallstones by means of the sonic output associated with tapping them. With the more refined techniques which have been described herein, new applications have become possible. Among those which had some success have been methods for outlining the cerebral ventricles in order to locate abnormal growths in the brain, methods of investigating cancers of the breasts and other portions of the body, and other similar approaches which are basically very much the same as the nondestructive testing used on metals.

DIAGNOSTIC EQUIPMENT. Ultrasonic ventriculography: Exploration of the ventricles for tumors has been carried out recently.[1] Basically this is a means for passing ultrasonic waves through the brain and picking them up on the other side by means of separate transmitters and receivers, as shown in Fig. 11-6a; the principle is similar to continuous-wave methods of testing materials. Water is used as a coupling medium, and the head is inserted in a special rubber housing which couples the water and the ultrasonic energy to it. The equipment is used to examine the different acoustic losses from different parts of the head both by reflection in it and by absorption. It has been found that ultrasonic waves are more attenuated in brain tissue than in liquid. However, problems of resolution which depend upon the amount of scattering, refraction, and diffraction still remain to be solved. Figure 11-6b shows a representation of a complete apparatus as used in one project for making a photograph of the subject. One of the major problems which still remains is a means of getting an adequate picture by some form of ultrasonic cell. The unit shown used a strip of barium titanate subdivided into 20 separate sections. Barium titanate when used as transducers has been found to show considerable variation in activity at different points on any transducer. Naturally this detracts from the picture. The 20 sections are switched by a commutator, and produce the vertical part of the picture. The transducer is moved horizontally to provide the horizontal section.

Ultrasonic-pulse-test methods have also been used by several investigators to get pictures of the body tissue for cancer diagnosis and other reasons. These methods are practically identical to material testing methods already described.[2]

Therapy. Ultrasonic therapy equipment has been widely used, especially in Europe, and is rapidly becoming an accepted method of treatment

[1] T. F. Hueter and R. F. Bolt, *JASA*, **23** (1951) 160.
[2] J. M. Reid and J. J. Wild, *IRE Conv. Record Pt.* 9 (1955) 68; D. H. Howry, *IRE Conv. Record Pt.* 9 (1955) 75.

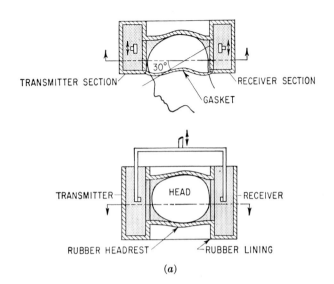

TRANSMITTER SECTION

RECEIVER SECTION

30°

GASKET

TRANSMITTER

HEAD

RECEIVER

RUBBER HEADREST

RUBBER LINING

(a)

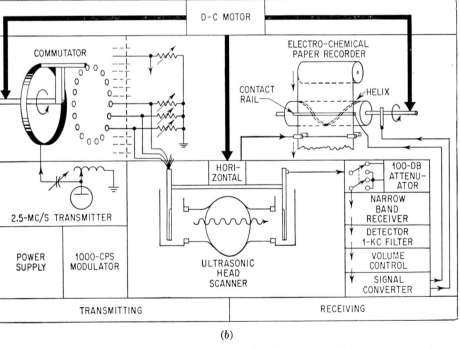

D-C MOTOR

COMMUTATOR

ELECTRO-CHEMICAL
PAPER RECORDER

CONTACT
RAIL

HELIX

HORI-
ZONTAL

100-DB
ATTENU-
ATOR

2.5-MC/S TRANSMITTER

NARROW
BAND
RECEIVER

DETECTOR
1-KC FILTER

POWER
SUPPLY

1000-CPS
MODULATOR

ULTRASONIC
HEAD
SCANNER

VOLUME
CONTROL

SIGNAL
CONVERTER

TRANSMITTING

RECEIVING

(b)

FIG. 11-6. Apparatus for ultrasonic brain examination: (a) transducer arrangement; (b) block diagram.

in this country. The applications of this equipment are not the topic of this book but rather one of medical study.[1]

The design of the equipment is comparatively simple and straightforward. Figure 11-7 shows a photograph, schematic, and picture of the transducer of such a piece of equipment. Most of such equipment is designed to operate in the vicinity of 1 Mc with a power output of about $3\frac{1}{2}$ watts/cm². In general, transducers having a diameter of $1\frac{1}{2}$ in. or less are used, and the total power requirement is the function of the crystal size. Transducers may be magnetostrictive, quartz, barium titanate, or other crystals, but quartz crystals have been most commonly used. The crystal may be cemented to the back of a metal face, which is usually a function of one-half of the wavelength; at these power levels, the back can be in air. A simple tuned oscillator is used to drive the crystal. The transducer is then coupled to the skin through either a liquid or grease-like material. Irradiation charts and treatments may be found in the medical literature.

An ultrasonic therapy oscillator is operated either continuously or with various pulsing means, and the output of the transducer is coupled to the skin. Treatments may be given under water. The general physical effects of ultrasonics may be divided in the living system in the following categories: (1) heating, (2) changes in pressure, (3) cavitation, and (4) various forces resulting from radiation pressure. There is some question as to exactly what causes the physiological changes under treatment. However, at present, ultrasonic treatment is recommended for a great many diseases such as bursitis, abscesses, and lumbago.

The frequency most commonly used is in the vicinity of 1 Mc. The maximum output of the head is recommended to be 3 to 5 watts/cm², and most units are between 5 and 12 cm² in size. This is the actual size of the crystal, and the head itself is usually two to three times this size.

Units have been made which were pulsed. The actual medical effect of pulsing does not seem to have been defined, although it may give greater mechanical effects with less heat. Transducers have been made either plane, that is, to generate plane waves, or focused.

Most units presently made are plane, but it should be realized that in the 1-Mc region (with a head diameter of $1\frac{1}{2}$ in. or greater) there will be some focusing effect about 6 or 8 in. from the transducer. The transducer is usually made by bonding a crystal to the back of a metal plate. The method of bonding is very important and of course must be done in such a way that the ultrasonics will travel through the bond without attenuation. The front plate is usually a function of the wavelength, that is, it is usually resonant at the frequency of treatment.

[1] J. M. Van Went, "Ultrasonic and Ultrashort Waves and Medicine," Elsevier, 1954; R. Pohlmann, "Die Ultraschall Therapie," Verlag Hans Huber, 1951.

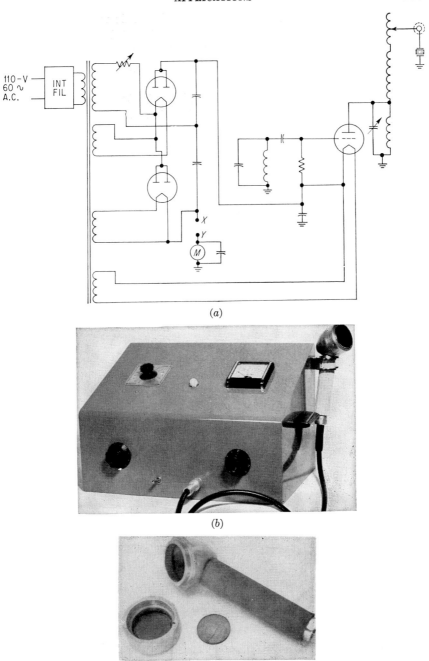

Fig. 11-7. Typical wave therapy unit: (a) schematic; (b) therapy unit; (c) therapy transducer.

Surgery.   It has been determined that ultrasonic waves may be used to selectively cut tissue.   A setup for experimental surgery using four transducers to produce a very-high-intensity focused beam for this purpose is shown in Fig. 11-8.   The transducers for this equipment are shown in greater detail on page 255.

Soldering and Brazing.   It has been shown that metals can be soldered or brazed without fluxes by subjecting them to ultrasonic vibration.   The ultrasound removes the oxide, allowing the solder to adhere.   In general,

FIG. 11-8. Electronic and transducer sections of apparatus for experimental surgery.

lower-temperature solders (up to about 600°F) have been more commonly used.

Several ultrasonic approaches to soldering have appeared, in which units have been built using a transducer with a tip which could be brought into contact with the material being soldered.   It has been found that cavitation then forms near the tip and removes the oxide from the material.   Heat can then be applied, and solder can be fastened to the bare material.

Once treated ultrasonically, material is solderable by standard means so long as a thin layer of solder remains on its surface.   Once solder is removed, the surface will rapidly oxidize and not take solder unless re-treated, so it is sometimes advisable to repeat the treatment at each soldering. However, coated surfaces tend to retain solder, even when wiped.

A number of approaches to the design of such equipment have appeared. In one case, the type of transducer chosen was a longitudinally excited magnetostrictive element. The choice of magnetostriction is usual as most ultrasonic crystal materials have poor temperature characteristics and are comparatively fragile, while magnetostrictive units are sturdy and will take heat.

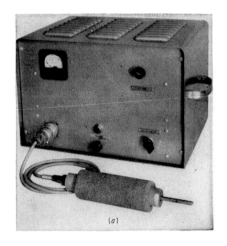

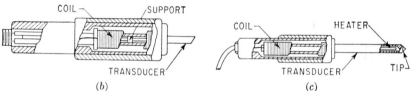

(b)   (c)

FIG. 11-9. (a) Soldering apparatus; (b) cutaway view of nonheater transducer; (c) self-heated transducer.

In certain cases, such as the soldering of small parts or wires, it is desirable to have a self-heated iron. In other cases, such as the soldering of large welds or materials which would require a great amount of heat, external heating is needed. In general, a self-heated unit requires more driving power for the same amount of ultrasonic output.

For all practical purposes, soldering is not improved by raising the amount of ultrasonic energy above a certain critical point at which soldering is completely satisfactory. With a nonheated tip, this is in the vicinity of 25 acoustic watts. The generator shown in Fig. 11-9 is designed

with an output between 35 and 50 acoustic watts. A cutaway view of
the transducer is also given. This unit is built of high-temperature materials, and has a rod assembly which can be removed so that various shapes
and frequencies of rods can be used. The self-heated unit may be plugged

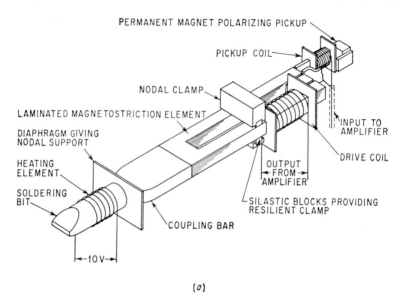

(a)

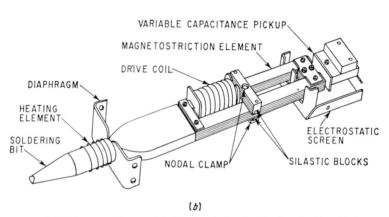

(b)

Fig. 11-10. Soldering transducer: (a) showing inductive feedback; (b) utilizing capacitive feedback. (*From Mullard.*)

into the same generator. This iron has a cartridge-type heater mounted
in a hollow-cylinder magnetostrictive element with a movable or separate
tip. The tip can be of any shape, and various heater elements may be
incorporated. Curie point of the transducer is not reached even with

continuous operation, so that the unit may be used for an indefinite period. In some cases air or water cooling is added.

Because the generator is tunable from 10 to 50 kc, shaping of the bits, wear, etc., do not cause loss of operation.

In this case, the transducers are designed to operate from a single coil with both the d-c bias and the a-c signal applied. Units have been made to provide 250 or 1,000 watts output (enough to drive even large pots).

Similar hand-soldering units have been designed in this country and abroad. Figure 11-10 shows two methods of stabilizing frequency, the first of which uses a head with a magnetic pickup, the second capacitive. This voltage is fed back to the oscillator to control its frequency (Mullard). These units are heated by a winding about the tip.

Most soldering units are air-cooled, although pots may be water- or oil-cooled.

Soldering Pots. Small soldering pots have also been designed; one of these can be plugged into the previously described generator or a similar one. One is 1 in. in diameter, and the other 3 in. in diameter, and both are $1\frac{1}{4}$ in. deep. The 3-in. pot is shown in Fig. 11-11. It consists of a nickel transducer of the slotted hollow-rod type driving a resonant pot. The transducer is cooled by a fan, and the pot is heated externally.

The resonant frequency of any magnetostrictive structure is influenced by rod dimensions and mass of driven structures. There is, therefore, a tendency for the frequency to decrease from that of a

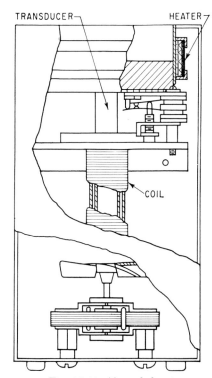

FIG. 11-11. Air-cooled pot.

simple rod with the same dimensions. It may be necessary to design other system elements to be resonant, and it is obvious that excursion of the solder is greater for a lower-frequency wave. These conditions lead to the design of a pot being somewhere under 20 kc. Since these units may be driven by a considerable amount of power, intense sources of sound result. A compromise must therefore result to raise the frequency above the audible range.

Larger pots using water-cooled stacks have also been designed (Fig. 11-12). These units require about 250 watts minimum for drive.

Applications. Applications for ultrasonic soldering may be found in the substitution of aluminum for copper or brass or in soldering wherever fluxes are undesirable. Tinning of aluminum-foil capacitors, aluminum wire, aluminum voice coils for speakers, etc., is an example. Filling casting holes, etc., on light alloy castings, sealing hermetically sealed containers, tinning printed circuitry, etc., are others.

Welding. Means for bonding materials by the introduction of vibratory ultrasonic energy has recently been proved to be a valuable new technique.

A single spot or series of overlapping spots or a continuous weld has been used to join a wide variety of objects. For example, one of the first successful applications was the welding of a small rib to heavy aluminum rod. Overlapping spots to produce a continuous weld were used. In addition to aluminum, other materials such as stainless steel, molybdenum, Inconel, and titanium have successfully been welded.

FIG. 11-12. Water-cooled solder-pot unit.

Welding Equipment. Ultrasonic welding equipment basically consists of the standard ultrasonic generator and transducer in addition to supports, clamps, etc., which are special and which are designed for holding the material to be welded. Welding can take place over a very broad frequency spectrum. However, frequencies in the low ultrasonic range have been most widely applied. Magnetostrictive transducers have been commonly used, although there is no reason why barium titanate cannot also be applied. A coupling system must also be used which will not be sensitive to the clamping force necessary to apply it to the weldment and which will not shift in frequency when so applied. In addition, a minimal amount of energy should be lost owing to inefficiencies in the coupling system. A number of systems have been worked out and may be considered to be special types of tools such as those described in Chap. 4. A number of these systems are shown in Fig. 11-13.[1] Special names have been applied to these, but the relationship to the basic type of transducer may be seen in the diagrams.

[1] J. B. Jones and W. C. Potthoff, *Am. Soc. Tool Eng.*, **58**, bk. 2 (1958) 152.

Generators ranging in power level from 400 to 4,000 watts have been used. There is nothing special in the design of these generators. The welding heads may be mounted to any convenient type of upright struc-ture or may be portable.

Cleaning. Ultrasonic cleaning seems to be due to a combination of cavitation and acceleration of the cleaning fluid. Experiments in the

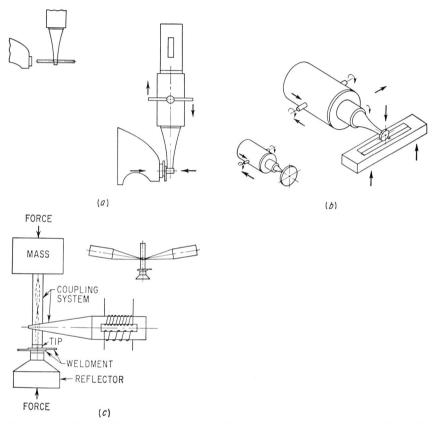

(a)

(b)

FORCE

MASS

COUPLING SYSTEM

TIP

WELDMENT

REFLECTOR

FORCE

(c)

FIG. 11-13. Types of transducers for welding applications: (a) lateral drive; (b) continuous seam; (c) mass-reed wedge. (*Aeroprojects.*)

cleaning of materials, particularly metals, have been carried out in both high and low frequencies. In this case, *high frequency* refers to a fre-quency in the vicinity of 1 Mc while *low frequency* refers to a frequency of less than about 100,000 cps (0.1 Mc). Equipment of both sorts will be shown. Cavitation is greater at the low frequencies, but the high-fre-quency units give more sharply beamed results. Figure 11-14a shows a low-power high-frequency unit which uses a barium titanate transducer to generate power. Magnetostrictive units have also been used. The unit consists of an oscillator–power amplifier of a conventional type. The transducer is coupled to the bottom of a tank either by being dropped into the tank or through a hole in the sidewall of the tank. It may also

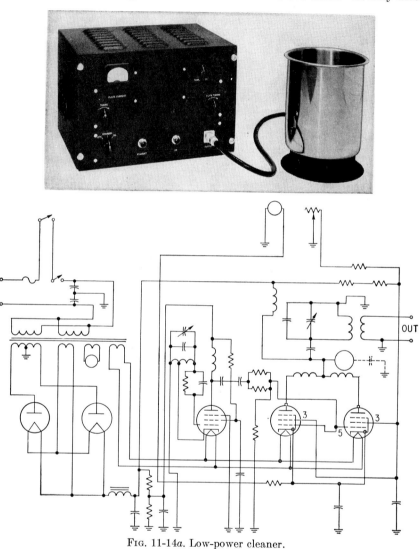

FIG. 11-14a. Low-power cleaner.

be fastened to the outside and will radiate through the wall of the tank, but the efficiency is much lower.

The same type of operation using a low-frequency generator and transducer of either barium titanate or magnetostrictive material may be used. Low frequencies have been found preferable for the cleaning of metals while high frequencies have been found advantageous in the treatment of fibers and certain other special parts. The basic design of the low-frequency generator is the same as the high-frequency one except for the considerations of frequency.

In general, the cleaning material is either a water-detergent solution, trichlorethylene, or Stoddard solvents. A great many parts have been satisfactorily cleaned, and ultrasonic cleaning is now becoming generally accepted. It does not completely do away with the necessity for other types of cleaning but, in general, adds to the effectiveness of the other types. Among materials which have been satisfactorily cleaned are a

Fig. 11-14b. A large industrial ultrasonic cleaning device. (*Circo.*)

wide range of airplane parts, motor parts, machine parts of all types having blind holes or presenting other difficulties in cleaning. Moreover, in certain cases, it appears likely that materials which have been atomically contaminated can be cleaned by ultrasound. In the normal use of ultrasound, it has been found to reduce cost of materials and labor and to satisfactorily clean parts which could not be cleaned by other means. In particular, it is valuable in the cleaning of delicate instrument parts either partially disassembled or completely assembled. Bearings have been cleaned both assembled and disassembled. Electronic assemblies, armatures, etc., have also been satisfactorily cleaned, and it appears that by the time this is printed, a wide range of uses will have been developed.

The procedure for ultrasonic cleaning consists in immersing the article to be cleaned in the cleaning fluid in which an ultrasonic field is generated by a transducer which is in the tank. It can be applied to existing equipment and has been widely used in automatic cleaning installations (Fig. 11-14b).

Evaluation of Cleaning. Methods for evaluating the efficiency of ultrasonic cleaning are not as yet generally set. However, some preliminary work has been done to set such standards. Comparisons have been made on stainless parts with radioactive dirt (Fig. 11-15).[1]

Surface Decontamination (Radioactivity). Several studies have been made in this country and abroad on the effect of ultrasonic agitation on surface decontamination of materials which have been exposed to radioactivity. One used an oscillator generator (shown in Fig. 11-16b) which produces a peak output power of about 400 watts. This unit drives an

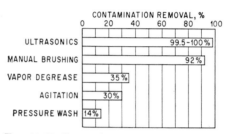

Fig. 11-15. Comparison of cleaning methods.

x-cut quartz crystal in a holder shown in Fig. 11-16a[2] and operates in the high-frequency range, that is, between about 460 kc and 1 Mc. The material to be decontaminated is held in a thin-walled glass test tube immersed in the water which is directly agitated in a beaker, and the energy is focused into the test tube by means of a Perspex (plastic lens). The power in 10 ml of water which was held in the test tube was measured and found to be 14 watts. Samples were cut to fit the test tube. The samples were contaminated with Ru[106] and aged mixed fission products. It was then counted by a Geiger-Müller counter before and after treatment. Solutions used were plain detergents and a number of standard decontamination solutions. Materials were aluminum, steel, rubber, glass, human skin, polythene, and others.

Results indicated that ultrasonic agitation greatly increased the speed and extent of decontamination in the cases where it was bound to the surface by adsorption, occlusion, and mechanical adhesion.

[1] T. J. Bulat, *Metal Progr.*, **68** (1955) 94.

[2] J. L. Linsley-Hood, The Effect of Ultrasonic Agitation on the Surface Decontamination Rates, *Ministry of Supply, Gt. Brit., Tech. Note* 113.

Similar work has been done at Oak Ridge using a section of a barium titanate cylinder operating at 400 kc and a standard ultrasonic generator.

Drilling.   Ultrasonic drilling consists in activating a transducer driving a tool while passing an abrasive such as boron carbide, silicon carbide, or

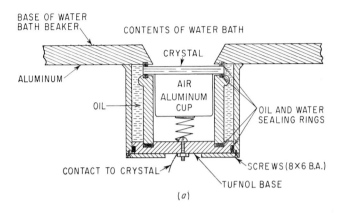

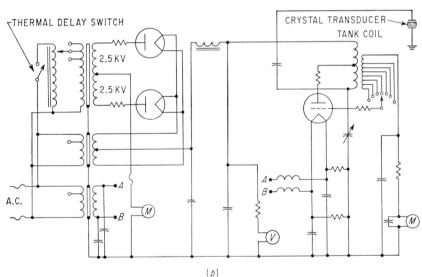

Fig. 11-16. Apparatus for decontamination: (*a*) crystal mounting; (*b*) schematic of driver.

aluminum oxide suspended in a liquid over the work.   Silicon carbide is used on glass, ceramics, quartz, etc.; boron carbide for hard steels; diamond dust to cut gems, etc.   The ultrasound being produced by the tool forces the abrasive particles against the material to be cut at an acceleration in the order of hundreds of thousands of gravities.   The abrasive

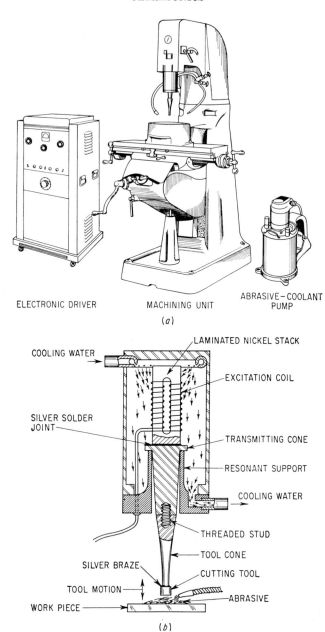

ELECTRONIC DRIVER   MACHINING UNIT   ABRASIVE–COOLANT PUMP

(a)

COOLING WATER

LAMINATED NICKEL STACK

EXCITATION COIL

SILVER SOLDER JOINT

TRANSMITTING CONE

RESONANT SUPPORT

COOLING WATER

THREADED STUD

TOOL CONE

SILVER BRAZE

CUTTING TOOL

TOOL MOTION

ABRASIVE

WORK PIECE

(b)

FIG. 11-17. Typical ultrasonic drill: (a) apparatus (*Cavitron-Sheffield*); (b) transducer (*Raytheon*).

may be maintained on the work surface either by placing the work in a pool or by pumping the slurry over the work continuously. The cutting tools are made by shaping them to either the male or female counterpart of the shape desired in the material to be cut and are made of cold-rolled or unhardened steel. They are then silver-soldered to the tip of the cutting tool. Generally, the cutting head is mounted on a milling machine which allows motion of the work as it is being cut. A typical unit is shown in Fig. 11-17, which shows the generator pumps and mountings. Figure 11-17b shows the inside construction of the transducer. Power output may be anywhere from a few hundred watts to a few thousand watts depending upon the cross section of cut to be made and the speed of cutting. Generally, the cross section satisfactorily cut to date has been limited to about 2 in. in diameter, and at this size speed of cutting would be quite slow. It would probably take about 10 min with the equipment available today to cut a $\frac{1}{2}$-in.-diameter hole in a $\frac{1}{2}$-in.-thick piece of glass.

The speed of cutting is also a function of the size of the abrasive. These are normally used in grit sizes between 180 and 600, since they are commercially available and feasible. Speed of cutting becomes greater as grit size increases and also as the abrasive hardness becomes greater. However, surface finish varies inversely as size of the grit. Various means of getting the grit to the part actually being cut have been tried, and it is apparent that certain problems may arise in the cutting of blind holes, etc.

The ultrasonic machine tool will, of course, cut materials at the expense of wear of the cutting tool, and it will be found that the tool will gradually wear as a cut is carried out depending upon what is being cut. In the case of tool steel and tungsten carbide, the tool will wear as fast as it cuts, but in the case of ceramics, glass, etc., the tool will only wear at about 2 per cent of the speed of cutting.

It is necessary either to change the slurry periodically or to remove the materials from the slurry which are being machined off into it. However, the slurry is not very expensive and is usually replaced after a few hundred running hours.

Boron carbide is superior to the other materials for cutting.

Tool Wear. In ultrasonic cutting, material is removed from both the material to be cut and the tool itself. If the tool is steel, the ratio of wear on the work to that on the tool is shown in Table 11-3, which has been experimentally determined. Side wear also takes place and affects the accuracy.

For this reason, several tools must be used where large amounts of material are to be removed. The tool is smaller than the hole to be drilled by about 0.01 to 0.025 in. Roughing tools may be used first. Accuracies of 0.0002 in. are possible with care.

TABLE 11-3. MATERIAL REMOVAL RATIO

Material	Ratio of stock to tool removal
Boron carbide	2.5:1
Carbon-graphite	100:1
Ceramic	75:1
Ferrite	100:1
Germanium	100:1
Glass	100:1
Glass-bonded mica	100:1
Mother of pearl	100:1
Mycalex	50:1
Quartz	50:1
Tool steel	1:1
Tungsten carbide	1.5:1

Finish. The size of the abrasive used in cutting controls the surface finish obtained. Average size of abrasives is given in Table 11-4. A fresh flow of abrasive is necessary during cutting. Figure 11-18 shows the surface finish (microinches) vs. grit size for cutting metals.

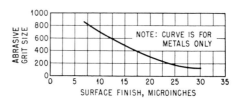

FIG. 11-18. Surface finish vs. grit size.

The size of abrasive also controls the rapidity of cutting, with speed in general directly proportional to size. However, so many other factors influence this that no reliable data are available.

TABLE 11-4. GRIT VS. PARTICLE SIZE

Grit number	Average particle size, in.
180	0.002163
240	0.001542
280	0.001394
400	0.001104
600	0.000402

Abrasive-to-Water Ratio. A ratio of abrasive to water is not critical, and is usually about 1:2 or 1:3 by weight. It is important that the abrasive be kept mixed evenly throughout the water.

Milling. The ultrasonic machine tool described is limited to drilling. Similar machines have been made for milling purposes.

Dental Cutting.   The development of ultrasonic cutting has naturally suggested the use of such instruments for dental applications since present instrumentation is not entirely satisfactory.   The ultrasonic equipment offers the following advantages:

1. It is largely painless.
2. It does away with the mechanical devices now necessary on dental drills.
3. It cuts hard material very easily.

The equipment, however, has the following disadvantages:

1. It requires the use of a slurry and to date cuts very poorly without any element of the slurry, that is, without either the water or the powder.
2. The operation is uneven.
3. It cuts soft material (such as decay) poorly.
4. The direction of cutting is largely in line with the tool.

The way in which a magnetostrictive head can be adapted for cutting is shown schematically in Fig. 11-19.[1]   A cooling jacket for circulating

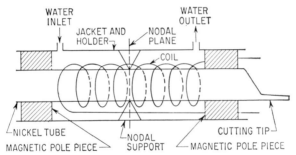

FIG. 11-19. Schematic representation of dental cutting tool.   (*From Nielson, Richards, and Wolcott.*)

water has been added.   The magnetizing system consists of a pair of magnets, one at each end of the tool.   A cutting edge has been added. A typical size for such an instrument would be about 5 in. long, about $3/4$ in. in diameter, and it would weigh about 5 or 6 oz.   Since the polarizing magnetism is supplied by permanent magnets, only the alternating current need be furnished by the generator.   This may be done by means of any of the standard oscillator–power-amplifier units, and the handpiece shown requires about 400 watts to cut rapidly.   It operates at 25,000 cps, which is above the hearing limit.   The slurry is fed to the tip and consists of a thick mixture of aluminum oxide (particle size, 30 μ).   The tool is held in the hand and guided with a light pressure at the point of cutting. Pressure is critical since either too light or too heavy pressure causes the

[1] A. G. Nielson, D.D.S., J. R. Richards, and R. B. Wolcott, D.D.S., M.S., *J. Am. Dental Assoc.*, **50** (1955) 392.

speed of cutting to be greatly diminished. Cutting appears to be mostly in the direction of vibration. However, tips may be bent to allow some cutting in other directions at a very much slower rate.

It is difficult to attach the cutting tip to the transducer. When the attachment is a removable one, a great deal of power is lost in the joint. When it is not, the entire transducer rod must be changed in order to change the cutting tip. Since the cutting tips have the tendency to wear at a rate which has not been completely determined as yet, this may become an awkward situation.

At the present time, equipment which has been made has been between 250 and 400 watts input power. Since the efficiency of the transducers is not known, it is quite possible that very much smaller equipment may be satisfactory in the future.

The thickness of the water oxide mix for optimum cutting has not been determined as yet. Since this mix has to be pumped to the tip of the tool, which is in the mouth, a thick mix is not too practical, although it appears that cutting is more rapid in such a case. The slurry must be disposed of after use by removing it from the patient's mouth in some manner, and this also has some effect on the ratio between liquid and solid in the mix.

Burglar Alarm.[1] It is possible to use ultrasonic waves in air for various signaling applications. One such application is for protective systems. The area to be protected has ultrasonic waves transmitted through it. Echoes are returned from the various objects which reflect the waves. If the object is moving, the frequency of the echo differs from the frequency of the transmitted wave echoing to the well-known Doppler relationships. The reflected echoes are then picked up and amplified and compared with the original wave in frequency. If the frequency is different, an alarm system is set off.

It is therefore apparent that anything that moves, such as an intruder or even the moving flame of a fire, will reflect these waves and set off the alarm.

Since ultrasonic waves are attenuated rapidly in air, a frequency must be picked which will allow coverage of an adequate area. This frequency has been found to be in the vicinity of 20,000 cps. At this frequency, attenuation of 1 wave/100 ft is about one-half. The sensitivity of a system to echoes is a function of the surrounding noise level and also of the transmitted power and attenuation. It has been found experimentally that in an enclosure 100 by 100 by 20 ft, an object of about 0.03 ft^2 is about the smallest to be detected with a radiating power of $\frac{1}{10}$ watt (for a single pair of transducers). However, this is an optimum condition

[1] S. Bagno, U.S. Patents 2,613,283 (1952); 2,615,970 (1952); 2,623,931 (1952); 2,655,645 (1953); 2,732,544 (1956); 2,767,393 (1956); 2,794,974 (1957).

in which there is only one moving object and there is no other appreciable noise generated.

The circuit of a commercial ultrasonic alarm system is shown in the block diagram of Fig. 11-20a and in the schematic of Fig. 11-20b. An oscillator is used to drive the transmitting transducer, and the received signal is amplified by several stages of amplification. It is then compared with the oscillator signal, and the Doppler signal separated by a low-pass filter.

The Doppler spectra of various signals have been experimentally determined and are shown in Fig. 11-20c. It will be noticed that spectra of various types of disturbances differ.

The transducers are magnetostrictive and are constructed of nickel fastened to diaphragms of aluminum.

Miscellaneous Devices. *Ultrasonic Trainer.* Ultrasonic waves have been used as the basis for equipment used to train in the operation of radar. The pulses of sound energy are transmitted in water in the same manner that radio energy is transmitted in space. The speed of these pulses is about 1/200,000 the speed of the radio waves, and thus a map may be built to this scale and provide the same relationship for echoes as is provided in the radar system operated in air. The energy is directed in narrow beams at the map, and the reflections are received and displayed on an indicator. This produces a realistic picture which has many of the same characteristics as a radar picture. Such trainers have been built using the operating controls of the radar system.[1] A number of such units have been built and are still being used.

Basically this device positions a transmitter over a scale model of the place to be simulated. The map is under water, which acts as the couplant. Pulses of high frequency (15 Mc) are sent in a beam through the water; the beam hits the map and is reflected. Electronic circuits introduce wind drift, change in aircraft speed, tuning marks, etc. The crystal transmitter-receiver is gold-plated x-cut quartz (Fig. 11-21).

Blind Guidance. A number of proposals have been made from time to time to use ultrasonic energy for guidance purposes. One such device has been equipment for guiding blind people by means of echo ranging. Such systems have been built and used, giving information for a range of maximum distance between 10 and 50 ft. The ultrasonic systems have been limited in certain ways, but in general the basic information appears to be present. Since this is a field which may become important, it may be advisable to give some general information. Among the questions to be answered are: What type of obstacle gives reflections, and how are the reflections identified?

Systems have been built which present this information either orally,

[1] *Radiation Lab. Rept.* 962 (1946).

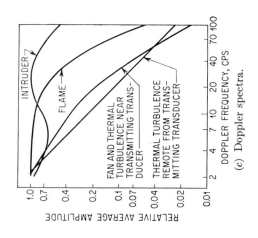

(c) Doppler spectra.

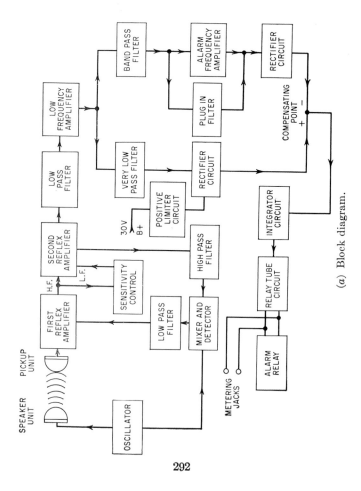

(a) Block diagram.

292

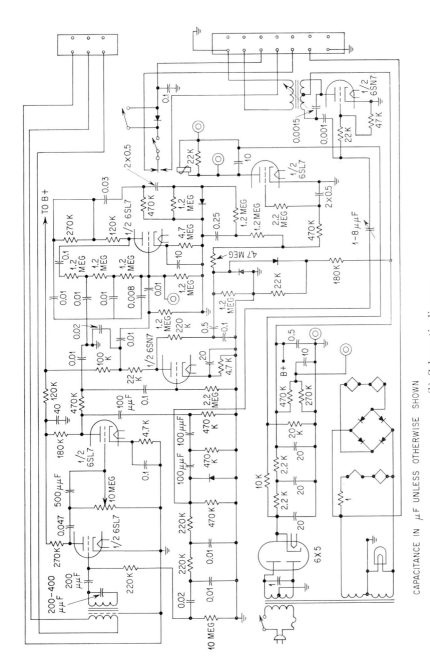

CAPACITANCE IN μF UNLESS OTHERWISE SHOWN

(b) Schematic diagram.

FIG. 11-20. Ultrasonic burglar alarm.

293

tactually, or by controlled shock. It is obvious that many of the problems in blind guidance are psychological and information problems, and not involved in ultrasonics.

The units described used magnetostrictive transducers operating at about 30 or 65 kc. The beam width is about 6.5 deg, and objects spaced about 1 ft apart can be distinguished. Several systems have been used of which the simplest is a pulse-echo range shown in Fig. 11-22. This is typical of such systems described in Chap. 9. Some differentiation must be carried out to indicate the information from the first pulse echo since

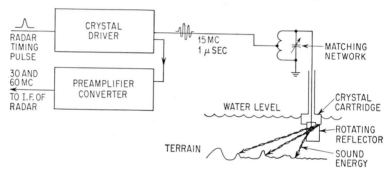

FIG. 11-21. Ultrasonic trainer.

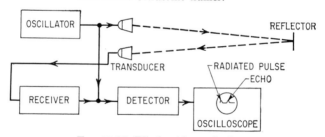

FIG. 11-22. Blind-guidance device.

multiple echoes occur, which cause difficulty in interpretation. For example, a system which responds to the first echo may be used which retriggers the transmitter, giving a frequency of operation which is a function of the distance from the echo.

Another system used was frequency modulated, and the frequency of the ultrasonic signal was varied as a function of time. The delayed echo occurs at another frequency which is a function of distance. The difference between these two frequencies is also a function of distance. This difference frequency may be made audible.

A third system known as pulse-frequency modulation has also been developed to use the good characteristics of both these systems. The oscillator frequency is varied in a saw-tooth manner. The received echo is a varying frequency pulse. The original transmitted signal and the received signal are mixed, and the audible note which results is the indication.

It is obvious that ultrasonics lends itself to all types of ranging systems in a manner very similar to that in which radar frequency waves may be used, so long as the transmission characteristics of the ultrasonic waves are borne in mind.

Microscopes and Telescopes. The devices described have served as the basis for an ultrasonic microscope or telescope.[1] The significant part of the apparatus is the cathode-ray tube shown in Fig. 11-23. In it there is a barium titanate plate which has a charge distributed over its surface, proportional to its exposure to ultrasound, and which is scanned by an electron beam produced by the gun. The scanning action produces secondary electrons proportional to the charge and therefore to the image. These are processed to provide a picture. This is essentially the same as other systems suggested. The significant point is that this apparatus appears to actually have been made. The quality of the pictures, however, is not high.

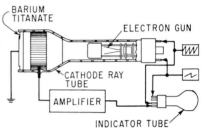

FIG. 11-23. Ultrasonic image tube.

The same principle has also been applied to a microscope. In this unit, the object to be viewed is irradiated with ultrasound by a crystal sender. The reflected ultrasound is focused on a quartz plate. This is scanned and collected. An indicator tube is synchronized with the scanner to view the image. Magnifications of tens of thousands have been claimed at frequencies of 10^9 cps (1,000 Mc), giving resolving powers close to those of optical units.

Ultrasonic illumination may be continuous or pulsed. Several versions of the basic principle have been suggested.

In Fig. 11-23,[2] a barium titanate plate with a diameter of 120 mm is connected to the bulb of the glass envelope by a vacuum seal. An electron beam is produced by the electron gun and strikes the target to produce secondary electrons which are collected by a plate connected to an amplifier. Sound waves striking the target from the outside produce charges of changing polarity to collect on the inside face. These charges influence the secondary emission and therefore modulate the collector current into the amplifier. The signal is then amplified and applied to the

[1] G. B. Devey, *Radio-Electronics*, **20** (1953) 8; S. J. Sokolov, *J. Tech. Phys., U.S.S.R.*, **19**, no. 2 (1949) 271.

[2] P. K. Oshchepkov, L. D. Rozenberg, and I. B. Seinennikov, *Acoustic J. U.S.S.R.*, **4** (1955).

modulator of an indicating CRT. The transducer output is synchronized with the CRT sweep by conventional means.

Fish and Depth Finders. Ultrasonic instruments have been made for measuring depth of water and locating schools of fish for small fishing vessels. Those units usually consist of a recorder or oscilloscope, a tuning circuit (usually mechanical), a pulsed oscillator, a sending transducer, a receiving transducer, and an amplifier which activates the recorder. The unit therefore has the characteristics of the pulse type, with suitable frequencies and time bases.

Since the pulse rate is comparatively low, capacitor discharge through the transducer may be used. A typical circuit is shown in Fig. 11-24.

Tank-level Indicator. One of the early uses of ultrasonics, very similar in principle to depth measurement, was the basis for tank-level-measuring devices. The system uses a transmitter which sends out a pulse of ultrasound, a receiver for the echo, and time-measuring circuitry (Fig. 11-25).

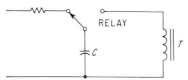

FIG. 11-24. Capacitor discharge circuit.

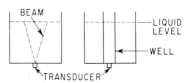

FIG. 11-25. Tank-depth-measurement devices.

The top of the liquid or the interface between two liquids may be indicated. A number of configurations are possible. The simplest has already been shown. In cases where liquid turbulence is a problem, still-wells may be included, either internal or external. Calibration stillwells may also be included if desired. One electronic unit may be used for several transducers. Accuracies of ± 1 cm are possible, but 10 to 50 cm is more likely. Contact transducers have also been used. These merely indicate if they are immersed in a liquid or not by their effect on the electronic circuit in which they are inserted.

Viscosity-measurement Devices. The use of ultrasonic devices to automatically measure viscosity has been suggested. One such device utilizes a magnetostrictive probe in the form of a longitudinally oscillating flat blade.[1] The damping of this reed by the liquid is determined by its viscosity. About 28 kc is used in the form of pulses. The transducer is pulsed and then allowed to ring until the amplitude falls to a certain value which causes another pulse. The rate of pulsing is calibrated in terms of viscosity. A block diagram of the system is shown in Fig. 11-26.

Flowmeter. The rate of flow of liquids may be measured ultrasonically by utilizing the Doppler effect. Two transducers are placed in the liquid

[1] S. R. Rich and W. Roth, *Bull. Am. Phys. Soc.*, **3** (1952) 59.

and are pulse-excited. One unit is used as transducer, the other as receiver, and alternately switched so that each in turn transmits and receives. The ultrasound thus travels first in the direction of flow, then against it, etc.; and its velocity is added to the velocity of flow, then subtracted, etc. From this the rate of flow may be computed.[1]

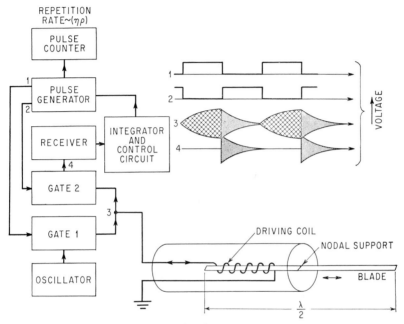

FIG. 11-26. Viscosity measurement.

Radar Targets. Ultrasonic units have been used to simulate radar targets for tuning a radar system. One such system is shown in Fig. 11-27. The glass rod takes the place of the medium in which the radar pip would travel. The reflected pulse may be used to calibrate time scales. This unit is essentially a special type of delay line.

Sonic Gas Analyzer. A very similar instrument to the flowmeter may be used to analyze gases.[2] An ultrasonic wave is transmitted through a gas and the velocity measured. The time interval between transmitter and received signals is expressed as a phase angle which is measured by electronic means.[3]

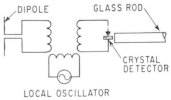

FIG. 11-27. Radar target.

[1] W. B. Hess, R. C. Swenzel, and S. K. Waldorf, *Elec. Eng.*, **69** (1950) 983.

[2] Grubb Parsons and Co.

[3] L. E. Lawley, *Chem. & Ind. London* (1954) 200.

Vibration Pickup. A vibration pickup based on ultrasonic Doppler effects has been built (Fig. 11-28).[1] A barium titanate transducer transmits a beam of ultrasonic waves at 110 kc onto a vibrating body whose velocity is to be measured. The body reflects the waves; when it is moving toward the transmitter, the frequency increases and vice versa. A receiving crystal picks up the varying frequency, and it is amplified, limited, and discriminated to produce voltages proportional to the vibration velocity. For best results the head should be positioned about 6 in. from the part. Its main advantage is that it does not load the part to be tested.

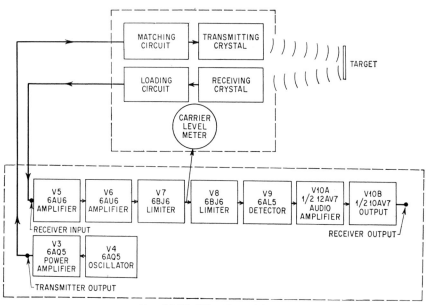

Fig. 11-28. Vibration pickup.

Ultrasonic Signaling in the Ocean. One of the chief applications of ultrasonic waves has been in submarine signaling, where they are widely used for the location of obstacles and of enemy ships. The pulse method is generally used, and the time between the sending and reception of the pulses is an indication of the position of the reflecting objects. However, a submarine signaling indicator commonly shows a series of reflections arriving at various times as well as the genuine signal, which is the important indication. These spurious indications may be reflections from the surfaces of the water, usually from the troughs of the waves.[2] Since very little absorption occurs during the transmission of ultrasonics in the

[1] H. C. Hardy, *Natl. Elec. Conf.*, **XI** (1955) 476.

[2] R. J. Urick and H. L. Saxton, *JASA*, **19** (1947) 8.

sea, a great many such reflections are likely. Besides this, there is a certain amount of reflection from the bottom of the ocean, although this is not so troublesome as that from the top. Difficulty is also encountered with temperature gradients and with movement within the body of liquid.

Ultrasonic Propagation in Air. A great deal of work has been done in the field of ultrasonic transmission through the atmosphere, since this application offers a method of sound ranging, communication, altitude determination, etc. Generally, the order of frequency is from 10 to 30 kc, and it is necessary to propagate within 10 ft of the ground.[1] Many problems make this type of work very difficult, specifically the fact that there is considerable scattering by the lower atmosphere and also by different kinds of various natural obstruction. In addition to this the waves are affected by winds and air-temperature gradients that exist close to the earth. Rain also attenuates sound, and for all these reasons the sound energy is sharply reduced.

Compressed air whistles are often used for the production of the ultrasonic energy, and the receivers may be either resistance coupled or heterodyne. Parabolic reflectors can be used to concentrate and direct the energy.

Ultrasonic methods have not been so successful when applied to this field as when used in the testing, seismic, and submarine signaling fields.

Propagation through Wires. Some work has been done in attempting to send ultrasonic vibrations through ordinary wires for signaling purposes. Low frequencies of the general order of 30 to 150 kc have been used. In order to couple the energy into the wire, one end is fastened to a crystal transducer for sending purposes and the other end fastened to a second transducer for receiving purposes. Such signaling has been done effectively over relatively short distances, but it has not been successful in long-distance communication. Bends and breaks in the wire will naturally interfere with the propagation of the waves and help dampen them quickly.

Television. It is possible to obtain a television picture by modulating a light ultrasonically. The basis of such a system is the ultrasonic cell, which consists of a body of liquid through which the ultrasonics pass and, in turn, modulate the light. By using the phenomenon of light diffraction, the ultrasonic system gives a much greater illumination than most other television methods. The design of these systems is a science in itself and will not be considered in detail here.

The amount of voltage exciting the unit controls the illumination directly; when this voltage is modulated, the intensity is also modulated.

The further design of the ultrasonic television system seems to offer great possibilities once the system becomes simple enough and entirely

[1] H. K. Schilling, Ultrasonic Signaling, *OSRD* 5012.

electronic.   However, ultrasonic systems are not popular to date in this country.   Figure 11-29 indicates a typical system of the ultrasonic type.

Ultrasonic Delay Lines.   A delay line is a component into which an electrical signal can be put and out of which at some later time an electrical signal is obtained.   The application of such lines is wide since they may be used in any type of computer which requires a means of storing information (commonly referred to as *memory*).   The amount of delay

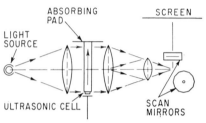

FIG. 11-29. Television system.

required depends upon the application and may be anywhere in the order from a few microseconds to a few thousand microseconds as commonly used today.   An ultrasonic delay line is a device on which electrical energy is impressed, usually in the form of a pulse, by means of a suitable ultrasonic transducer such as any of those described herein which then changes the electrical energy into sound.   This sound then travels in the delay line for a time determined by the length of its path and its velocity in the material.   It then hits a second ultrasonic transducer which changes it back into electrical energy.   A typical ultrasonic line is shown in Fig. 11-30 and consists of one or more transducers (usually quartz crystals,

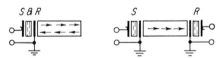

FIG. 11-30. Simple delay line.

but not necessarily so), a piece of material through which the ultrasonic waves travel, an absorbing medium usually placed around the ends of the material to do away with reflections, and some material for bonding the crystal to the line.

A common frequency used in ultrasonic lines is 15 Mc, although recently 30 Mc has become widely accepted.

It is obvious that the first indication from the input pulse indicates the delay desired (after it has traveled through the delay lines).   A number of additional pulses may be present.   These pulses are sometimes referred to as secondaries and may consist of reflections which have traveled either in other paths than the original pulses or have been reflected in the line more than once. They may also be produced by conversions of the type of ultrasonic wave known as *mode conversion*, or by scattering, by inclusions in the material, etc. In the case of a folded type of delay line such as the rather sophisticated one shown in Fig. 11-31 (known as a *symmetrical* type), in which the waves hit each of the facets a number of times as they progress around through the delay line, secondaries can arise from the fact that the sound beam produced by the transducer spreads, allowing portions of the energy to hit these walls and be reflected.

The simplest form of delay shows two common types of units. In one a single crystal is used and the energy sent out into the piece. The delay is the time of travel of the energy from the time it leaves the crystal until it hits the reflecting end of the path and returns to the crystal. A second elementary form is a separate sender and receiver in which the energy is

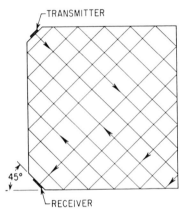

FIG. 11-31. Delay line—rectangular symmetrical.

transmitted from the sending crystal and travels through the part and is received by the receiver. The reflecting faces of the path are called facets. In a simple line of this type, the energy will continue to be reflected back and forth in the line, and pulses will be received at multiples of the time of travel. Thus, these pulses may be used as time markers or for other uses requiring precisely separated pulses. If the material from which the travel path is made is wide enough, no energy will hit the sides of the path and therefore the types of spurious signals generated by that means will not be important. Units of this type may be used up to about 100 μsec. As units become larger, it becomes obvious that some means must be used to keep the physical size of the path from becoming unwieldy. The first type of unit shown, that is, the reflected single transducer type, is an elementary sort of folded unit since the same material is used to generate a delay twice that which would be experienced by passing through the material once. It is therefore apparent that units could be made in which the travel path was made longer by having the energy bounce around inside the material. Such a unit is shown in Fig. 11-31, which consists of a rectangular piece of material with two corners removed and transducers placed on them. This unit is known as one of simple rectangular symmetry, and the path which the energy will travel is traced out in it. The total length of the path is much greater than any dimension of the part itself. Such units will accordingly give much greater delay than a simple bar.

The folded lines have the very great advantage of long paths, but of course they offer more difficult design problems. Spurious or secondary responses will be generated in them due to the diffraction pattern of transmitting, and receiving crystals and the resulting energy will be reflected from the sidewalls along the path.

As lines become longer, the question of the optimum geometric shape becomes important, and the use of polygons with multiple facets have become common. Such a unit is shown in Fig. 11-32.[1]

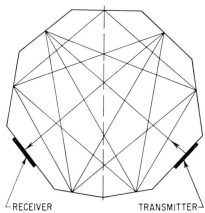

RECEIVER   TRANSMITTER

FIG. 11-32. Delay line—polygon; multiple symmetry.

Originally x-cut crystals were used, and longitudinal waves resulted, but it was discovered that shear waves have lower velocities as well as lower insertion losses. Therefore, y- or ac-cut crystals are ordinarily used with solids. When the crystals operate at their fundamental, they can be ground to frequencies up to about 60 Mc. Above this frequency, they have to operate on a harmonic. Barium titanate has also been used as a transducer.

Among the materials used for ultrasonic lines are liquids, such as mercury, which was used in both straight and folded lines, and solids, such as fused silica or quartz, which have become widely used in both types of lines. A number of ultrasonic delay lines using mercury have been

[1] D. L. Arenberg, Ultrasonic Delay Lines, *IRE Conv. Record* (1954).

described in the literature but are not as widely used today as the fused-quartz type. In general, fused quartz may be said to give less insertion losses (about 45 db), a smaller size, and no mechanical vibration sensitivity.

Miscellaneous Considerations. INSERTION LOSSES. The signal traveling in an ultrasonic line will be attenuated owing to mismatch at the terminals. It will also be attenuated owing to absorption and other effects within the material as well as the bonding between the crystal and the line. Typical losses in solid lines are between 10 and 65 db. Maximum voltage input to these lines is in the vicinity of 100 volts.

DELAY TIMES. Units of this type have been built giving delay time of a fraction of 1 μsec to several milliseconds.

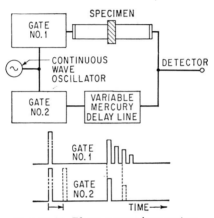

FIG. 11-33. Phase comparison system.

FREQUENCY. Frequencies in the vicinity of 30 Mc have been commonly used although lines have been built operating from a few megacycles to about 100 Mc.

BANDWIDTH. The bandwidth is usually determined by the transducers and their circuitry. A bandwidth of about 25 per cent of the carrier frequency may be obtained in common lines. The lines are terminated by a receptive load shunted by an inductor which resonates with the capacity of the crystal.

TEMPERATURE. The velocity of propagation of shear waves in quartz changes with temperature by about 70 ppm/°C negatively. Compressional units have a slightly higher temperature coefficient. Thermostatically controlled lines have been built where better temperature control is necessary. Circuitry for driving delay lines is conventional and may be found in the literature.

Phase Systems. In a reflective system the accuracy is limited by the sharpness of the leading edge of the pulse. Phase analysis has accordingly been used to get more accurate measurements.[1] The system is shown in Fig. 11-33.

Basically the system compares the time of travel of a pulse in a material and in a delay line with known characteristics. Pulses may be either added, subtracted, or compared.

Miscellaneous Pulse Applications. Pulsed energy at high powers has been used for medical and industrial apparatus. Most of this is simply 60 cps used as power supply (unrectified), giving a modulated r-f output. However, some high-power pulsed apparatus (high-frequency) has also appeared.

[1] H. J. McSkimmin, *JASA*, **22** (1950) 413.

INDEX